# THE SELFISH
# SOCIETY

*Also by Sue Gerhardt*

Why Love Matters: how affection
shapes a baby's brain

# THE SELFISH SOCIETY

## HOW WE ALL FORGOT TO LOVE ONE ANOTHER AND MADE MONEY INSTEAD

### SUE GERHARDT

**SIMON &
SCHUSTER**

London · New York · Sydney · Toronto

A CBS COMPANY

First published in Great Britain by Simon & Schuster UK Ltd, 2010
A CBS COMPANY

1 3 5 7 9 10 8 6 4 2

Simon & Schuster UK Ltd
1st Floor
222 Gray's Inn Road
London WC1X 8HB

www.simonandschuster.co.uk

Simon & Schuster Australia
Sydney

Diagram of the brain on p.60 © Liane Payne

A CIP catalogue record for this book
is available from the British Library.

ISBN: 978-1-84737-571-1

Typeset by M Rules
Printed in the UK by CPI Mackays, Chatham ME5 8TD

To my children and their generation

And in loving memory of
Ros Peers, 1951–2000

# CONTENTS

# ACKNOWLEDGEMENTS

Many friends and colleagues helped me think about the issues in this book.

I am particularly grateful to those friends and colleagues who found the time to read the whole manuscript, and give detailed comments. They really helped to clarify my thinking: Adam Swift, Mike Crosse, Harry Hendrick, Jane Henriques, Leo Boyes, and Diana Goodman.

In the early stages, John Phibbs, Leslie Sklair, Paul Gerhardt, John Edginton, Fiona Duxbury and Martha Sweezy helped me to shape the proposal, though it was my agent Sam Copeland who guided the process and pointed me in the right direction.

I also received helpful input from Andrew West, Paul Gerhardt, Julia Shay, Jennifer Browner and Stuart Mealing.

Thanks also to my editors: Mike Jones for his good judgement and support for the project, and above all to Victoria Millar for making such a creative contribution and for taking such pains with the nuances of my argument. I'm also grateful for the editorial assistance of Rory Scarfe and Karl French.

Roz Taylor and other staff at the Summertown Public Library in Oxford have regularly, over a number of years, helped me to track down books and papers from the British

Library, which enormously helped my process of research. Thanks to them.

During the years of writing this book, fitting it in around my clinical practice, I benefited from stimulating links with the Association of Infant Mental Health (AIMH), and in particular with my colleagues on its Advocacy group: Sarah Stewart-Brown, Clive Dorman, Penelope Leach and Amanda Jones. Oliver James, whose thinking runs on close tracks to my own, has been an encouraging and stimulating friend. Thanks also to Tim Kasser, Bill McKibben and Fred Previc for their helpful responses to my questions.

I have enjoyed a sustained conversation with my colleagues at the Oxford Parent Infant Project (OXPIP) over the last ten years, which has enriched my working life. I particularly want to thank my clients themselves, both at OXPIP and in my private practice, especially those who gave permission for me to draw on their experiences in this book.

Thanks to my dear Laurie and Jess, who enlivened and distracted me and kept my feet on the ground during the long haul of organising a book. Thanks also to the Oxford Mindfulness group and my fellow meditators who helped me to keep practising. Most of all, I owe a great deal to my friends Jean Knox, Chris Shingler, Jane Henriques, Doro Marden, Mollie Kenyon-Jones, Celia Fry, Karey Taylor, Joanna Dennison, Anne and Rob Burns, Joanna Tucker and Fiona Duxbury who took good care of me along the way. And a special thank you to Margaret Landale.

# PART I

Defining the Problem

# INTRODUCTION

When people write books, they often project aspects of their own experience into their ideas or characters. The personal story of Ayn Rand, the best-selling American novelist and philosopher of selfishness and self-sufficiency, reveals how key aspects of her own life drove her thinking and writing. As a child in Russia, she had seen her father's chemist's shop expropriated by the revolutionary communists and was turned passionately against state power for the rest of her life. Later, as a young woman, she used her initiative and independent spirit to make her escape from the Soviet Union on her own. These experiences formed the backdrop to her lifelong, one-woman campaign against dependence on others or on the state. She argued that we should all do as she had done: take care of ourselves. In her view, selfishness was a virtue. Rand promoted her ideas in many public appearances, coming across as a cool, self-possessed yet intense woman with a piercing dark-eyed gaze and anxious frown, fiercely arguing that it was 'immoral' for people to be guided by their emotions, which she saw as the antithesis of rationality.

My own 'campaign' has been driven by different experiences. I had a more peaceful childhood than Ayn Rand's, but one in which I experienced both hostility and neglect in various ways and felt compelled not to depend on others' care. Although I found myself using my intellect to survive, my childhood left me with a conviction that what really matters is not rationality or self-sufficiency, which were thrust upon me, but the emotional understanding that was missing from my experience. Sensitised to that lack of emotional connection, just as Rand was sensitised to feeling subjugated and dependent, that lack is what I now perceive to be 'out there' in our current society. In many ways, this book is my attempt to influence public awareness to move in the opposite direction from Rand's, to embrace the pleasures of belonging and depending. My argument is that emotion, rather than rationality, is central to morality and at the heart of our politics and our culture.

My vision of the state of things has been further shaped by my adult professional experiences as a psychotherapist. For over twelve years, I have worked as a 'relational' psychotherapist, an approach rooted in the understanding that our sense of self is based on our actual relationships. Like many relational psychotherapists, I draw on my awareness of the significance of early attachment relationships as well as – in recent years – of brain development, to make sense of adults' individual personal difficulties. However, I have come to believe that this body of knowledge has a wider application to society as a whole. It can also throw light on social mores more generally, by explaining how our moral values are established and guiding us towards what really matters in bringing up children to be constructive and co-operative members of society. My experience of working with a wide variety of individual clients from many different backgrounds – both in private psychotherapy practice as well as with those clients referred by public agencies such as social services and health services – has made me aware of how much parenting contributes – positively and negatively – to the creation of our society. It has strengthened my conviction that our ability to care and have concern for others is as much a function of our early development as an indication of individual moral failings or lack of will. This is a departure from previous accounts of morality which have relied on ideas of sinful or irrational 'human nature'. Instead, this book presents a more developmental view of morality. It suggests that modern research in developmental psychology and neuroscience tells a different story from the old account of original sin, a story that the public needs to hear, not least because it can also help us to understand how society works. Contradicting Ayn Rand's view of a world full of self-sufficient individuals, this research makes it clear that we live instead in an interdependent world in which our moral values are created through the way we relate to each other, starting as early as babyhood.

Many years ago, my studies in early childhood observation under the auspices of the Tavistock Clinic in London gave me my first insights into babies' mental development. Although already a mother twice over, watching babies on a weekly basis for over two years enabled me to see the process of development more objectively. It stimulated my interest in the impact of those early experiences on the baby's brain, so I immersed myself in reading widely in the literature of neurobiology. I found myself in an Aladdin's cave of fascinating material which confirmed that the brain is not a machine which operates in glorious isolation, but a nervous system which is designed to respond to the environment in which we find ourselves, and to help us to predict what will happen in that environment. Brains are shaped by experience, and the quality of care and attention we receive as babies affects the neurobiology of our brains. Early brain development, in particular, is very rapid and sets up many biochemical systems and neural pathways that we will continue to use for the rest of our lives

This view contrasts with the popular notion that our genes are all-powerful directors of our behaviour. Although it is true that we are born with a genetic make-up which may determine the colour of our eyes, our basic temperament or our susceptibility to various mental and physical health conditions, it is vital to understand that the genes involved in social behaviour don't turn themselves on or off, but – according to recent epigenetic studies – are triggered into activity by the environment. Even the psychiatrist Sir Michael Rutter, a staunch advocate of the importance of genes, acknowledges that genes do not *determine* 'either psychological characteristics or mental disorders'.[1] His analysis is a sophisticated one, which argues that genes play their part in complex reciprocal interactions *with* the environment. Nevertheless, our brains lay down neural pathways generated by the experiences that they have. This opens up the possibility that it is not only parenting which affects our psychological development and our brain structure, but also the society and culture in which we live.

When I wrote *Why Love Matters: how affection shapes a baby's brain* (2004), my purpose was to explain what I had learned about the importance of babyhood as the foundation of individual emotional well-being, mental health and good character. I demonstrated the links between the quality of early care and the later incidence of depression, personality disorders and anti-social behaviour – issues that specifically concerned me as a psychotherapist working with individuals who were struggling with their relationships, their unfulfilled potentials, or their destructive and self-destructive behaviours, as well as reflecting my work as a parent-infant psychotherapist helping families to bond with their babies. My goal was to encourage parents and policy-makers to become more aware of the importance and significance of early child-rearing, in order to prevent further individual suffering and poor emotional development.

Since then I have become more interested in the way that these babyhood experiences are not just an issue for individuals, but also matter to society. Particularly in the current economic crisis, when we are beginning to question many assumptions about ethical standards, I believe that it is important to understand these connections between our infancies and the kind of world we create. So in this book, I am casting my net wider and investigating the ways in which early child-rearing plays its part in determining social values as well as reflecting them and being shaped by them.

In my work with individuals, understanding someone's early developmental history is central to understanding the person. In this book, I wanted to apply a similar developmental perspective to the bigger social picture, to discover whether psychology could help to throw light on our social and historical processes and the problem of how to achieve a more empathic society. This book is a record of those explorations, which have taken me down different paths, applying what I know about early emotional and brain development to the fields of history, economics, politics and social anthropology. In weaving together these different perspectives, my aim has been to create an overview, using broad brushstrokes rather than the detailed analysis with which specialists within these disciplines are necessarily preoccupied. Even when I am taking a detour into the transition to capitalism or the cross-cultural aspects of child-rearing, my goal is not an academic one, but is always ultimately focused on what these sources can tell us about the present.

Currently, Western culture is much closer to Ayn Rand's vision of a society of self-interested and self-sufficient individuals than to my vision of an empathic, emotionally literate society. After all, most people assume that it is simply 'true' that we will all put our own interests ahead of those of other people, and these beliefs underpin their acceptance of industrial capitalism as an economic system. However, the eighteenth-century theorists who advanced the 'self-interested' view of human motivation did not have access to the information that we now have, especially the great advances in psychological knowledge that have taken place. Their theories rested on Enlightenment ideas of rationality, uninformed by modern awareness of unconscious processes, group behaviour or emotional development. These old forms of thinking tend to be based on assumptions that people respond to rational argument and can change their behaviour by using logic or willpower. Yet time and time again, experience proves this pervasive belief wrong. For example, in 2005 there was a rise in teenage pregnancies despite a government campaign for better sex education and information about contraception. The British Minister for Children at the time, Beverley Hughes, made a comment that conveyed her bewilderment. 'We've reached a sticking point,' she said, 'people for one reason or another don't think through the consequences.'[2] The implication is that teenage pregnancy was a failure of rationality on the girls' part, as if their need to be loved, or to find meaning in a life that was devoid of other opportunities, could not be taken seriously as salient factors. Our economic and political thinking is still locked into these old belief systems, unaware of many of the core factors that drive our behaviour – in particular, the crucial role that early experience plays in setting up our emotional behaviours, and the importance of the inner life of feelings and implicit beliefs in our decision-making.

In practice, our 'moral values' are often not so much the conscious ideas that we express when we reason with our children, although that may be an important aspect of parenting, but the unconscious assumptions that we all live by in our everyday relationships. Of course, it is hard to see these things clearly. They take us out of the realm of verbal knowledge to the invisible realm of emotional experience, the more mysterious, unseen aspects of reality that guide us and drive our behaviour.

Although it is largely parents who convey many of these unconscious messages and practices to their children, our moral behaviour – selfish or unselfish – is not just about the values of individual parents. Parents themselves are heavily influenced by their social relationships. Without necessarily being aware of it, they pass on the culture in which they are immersed. Just as children don't choose the family they are born into, so too parents don't choose their society. They respond to it and adapt to its norms, often unwittingly. If everyone around you is behaving selfishly, it is difficult not to join in. Each society or culture is a sort of mega-family which transmits many underlying beliefs and attitudes, simply through the way things are done and the way things are.

This 'social unconscious' mostly arises from the current power structures, which shape our values and expectations without our being aware of it. Many of our social structures and practices – such as the allocation and control of resources – are difficult to discuss or question because they seem to be inevitable. We experience them as a given 'reality', not as a social context that we create together. In the West, our 'reality' has been a culture focused on material and technical progress; we take it for granted that human relationships will in many ways be subordinated to our concern with expanding productivity and growth. So ingrained is this attitude that it is hard to perceive the underlying assumptions we make that material well-being should take precedence over emotional well-being.

Even those who have the most power to define our social reality are not necessarily aware of it. The early pioneers of industrial capitalism did not foresee the potential impact of their economic system and its 'self-interestedness' on people's relationships. They were simply excited by the creative energies that were being released and their potential for greater material benefits, and took it for granted that relationships would continue as they always had. The early philosopher of capitalism Adam Smith still lived in an age when he could assume that humans had a natural 'sympathy' for each other which was beyond question. As he said, even the 'greatest ruffian' can 'feel for the misery of others' as well as finding pleasure in others' happiness.[3] He could not have imagined the extent to which his concept of a '*Homo economicus*', driven by self-interest in his business dealings, would come to stand for the whole of human nature and convince many people that a selfish way of life is the only way of life.

   These notions of the inevitability of self-interest have prevailed for more than two centuries. However, even before the
recent economic crisis, such ideas were beginning to look a
little worn and threadbare. There was a gathering consensus
that our materialism and our self-centredness had become a
problem because those values had taken over in every sphere
of our lives. I was alerted to this emerging view a few years
ago when I read an opinion piece by the *New Statesman*
columnist and academic Martin Jacques deploring the sad
decline of family, community and caring. We were living,
Jacques said, in 'the age of selfishness': 'The credo of self,
inextricably entwined with the gospel of the market, has
hijacked the fabric of our lives.' His thesis was: 'Our social
world has come to mirror and mimic the rhythms and characteristics of the market, contractual in nature. Meanwhile,
the family – the site of virtually the only life-long relationships we enjoy – has become an ever-weaker institution:
extended families are increasingly marginal, nuclear families
are getting smaller and more short-lived, almost half of all
marriages end in divorce, and most parents spend less time
with their pre-school children.'[4] Yet although I found myself
endorsing much of what he said, Jacques offered little sense of
what should replace these trends, other than, implicitly, a
return to more traditional forms of the family. His conclusion
was hopeless and pessimistic: 'What is to be done, I hear the
policy-wonks say. Nothing much, I guess.'
   We have become used to hearing that we are living in a
'broken society'. In 2008 the Conservative leader David
Cameron described the United Kingdom as a society characterised by knife crime, poverty, ill health, family breakdown
and worklessness. He called it 'a de-moralised society' where

'children grow up without boundaries, thinking they can do as they please'. Seeing the problem as a disciplinary one, he bemoaned a society where there has been 'a decades-long erosion of responsibility, of social virtue, of self-discipline, respect for others, deferring gratification instead of instant gratification'.[5] In his view, this was the result of a national culture in which people saw themselves as 'victims' of drug addiction, obesity, or family breakdown, instead of recognising that they had choices and should take responsibility for themselves. According to a representative poll of 1,832 adults taken shortly after this speech, the vast majority of people agreed with him.[6]

Cameron identified something which, regardless of their political persuasion, people could recognise in the world around them: a carelessness about child-rearing, and a lack of responsibility for long-term well-being. However, both Martin Jacques and David Cameron diagnose the causes of these ills in terms of a lack of individual discipline or commitment. This is only half the story. *Why* are people like this? If they are, it is not just because they are weak or selfish, but also because they live in a society which does not help them to flourish and to care for each other. The heart of the matter is that we are living in an impoverished emotional culture, the end product of decades of individualism and consumerism, which have eroded our social bonds. This emotional impoverishment may look very different at different ends of the social scale – for the poorest socio-economic groups, it can result in being caught up in violent crime or in the benefits culture, whilst for the rich, it is more likely to result in being caught up in excessive consumption or fraudulent financial dealings – but whatever form it takes, I see materialism and social breakdown as the culmination of a value system which by definition does not take other people into account. This is manifest at every level, from the individual to prevailing social policy.

In the middle of the recent 'flu pandemic, I heard a story about a woman going to the hairdressers determined to make herself feel better by having her hair done, despite the fact that she felt ill and was sneezing and coughing within reach of half a dozen other people. When she left the hairdressers, the other customers looked at each other, raised their eyebrows and said, 'What a selfish woman.' My own understanding of selfishness correlates with this anecdotal example. I would define selfishness as the pursuit of self-interest without regard for others' needs or interests. Of course, we all act like this at times. As individuals, our ability to hold other people's needs and interests in mind is a capacity that wobbles and wavers depending on our own state of mind and current circumstances, as well as on our emotional maturity. I am sure my own tendencies to selfishness are as great, if not greater, than anyone else's. I suspect that each of us tends to think that selfishness is our own guilty secret, not a social issue. But selfishness is not just an individual failing. It is equally possible to have a selfish society, a society which sustains individualism, greed and materialism at the expense of collective interests and the needs of the social group as a whole. For me, all of these issues are intertwined, and will be discussed as aspects of selfishness in this book, because they all involve an element of disregard of others' needs and others' claims.

Although I would endorse Jacques' view of our times as an 'age of selfishness', I would, however, question whether the way forward is to strengthen the traditional family, as Jacques and Cameron suggest. Nor do I think it is a matter of attempting to be 'better' people by voluntarily adopting new moral values. Instead of reaching for familiar moral guidelines from the past, a more helpful starting point might be first to reach a thorough understanding of how and why selfishness arises. By looking at both social and family contexts, using all the current knowledge at our disposal across the various disciplines of history, neuroscience, sociology and psychology, we might arrive somewhere new.

Unlike Martin Jacques, I believe that there is much to be optimistic about. Major scientific advances in recent years can help us to understand how we develop both as individuals and as societies. Neuroscientific understanding may even be able to explain how the wider culture has an effect not just on our ideas, but also on our very brain structure and function. The evidence is now stacking up that among industrial capitalism's unintended side effects is the way that it has shaped our brains as well as our moral attitudes. As Fred Previc, a former US government research scientist, observed: 'Just as it was once thought that human activity could not dramatically alter the world's climate, so would it have once seemed unlikely that modern societies and lifestyles could produce widespread and serious neurochemical imbalances and associated impairments in brain function.'[7]

According to Previc – now no longer carrying out research for the government and perhaps freer to say what he thinks is really going on – the highly stressful, competitive environments which we have allowed to prevail in Western societies have re-shaped certain aspects of our brain development. He argues that our pressurised way of life alters the behaviour of the brain's neurotransmitters – the vital substances which are like a variety of biochemical lubricating fluids that help the different parts of the brain to connect. When humans are stressed, the calming neurotransmitter serotonin gets used up and as its level sinks, the level of the motivational neuro-transmitter dopamine tends to rise, producing more 'active coping', driven and self-willed behaviour. Previc believes that many of these effects are passed on pre-natally. In societies where mothers are under stress, their babies' brain biochem-istry – either in the womb or in the delicate post-natal period of development – can be affected. The more stressed she is, the more sensitive to stress the baby's brain may become.[8]

Whilst scientists can illuminate the damage we cause our-selves by living in a competitive and emotionally unsupportive environment, and can demonstrate the effects of poor rela-tionships on our bodies and brains, philosophers can illuminate new ways of thinking which may help us to achieve a more caring and co-operative society. Looking towards the future, I have found inspiration not amongst politicians, but amongst feminist thinkers who have put for-ward their ideas for a new 'ethic of care'[9]. Their vision is not a sentimental ideal of a caring world, but a more down-to-earth analysis of what care means in practice. They emphasise that care is an *activity* not a set of principles or feelings. It is an activity that all human beings are involved with because we all receive care and give care in different ways. Yet although it is very much about how we relate to other people and how well we pay attention to them, it does not have to be based on per-sonal emotion but 'includes everything that we do to maintain, continue, and repair our "world" so that we can live in it as well as possible'.[10] It is highly practical.

This doesn't mean that it is easy to meet everyone's needs. Thinkers like Joan Tronto, Professor of Political Science and Women's Studies at the City University of New York (CUNY), are realistically aware that 'there will inevitably be more care needs than can be met'.[11] There will always be difficult issues to face about which needs should take priority. For Tronto, these must be decided through collective political debate, not by relying on the 'false security' of abstract individual rights and idealistic moral universalism – views which originated with the Enlightenment in the seventeenth century, but which fail to recognise the reality of unequal social power and our differing needs for care at any one time. Instead, she advocates a more pragmatic ethic based on paying attention to actual people living specific lives and striving to take their needs as seriously as we take our own.

In this sense, the 'ethic of care' is closely related to the influential concept of 'mentalisation' developed by the British psychoanalyst and academic Peter Fonagy.[12] This is a concept that is gaining many adherents amongst psychotherapists, because it helps us to understand how good relationships with other people work. In essence, mentalisation is about the ability to grasp that other people have minds and feelings of their own which motivate their behaviour, just as our own do, and to understand that other people may experience things very differently from ourselves. It's a capacity which depends on openness to one's own experience, since it is difficult to be open to other people's emotions and to respect their different points of view if one cannot tolerate and fully experience one's own emotions. In many ways, the success of an ethic of care depends on people being able to 'mentalise'.

Developing a new politics based on practical caring and mentalising is an urgent task. We're currently facing hugely demanding problems such as the prospect of devastating climate change combined with the weakening of Western economies. Finding solutions to such problems will require global co-operation and foresight. Yet in recent decades, instead of bringing maturity and wisdom to the task, we regressed to a more self-indulgent collective mentality which convinced us all that we could have anything we liked without really paying for it. In our time Western industrial capitalism has reached a level of decadence that has encouraged many of us to become less emotionally aware of others rather than more so.

Like children let loose in the sweet shop, we have gorged ourselves on everything we could get hold of, blissfully unaware of the true cost of our activities. We have been careless or ignorant of the impact of our behaviour on the poorest and most powerless inhabitants of the planet, on our own children, and on the environment itself. As almost everyone now acknowledges, there is mounting evidence that our industrial activities have poisoned our water, air and soil, have destroyed the rainforests and are heating up the planet to a dangerous degree. Childishly, we have failed collectively to take responsibility for these consequences, or for the consequences of unfairly taking advantage of those who have not been able to play the capitalist game and ignoring their distress, malnutrition and disease.

Many of us would like to move towards a more caring society, but few people have any idea of how this could be achieved. Although science hopefully will continue to deliver technical and material discoveries which may help us to solve some of our current practical problems, it is equally important to recognise that many of our problems lie in the arena of relationships. We may know what we need to do to redress international poverty, but lack the empathy or the social skills to bring about change. We may be against war, but lack an understanding of how to resolve emotionally driven conflicts. The challenge now is to integrate the scientific knowledge that psychology and neuroscience offer us, information about how people develop and how their emotions are played out in the public sphere, with action: only then will we have a chance of moving towards the right solutions.

In practice, if we want to have a more caring society, we need people who are equipped to care for others. This, in turn, means that we will have to address the culture of early child-rearing, which is where the ability to mentalise and to respond to others' needs begins. However, even in sophisti-cated Western societies, we are still relatively psychologically unaware and nervous of taking such issues on board. When addressing issues around parenting, the political left still tends to avoid talking about feelings as such, preferring to focus on more neutral issues such as child poverty or employment poli-cies, whilst the political right tends to argue for a return to the traditional family as the way to recover society's emotional balance. To me, both of these approaches seem a little dated and uninspiring. Although I am concerned that current poli-cies are pushing mothers of very young children into the labour force, I am not convinced that re-creating the old tra-ditional division of labour would do anyone a service. I am happy to acknowledge the value of family life, but I am more interested in finding new ways of supporting good emotional development, whatever form they may take.

Whilst this book engages with these contemporary concerns, and the need to develop better policies for employment and child-rearing, its focus is on how we can integrate up-to-date psychological knowledge with social and political thinking and policy making. As a psychotherapist, I argue that we must bring a deeper understanding of the role of emotional development into our political awareness, and recognise that political behaviour in general is not something separate from other forms of human relationship and is influenced by the same emotional dynamics. For example, the way that our public figures behave in positions of leadership, as well as the policies they espouse, are influenced by the moral framework they themselves acquired in infancy. I want to make it clear that family life is not just a private sphere but is centrally important in passing on and sustaining our public emotional and moral culture. Parents, whether they are aware of it or not, reproduce current cultural values and shape their offspring for a particular way of life. Infancy, it turns out, is the hub of cultural transmission; unselfishness is not just an individual developmental achievement (which it is), but at the same time is a *cultural* achievement. The question asked by this book is: can we use developmental thinking to help to change our social and political culture?

# 1. The Current State of Things

In those years, people will say, we lost track
of the meaning of *we*, of *you*
we found ourselves
reduced to *I*
and the whole thing became
silly, ironic, terrible:
we were trying to live a personal life
and, yes, that was the only life
we could bear witness to

But the great dark birds of history screamed and plunged
into our personal weather
They were headed somewhere else but their beaks and
   pinions drove
along the shore, through the rags of fog
where we stood, saying *I*.

*Adrienne Rich, from 'In Those Years'*

We are living through a time when major changes in our way
of life seem inevitable. Although there are urgent problems to
solve, I personally feel as if a heavy weight is lifting: at least the

suffocating values of the last thirty years are now being questioned and many people are hoping for fresh air and new
beginnings. Few people kid themselves that 'greed is good'
any more and it is becoming less acceptable to assume that
society must continue to be run for the benefit of a few. But
are we capable of change? At the moment we seem to be
poised on the brink of new ways of doing things, unable to
jump in because we don't quite believe that it is really
possible.

One of the challenges we face is to become the kind of
people who are capable of creating a more ethical way of life.
This is difficult because our culture currently provides little
support for such a project. Although I would suggest that
people today are no more selfish than they have ever been,
and arguably are perhaps more aware and considerate of others
than in previous historical periods, we are emerging from a
particular period of a few decades in which we were encouraged to abandon our *aspirations* to unselfishness. In fact, the
culture that was unleashed by neo-conservatism positively
promoted selfishness. It celebrated individual acquisition and
gain, without regard for society as a whole. People were urged
to buy their council houses even though it depleted the stock
of public housing for those in need; an idealised celebrity culture fostered new aspirations – perfect bodies, perfect décor
and dazzling wealth – without concern for the standard of
living of the rest of society. The modern ethic became one of:
take what you can for yourself, look after number one.

However, that doesn't mean that we are comfortable with
our own selfishness. In many ways, we are all constantly preoccupied with exploring the boundary line between our own
wishes and needs and those of other people. In fact, much of

what we regard as newsworthy is the way that people cause harm to others by pursuing their own interests without regard for others. Although the revelations about corrupt practices in public life come thick and fast these days, we can still be shocked at hearing of someone defrauding public finances or lying to the public. On any day of the week, we can read in our daily newspapers horrifying stories of misconduct; in recent memory, there have been tales of a gang of children attacking a disabled teenager, a father who killed his children to punish his ex-wife, and a large corporation which dumped its toxic waste in foreign countries. Who could doubt that we are living in a selfish society?

The knowledge that most of us have acted badly at times confirms our guilty identification with selfishness. It is almost reassuring to be told by the scientist Richard Dawkins that such behaviour makes sense because our genes are 'ruthlessly selfish'.[1] Although he hedges his bets by suggesting that we don't have to obey our genes, the odds are stacked against us. Clearly, we are low, wily creatures who are bound by nature to put ourselves first, and to give less value to others.

Actually, we are not as cold-blooded as all that. Even though the most ancient part of our brain is a survival machine similar to the brain of a reptile, humans have a dramatically extended brain and with it, a whole range of other possible ways of being. Our reptile brain may be rigid, driven by habits, with only a very basic social awareness – dominate or be dominated – but we have acquired a whole range of new possibilities with the mammalian part of our brains. This gives us social instincts for nurturance and co-operation, along with the biochemical responses that enable us to play and enjoy being with others. Finally, humans have evolved even higher layers of the brain, which enable us to communicate our feelings and think about our social relationships, giving us much greater flexibility and social adaptability.

The connections between these different parts of our brains cannot be taken for granted. It isn't easy to integrate these different aspects of ourselves. There is always a balancing act between the basic urge for individual survival and the more sophisticated ability to maintain social connections to survive in a complex human society. As psychoanalytic thinking makes clear, we always have mixed motives and ambivalent feelings. We are 'both/and' not 'either/or'. In particular, as social beings we have to make the constant attempt to keep both self and other in mind.

## Collective or individualist values

This difficult juggling act is strongly influenced by the cultural context in which we live. If we create a culture that encourages selfishness, it will flourish; if our culture encourages concern for others, that can flourish too. During the Second World War, for example, people re-discovered their ability to collaborate for the common purpose of survival. Although not everyone behaved co-operatively and conflicts still occurred, many people testified that they felt a sense of good will and that although they were 'the worst of times' they were also 'the best of times', as one Land Girl, Pat Parker, experienced it.[2] The British poet Louis MacNeice was taken with the colourful Bank Holiday atmosphere on the underground railway platforms where people sheltered against the bombs. As he described it, people had their sandwiches and played their mouth organs, then slept in their patchwork quilts under a blaze of lights: 'Someone remarked to me that this was really Back to the Village, a revival of the archaic communal life . . .'[3] It felt to many people as if they were 'all in it together', and this motivated them to work together to achieve collective goals. Clearly, when social aims are clearly identified, they can inspire people to action just as much as the pursuit of individual glory.

It is the social context that determines what is regarded as normal behaviour. The collective spirit which occasionally surfaced in wartime was an interlude and has made only brief reappearances in our own era of advanced capitalism. For most of the period since the rise of industrial capitalism in the early nineteenth century, collective values such as solidarity and co-operation have been unwelcome to the authorities, although they were sustained by the socialist and trade union movements until the late twentieth century. Eventually, however, such values were eroded by rising prosperity and the pursuit of material security above all else – a project that spread from the middle class downwards, as wealth increased. The new culture developed the 'I' at the expense of the 'we', as the American poet Adrienne Rich suggests in her 1991 poem.

The apologists of capitalism have always insisted that self-interest was the motor of wealth creation and, as such, to be welcomed. The tremendous success of mass production in raising the level of material well-being and in supplying commodities to the whole population seemed to support this view. A wealthier society was also able to afford to finance astonishing advances in scientific and medical knowledge. These gains were so impressive that they seemed to justify the human casualties along the way. They made it very difficult to question the validity of naked self-interest and made many people genuinely feel powerless to demand a more moral basis for society. If narrow self-interest is what makes the economy tick, enabling a higher quality of life for so many, how can we ask people to be responsible, unselfish or considerate of others? This has led us into an impasse. The aspiration to be 'good', promoted and shared by most religions, has become a rather abstract and lofty goal divorced from the 'reality' of getting and spending. Morality then becomes an anaemic sideshow, an optional extra, whilst the real action lies in the red-blooded pursuit of selfish goals.

Today, religious leaders such as the Archbishop of Canterbury valiantly argue for their vision of the good, to inspire people to recover moral values. Secular organisations like UNESCO have also tried to take a moral lead, hoping to evoke a sense of social responsibility and to counter the focus on 'human rights' of the prevailing individualist mentality. Instead, they have proposed a Declaration of Human Responsibilities,[4] reaching for an agreed moral standard within a rationalist framework – as if all that were needed to achieve social harmony was to agree on our goals. These efforts may have some effect in changing the cultural land-scape, but they don't address the deeper roots of the problem. First, they don't acknowledge the all-pervasiveness of eco-nomic power, which currently determines our social practices in ways that we can't always see clearly. In a world which spends more on pet food, cigarettes or ice cream[5] than on ensuring everyone has access to water and sanitation, a world where the budget for international co-operation and peace (via the United Nations organisation) commands only 1.5 per cent of international military spending,[6] it is pious to hope that individuals can simply adopt new and better behaviours. When people want ice cream they are not *aware* of the collective priorities their choice reflects.

Second, a rationalist approach obscures the fact that social values are not determined by conscious deliberation, but are largely passed on at an unconscious level, through our relationships with each other. After all, why do people behave unethically – why don't they behave humanely, non-violently, with integrity and truth – as this Declaration would like them to? Is a Declaration going to make them behave differently? The answer is likely to be 'no'. Qualities such as the ability to deal with conflicts non-violently, or to be self-aware and congruent, come from inside the person – they reflect genuine moral development and cannot be conjured up by people who are traumatised by their experience of maltreatment of various kinds.

The impact of early childhood is particularly strong. When children experience a lack of care and attention, or are on the receiving end of hostility, they will struggle to develop into unselfish and caring people. Yet this knowledge that it is our experiences, particularly our earliest experiences, which have the strongest influence on our values and relationships to others, has not yet become part of our culture. Although it has long been understood that children are the adults of tomorrow, and that it matters how we bring them up, in societal terms we are still not taking the impact of early childhood seriously enough. We have not yet achieved the same degree of recognition that it is the pre-verbal stage in particular which shapes our values. There are still too many people who think that their behaviour towards babies has no impact because babies 'don't understand' or 'won't remember'.

This knowledge of the crucial nature of pre-verbal experience is still relatively new. It began in the 1950s and 1960s
with the huge body of experimental research generated by the
psychoanalyst John Bowlby's powerful and influential 'attachment theory'. Bowlby courageously stood up to the entire
psychoanalytic profession of his day to insist that a child's
actual early attachment experiences were the key to his or her
healthy emotional development. His once controversial thinking is now taken for granted in developmental psychology and
in developmental approaches to psychotherapy.[7] The research
that has built on his foundations is a wonderful resource
which has helped us to achieve a deeper understanding about
how individuals develop and the psychological sources of our
behaviour. And the more that we know about the formation
of individual selves, the clearer it becomes that our social and
moral development is strongly shaped by the unconscious
learning of how to be human which takes place in infancy. If
we want to understand the psychological factors which drive
us to be materialistic or selfish, we need to look at how we
care for babies and the kind of values that care passes on to
them.

A new baby is not born with a burning desire to wear a
Gucci T-shirt, even though his parents – and the T-shirt manu-
facturers – might find it the fulfilment of their dreams. Nor
do the number of teddy bears in the baby's cot have any
impact on the baby's well-being. On the other hand, the
infant's emotional experience of dependence on others in
these early months does have a very powerful impact on his or
her subsequent behaviours and beliefs. Babies very rapidly
learn to channel their needs in a socially prescribed fashion.

As a specialist in this field, I have over the years found

myself talking to a wide range of people about the importance of infancy, from parents to lawyers to electricians and artists. No matter what their background, it is rare to find people who are aware of the importance of pre-verbal relationships, or of the powerful cultural messages that can be inadvertently conveyed to babies. Although we have become so rich that we have been able to invest in expensive experimental research into early psychological and brain development – research that has consolidated the insights of attachment theory – we are not making use of this vast store of knowledge. Even in the affluent countries of the world, this information has not yet reached the population at large. As Meredith Small, a professor of anthropology at Cornell University, put it: 'It is ironic that while research on the critical role of attachment relationships for healthy infant development emanated from the West, Westerners alone do not put this research into practice.'[8]

## Caught up in capitalism

Instead, psychological discoveries have more often been used to manipulate consumers, and to increase our consumption through advertising, with its empty promises of sexual fulfilment. In other words, like so much else in this phase of human history, psychology has been subordinated to material pleasures and comforts. We have been mesmerised by the ease and enjoyment offered by the technological feats of the last century – electricity, telecommunications, health care, entertainment, rapid transport and domestic conveniences – yet our consumer sophistication has not yet been matched by our psychological maturity or understanding.

Nor have the conveniences themselves – while pleasurable and superbly clever – helped us to become more human or enhanced our relationships in any way. Even though dish-washing machines, DVD players or iPods – to name just a few – demand complex social organisation and sophisticated technology to bring them into being, no active participation in the production process is required from us, the user. Mentally they engage only the most basic programmes of the brain – those set to achieve immediate and short-term pleasures and to avoid painful experiences, which are neuro-logically speaking our most 'selfish' instincts.

Lately, however, there has been a growing interest in the value of relationships as well as things. It is tempting to hope that this shift is driven by a new-found concern and respon-sibility for others, but the evidence suggests that it is more likely to be a new form of self-concern. In affluent societies, people now expect capitalism to deliver on the promises of its advertising and provide happiness as well as material comforts. We yearn for the real satisfactions that relationships of various kinds bring. Yet the richer we get, and the more apparent it is that capitalism cannot deliver this kind of fulfilment, the more dissatisfied and preoccupied with our own increasing psychological ill health we become. Some recent studies, notably by the psychologist Daniel Kahneman, have shown that people in the wealthiest consumer societies have become no more happy or fulfilled over the last fifty years, despite their increased wealth. Kahneman won the Nobel Prize for Economics for his work in 'behavioural economics', which demonstrated that there was a 'weak relationship between income and global life satisfaction'.[9] According to his research, if we really wanted to be happy, we would sleep more and spend more time with friends, not pursue greater income and buy more consumer goods.

Despite all the immediate gratifications that have been on offer – the sexual freedom, easy credit, labour-saving devices and on tap personal entertainment, all of which are still only aspirations for those in less developed economies – we have not got happier. In fact, depression is now classified as one of the world's most prevalent illnesses. As Richard Layard, an economist at the London School of Economics, put it: 'Depression has actually increased as our incomes have risen.'[10] In the USA, statistics reveal that over a quarter of the population suffers from a diagnosable mental disorder in a given year.[11]

Such figures are shockingly high. However, there are valid questions about whether this is an objective change or the result of changed perceptions in a medicalised, therapeutic culture which tends to define everyday problems of living, such as feeling unhappy, as aspects of mental 'disease'. The psychiatrist Derek Summerfield, the sociologist Frank Furedi and others linked to the Institute of Ideas have argued that labelling problems in this way undermines people's natural coping resources. Summerfield is outraged at the World Health Organisation's claim that depression 'is a worldwide epidemic that within twenty years will be second only to cardiovascular disease as the world's most debilitating disease'. He sees this as 'a serious distortion, which could serve to deflect attention away from what millions of people might cite as the basis of their misery, like poverty and lack of rights.'[12]

Poverty is of course a source of acute misery for those people who live and suffer in the undeveloped areas of the world where they have yet to reach adequate fulfilment of even their most basic needs, but in the richer nations, it is a relative concept. The poor in the USA have cars and air-conditioning. In practice, poverty in the affluent nations often has less to do with physical conditions such as extreme hunger, disease or lack of shelter, and more to do with psychological hopelessness. Although I don't want to downplay the despair of living in the worst communities which are blighted by unemployment, crime and a lack of purpose, recent evidence emerging from a large study of 8,000 children in Britain is finding that socio-economic circumstances are not the key determinant of a child's mental or physical health; what is more crucial is their mother's and father's own mental health and ability to be an effective parent.[13] Nor is poverty – though it restricts life and can cause unhappiness – the only source of mental illness. Depression and psychological illness frequently affect those who are better off, too. Very often, poor mental health is due to early life experiences that have undermined the sense of self and ability to manage feelings and relationships well. In affluent countries, it can also be exacerbated by our tendency to compare ourselves with others, and to find happiness or satisfaction in our social standing and material wealth relative to others.

In the West, we are trapped in these cycles of endless striving and dissatisfaction, trying to keep up with the ever more elaborate displays of consumption we see on television and on the internet. This drive to accumulate material goods and services appears to have addictive qualities: it is a powerful appetite which has no inbuilt mechanism to alert us when we have had enough; we want more and more – especially, it seems, just that little bit more than everyone else. This is partly a natural aspect of the human brain's dopamine reward systems, which are more active in response to unexpected gains than to getting the same old things (they are primarily designed to help us to adapt to new experiences). However, this human tendency has also been exploited by our economic system, which delights in stimulating new needs and in creating a momentum for the development of new products. After all, it would not be helpful to capitalism if we were satisfied with what we had.

What is less natural is the addictive quality of so much of our current behaviour. Even in the midst of material comfort and physical security that our forebears could only dream of, we continue to act as if we were deprived and must compete with others to get as much as we can. The reason for this may be that although we have relative material abundance, we do not in fact have emotional abundance. Many people *are* deprived of what really matters. Lacking emotional security, they seek security in material things.

This psychological message has been elaborated by Tim Kasser, a professor at a liberal arts college in the USA who himself espouses an anti-consumerist lifestyle of 'voluntary simplicity'. He lives in the countryside, grows his own vegetables, produces his own milk and eggs, and has no television (a tempting way to avoid the mind pollution of advertising, yet in my view a somewhat dubious strategy since television is the source of so much of our shared culture). Kasser is building up a body of research which begins to show that there is a link between the materialistic attitudes of the younger generations and their mental health. He has found that the more materialistic young people were, the less satisfying their relationships. This confirmed previous research by his colleague Ken Sheldon, professor of psychology at the

University of Missouri, showing that those teenagers with the most materialistic attitudes had the most conflict and aggression in their dating relationships, and demonstrated the least empathy and satisfaction in close relationships of all kinds. Kasser's research also showed that this was related to the early care they received in their families: 'Individuals who have not had their needs well met in the past come to think that wealth and possessions will bring them happiness and a good life'.[14]

In other words, they confuse material well-being with psychological well-being. The way this may have come about is illustrated by the story of some very young, sick children with tuberculosis observed by James Robertson, a social worker linked to John Bowlby, over a period of two years in the late 1940s. The treatment of tuberculosis at that time demanded that the children must endure prolonged separations from their parents whilst they were in hospital. Robertson described how the toddlers went through stages of adapting to their emotional deprivation – first protesting and looking for their lost mother, then becoming despairing and listless, and finally becoming emotionally detached. As Robertson described it, once they had reached this stage, the children seemed indifferent to their parents when they visited on Sundays: 'They were more interested in what their parents had brought than in the parents themselves. They searched bags and stuffed chocolate into their mouths.' His impression was that the children had numbed their feelings because of their repeated disappointment at not being taken home, and had replaced those longings with a 'hunger for sweet things which did not disappoint'.[15]

So many of us are now like these children. Billion-dollar industries exist to provide us with the comforts we crave when people let us down, whether that is sweet things, alcohol, or the latest consumer toys and fashions. All too easily, these sources of satisfaction become more desirable than unreliable close relationships. Experimental research on monkeys and rats suggests that the key once again lies in very early childhood. This research has shown that social isolation, emotional deprivation or stress in infancy alters the dopamine pathways, particularly in the 'social brain'. This can increase impulsive, 'grabby' behaviour, and can create a predisposition to addiction. The current research of Dr. Gene-Jack Wang, at the University of Florida, is finding that compulsive overeaters and compulsive drug-takers both have decreased dopamine D2 receptors.[16]

Not everyone is hooked on particular substances, yet 'things' still seem to provide real psychological benefits for many people. In the absence of a feeling of confidence about the social world, it is easy to become selfishly preoccupied with acquiring things and ignoring the relationship between your own desires and the needs of the wider society. Things can provide security of various kinds: owning your own home enables you to feel confident that it will not be taken away, owning a car means you don't have to depend on unreliable public transport. Things can even become a source of individual identity, since 'brands' sometimes appear to deliver a sense of self that people have not been able to derive from their family relationships. Equally, 'retail therapy' can sometimes provide a sense of power and choice that is lacking in everyday life – often, the only power many people will ever experience is purchasing power.

Whatever the psychological drivers are, consumerism has become a kind of 'mania', as the psychiatrist Peter Whybrow

calls it.[17] Massive overconsumption has become the norm –
most notably in the USA, where the majority of sixth-grade
children have a television in their bedrooms, and where huge
portions of high calorie food have led to an obesity crisis. The
powerful and successful seem just as driven to acquire more,
no matter how much they already have. The overpayment of
chief executives and the overspending of the poor are the twin
poles of the same phenomenon. In fact, the mania has been
at its most extreme in the corporations. In the UK, between
2000 and 2007, top chief executives' pay rose by 150 per
cent,[18] whilst in the USA in the same period, it rose around
313 per cent.[19] By 2007, a typical chief executive officer
earned more in one working day 'than the typical worker
earned all year', according to the American politician Joe
Biden.[20] These kinds of behaviour have almost come to seem
natural – just another demonstration of good old oppor-
tunistic human nature. But this is the explanation that we fall
back on when we can't make sense of our behaviour.

## Money not relationships

Driven by our dopamine reward systems, this behaviour has
set us on what Richard Layard, in his book *Happiness*,
describes as a 'hedonic treadmill'. In his view, happiness has
little to do with being on that treadmill, and endlessly seeking a new material 'fix' to stimulate our senses. In a bold
challenge to traditional economics, he claims that even perfect markets would not lead us to the best possible life or the
greatest happiness for all. Unusually for an economist, he suggests that what actually makes people happy is, above all, 'the
quality of our relationships with other people'.[21] Layard argues

that since we can now measure happiness, using brain scans, there is no longer any excuse for excluding it from our economic deliberations, and he has been remarkably successful in persuading the British government to consider the importance of 'happiness' as a goal rather than focusing purely on gross domestic product.

Layard has promoted the idea that we can bring about change by re-thinking our values and training ourselves out of negative and unhappy thoughts using very short-term 'cognitive' therapies and 'positive psychology' strategies. The UK government has taken up these proposals, since they are relatively cheap compared to other therapies, which invest in a longer-term therapeutic relationship as the source of change. However, the strange contradiction in Layard's thinking is that although he urges us to give more value to relationships as a source of happiness, he fails to appreciate those relationships' vital function in shaping the brain's emotional capacities in the first place. In practice, we can't maintain 'positive thinking' about ourselves, or create better relationships on our own; we need the consistent help and support of others. Although 'quick fix' therapies have indeed been shown to help people with particular anxieties or phobias to look differently at the world,[22] there is little evidence that they can help those who suffer from an uncertain sense of self originating in early life. For these people, help is needed over a sustained period of time,[23] to restore confidence in relationships and to enable new brain pathways to be established.

Although I share Layard's desire for a better society which he describes as one that devotes more of its wealth to security – in employment, in old age and in the community – a society which spends more on redressing imbalances of wealth for the global poor as well as helping the mentally ill, I am disappointed that he doesn't question the basic structure within which we live, a capitalist economy devoted to perpetual growth and to increasing profits year by year. I find it hard to see how our collective values can shift towards friendship, care for others and sustainable ways of living, while society continues to drive us to consume more and more.

The consumer culture is not organised around psychological needs. Its primary goal is to establish a vast market with an unlimited choice of goods to meet individuals' material needs and wishes. It is a culture founded on the idea that strong, independent individuals can make contracts with each other, and are free to choose what work they do and what they own, and can achieve it in competition with others. It rests on an ideology of 'freedom', 'choice' and, above all, individual property protected by legal 'rights'. It is an energetic ideology focused on promoting individual creativity and productivity, and protecting the material rewards for those efforts, but it is largely blind to other aspects of human existence such as dependence and emotional need.

In this 'marketised society', money shapes and directs our relationships and intimate lives to an unprecedented degree. Relationships and services from other people can be bought: we can pay for an escort to accompany us to dinner, a childminder to rear our children, someone to paint our nails, do our shopping, cook our food, or amuse us (and most of these people are women). When we are distressed, money buys someone to tell our troubles to and chocolate, alcohol or drugs to dull the pain. Some of us even find that the act of consumption itself provides emotional comfort and affirms a sense of identity without direct contact with other people.

This leads many of us to believe that money is essential to meet our emotional needs, and that if we had more money, and could buy the latest goods or services on offer, we would be happier. In this scheme of things, the chief route to happiness is to make enough money to buy everything you need and not depend on anyone else; true security is total control of one's life, total self-sufficiency through money. It then becomes easy to overlook or devalue the needs for community, connection and care that consumption cannot meet – the collective or non-material needs – the 'we' as opposed to the 'I'.

The positive side of the quest for self-sufficiency and continual economic growth is that it may inspire entrepreneurship and self-actualisation. But in its most negative form, it seems to come out of a sense of despair that people might support and care for one another. The belief that we can be fully autonomous is a desperate attempt to deny the fact that we are not in control of our lives, that we are born helpless, we may have accidents or misfortunes, and we may have to face chronic illness and inevitably the dependence of old age. In all these phases of life, when we are unable to contribute economically to society, we need sensitive care from other people. This requires a very different ethic from the go-getting entrepreneurial mentality.

In reality, capitalist societies have never managed to sustain the pure free market ideal. It has always been a myth, albeit a very potent one. In practice, there have always been people who could not ignore human distress. Poor communities have supported each other, co-operative societies have been formed, philanthropists have donated money, and eventually more organised forms of protection such as insurance and the welfare state have come forward to provide fluctuating levels of support. However, the ideology of self-sufficiency remains a powerful goal and a disincentive to trust others or depend on them.

## Are things getting worse?

A lack of trust in a supportive social world will inevitably lead to people turning inwards. When individuals don't feel connected to others, their social behaviour often deteriorates. It appears to many people that this lack of connection is increasing – is it?

Certainly there has been a sharp decline in social trust over the last fifty years or so. If children are the barometer of our well-being, the Western nations are clearly in trouble. Astonishingly, children in the UK and the USA have the worst outcomes on various measures of 'well-being' compared with other rich nations.[24] Since the 1990s, British teenagers have been reluctant to agree that 'most people can be trusted', although three-quarters of those born in the years before 1930 confidently agreed with the statement.[25] Today, 35 per cent of British children say that they don't feel loved and cared for by their parents and only 56 per cent feel able to talk to their parents about their problems.[26] It would not be surprising if such children turned away from shared activities and retreated into the immediate individual gratifications of video games, eating and shopping – or to gang membership to create a sense of identity and belonging.

This lack of connection to others is becoming manifest in the way people behave in public. In recent years there has been a host of voices arguing that that the standards for public behaviour in ordinary social life are becoming increasingly casual and self-centred: the poet and social commentator Robert Bly, for example, was already suggesting in 1997 in his book *The Sibling Society*[27] that manners have gone beyond informality to outright rudeness. Martin Jacques has also referred to a 'coarsening of tone' which he found 'difficult to give expression to'.[28] These experiences are subjective, but there is perhaps a growing sense that there has been a subtle shift towards a lack of regard for others in public behaviour, a carelessness about other people's feelings – for example, disturbing others with music or mobile phone conversations in enclosed public places such as trains, or parking inconsiderately on a pavement – often demonstrating a lack of awareness of others' needs or any distinction between public and private spaces.

The availability of easy credit from the 1980s onwards played a part in this trend towards disconnection from others. It fuelled the illusion of independence, enabling people to pursue their desires without needing to defer to authority figures such as bank managers, or older relatives, to obtain a loan. I remember the early 1980s as a turning point. One day a young couple living next door to our home – despite having very little income – took delivery of a three-piece suite, a brand new television (most of us were renting TVs in those days) and even an air-gun, suddenly able to have the things they wanted.

In many ways, these changes have been positive, enabling people to live more comfortably and breaking down the old authoritarian class culture. But at the same time, they have encouraged people to persist in the infantile perception that all their needs could and should be met. As our culture has rapidly adapted to these new financial opportunities, it has begun to seem as if the higher brain qualities of self-restraint, deferred gratification and concern for others are redundant values. Popular culture – from reality television shows to the vast internet porn industry – is now dominated by an adolescent, self-centred mentality. Robert Bly denounced these changes, declaring in his prophetic and somewhat doom-laden voice that we were losing our ability to mature. Young people are 'unparented', he says; they are no longer taught how to behave with honesty, self-control and integrity.

## The culture of narcissism

The American historian Christopher Lasch identified what he termed a 'culture of narcissism' in the USA as early as the 1970s.[29] In his ground-breaking analysis, he described how the individual self had become weakened and infantilised by the consumer society. Ironically, whilst capitalism pushed us towards independence and self-sufficiency, in many ways the rise of consumerism had the opposite effect. It prolonged the experience of dependence into adult life, surrounding us with 'fantasies of total gratification', a trend which has accelerated in the last thirty years, epitomised by the Hollywood actress Carrie Fisher's witticism: 'Instant gratification takes too long.'[30] Yet Lasch noted that without self-control and deferred gratification, it becomes much harder to develop the real satisfactions of learning skills, competencies and care for others. In Lasch's view, people were becoming less well-equipped to deal with the difficult aspects of life, such as the need for self-sacrifice or the pain of loss. Stuck in an infantilised state, grown-up people imagined that they would be cushioned from reality, from what Bly called 'a complicated web of griefs, postponed pleasures, unwelcome labour, responsibilities and unpaid debts to gods and human beings.' Long-term goals that required effort and sustained commitment became increasingly unattractive.

The essence of these phenomena is that they reflect a shallow form of relationship to others, based on appearances rather than on a real appreciation of the complexity of other people, including their flaws. More recently than Lasch, two American professors of psychology, Jean Twenge and Keith Campbell, have painted a chilling picture of the way this narcissism has now spread like a virus into every aspect of modern life: 'We have phony rich people (with interest-only mortgages and piles of debt), phony beauty (with plastic surgery and cosmetic procedures), phony athletes (with performance-enhancing drugs), phony celebrities (via reality TV and You Tube), phony genius students (with grade inflation), a phony national economy (with $11 trillion of government debt), phony feelings of being special among children (with parenting and education focused on self-esteem above all else) and phony friends (with the social networking explosion).'[31]

Christopher Lasch believed that modern capitalist society reinforced narcissistic traits in everyone, and allowed 'celebrities' with narcissistic personalities to set the tone of public and private life. However, his analysis was unusual because, unlike many social critics before and since, it did not assume that people's selfishness or superficiality was the natural state of humankind. Instead, for Lasch, narcissism is actually the psychological outcome of our *lack* of power: 'In its pathological form, narcissism originates as a defense against feelings of helpless dependency in early life, which it tries to counter with 'blind optimism' and grandiose illusions of personal self-sufficiency.'[32]

## Narcissistic leadership

In the last few decades the US and the UK, in particular, have given a free reign to narcissistic illusions and addictive materialism. As a result, the gap between the rich and poor has widened. Those at the top of the social scale, such as the senior bankers and lawyers interviewed by the liberal journalists Polly Toynbee and David Walker for their book *Unjust Rewards*,[33] revealed a strong sense of entitlement to their luxurious lifestyles and a staggering ignorance about the amount of money most people have to live on. These interviewees fiercely resisted the prospect of redistributing income, calling such measures 'bullshit crap which doesn't help the people', but they demonstrated little interest in 'helping the people' themselves, describing them for the most part as 'lazy' and undeserving.[34] Clearly, when there are extremes of wealth and privilege, within one nation or between nations, the stage is set for resentment and fear, not for empathy and mutual understanding. For this community of the rich, the claims and concerns of other – poorer – people did not have equal weight and value. The global poor are unlikely to merit much of their sympathy either.

The self-advancement of those at the top of the social scale turned out to come at a huge cost to others. We now know that the risk-taking that bolstered the exaggerated salaries and bonuses of the world's top financiers and chief executives has had a major impact on both their own societies as well as globally, threatening the collapse of the banking system and the well-being of millions. In less dramatic and obvious ways, their wealth has also been achieved at the cost of spending on public, social goods, both at home and abroad. For example, when poorer nations are in relationship with the richer, narcissistically self-centred countries, they are often prevented from spending money on social goods and welfare support for their own desperately needy peasantry or urban poor by economic policies dictated by the rich nations. When loaning money to developing countries, the international financial organisations, led by the US, demand 'structural adjustment programmes' which insist that poor countries pursue policies such as privatisation, deregulation or reducing trade barriers – policies which reflect Western ways of operating and which often benefit the donor countries more than the recipients.[35]

Narcissistic societies often behave in much the same way as narcissistic individuals. There is no neat divide between 'private life' and 'public life', since the people who lead the banks, governments or corporations bring their psychological attitudes and values to their public tasks. They shape the culture in their own image, often demonstrating the same problems in facing difficult realities as do narcissistic individuals. The demographer and historian Emmanuel Todd anticipated the current economic crash many years ago, based on his observation that American productivity was in decline, and US companies were performing badly compared to their competitors: for example, Nokia – a Finnish company – was outperforming the US company Motorola. But he also anticipated that a society which was so used to rampant unlimited spending would not be able to face up to its economic weakness. Instead, Todd argues that the US administration turned to military adventures (in Iraq and elsewhere) to avoid facing the humiliations of 'a reduction of their power and, most likely, of their standard of living'. In America's weakened economic state, military action conferred an image of strength (as well as safeguarding US access to Iraq's oil).[36] In other words, a narcissistic society with a sense of entitlement reached for grandiose solutions at other people's expense rather than deal with its own limitations.

As a psychotherapist I am often struck, when observing the behaviour of those in power, by their remarkable similarity to those less powerful people who are designated as 'patients'. Whether people are depressed, unhappy or could even be diagnosed as having borderline, narcissistic or anti-social personality psychopathology, the bottom line is that they have difficulties with the quality of their attachments to other people and often find it a struggle to think of others' needs. The same lack of emotional connection to other people is often seen on the public stage.

Yet we rarely address the underlying psychological and emotional dynamics of our public figures, or our culture as a whole. Public commentary is usually restricted to economic or political analysis – together with a sprinkling of gossip. I believe this undermines our attempts to understand the forces that are at work in our lives. At a time when we need to adjust our values and expectations away from a world economy based on growth and the exploitation of fossil fuels towards a world based on greater empathy for others and care for our natural resources, we will need to understand why we behave as we do and what drives us.

In my view, the hidden source of both selfishness and materialism, those unholy twins, is a feeling of deprivation. This is rooted in the actual experiences that people have had, and the way that they have been treated in their childhoods, particularly their infancy. With a poor experience of early dependence, children grow up longing to feel emotionally secure and accepted, yet lack the understanding of how to achieve satisfying relationships with others. Instead, they turn to materialism, status or power, because these are the values endorsed by our culture.

We now stand at a crossroads. The pursuit of 'rights' and 'enlightened self-interest' no longer seems up to the job of investing our lives with meaning and purpose. As Adrienne Rich's poem suggests, our obsession with the 'I' has become 'silly', and even 'terrible', in the face of the powerful changing circumstances with which we must inevitably deal. We may indeed be reaching some kind of saturation point which will reveal the limits of materialism.

Instead, we need a new ethic to take us into the future. I would suggest that we need the more collective values of empathy, care and thoughtful collaboration, if we are going to solve the problems that face us. But these qualities and values can't be willed into existence; they come about through lived experience – most of all through having experiences with other people of being cared for, empathised with and consulted. In particular, the roots of human moral behaviour are based in the emotional culture that is largely transmitted in early childhood. What does this mean in practice? How exactly do values get passed on?

# PART TWO

The Impact of Parenting

## 2. LEARNING HOW TO FEEL

If you plant two identical tomato seeds in two different environments, you will have two plants of strikingly different size and overall shape, but they will still be discernibly tomato plants. There is no longer any question that brain tissues create the potential for having certain types of experiences, but there is also no doubt that the experiences, especially early ones, can change the fine details of the brain forever.

*Jaak Panksepp, 1998*

We live in an age that is acutely concerned with 'parenting' and the values that we pass on to our children. How can it be that children in affluent societies should be depressed, suicidal, harming themselves, giving birth to babies at the age of thirteen or fourteen, or killing each other with knives? The liberal response is to blame society and to criticise the 'toxic childhoods' we now give our children; to focus on the evils of childhood poverty and the commercialisation of childhood. More illiberal commentators tend to blame the parents and concentrate their anxieties for children on their lack of parental 'discipline'. However, it is rare to hear anyone single out the impact of babyhood or early emotional development.

Although both camps assume that adults are failing to pass on moral values, this is almost always seen much more in terms of disciplinary issues than in terms of the quality of the child/adult relationship, let alone the early parent/infant bond. The liberal camp tends to focus on the difficulties that many parents have in raising children in an extremely consumerist society, where so many children are bewitched by the images they see on television or on the internet. Recognising that parents often cannot control the penetration of consumer culture into their children's lives, the liberal debate notes parents' confusion and helplessness: do parents have the right to interfere with their child's wishes to play the violent video games that everyone else is playing, or to watch the sexually charged clip on YouTube that everyone is talking about? In an individualistic society based on 'rights', parents are sometimes uncertain how to negotiate between the parent's 'rights' and the child's 'rights'. They may even believe that they are letting down their child if they don't provide the latest consumer item, since consumption seems to be of such great significance in the child's world, an integral part of fitting in.

On the other hand, some liberal critics have noted that there is a temptation for parents to use these modern media themselves, as a way to avoid more active parenting and engagement with their child. Diane Levin, parenting expert and professor of education, describes a typical scene in a restaurant where a child comes for a meal with four adults who look like her parents and grandparents. 'As soon as the child sat down, she started to fidget. Her father quickly whipped out a battery-operated DVD player, put it in front of her, and started a Disney movie. The child stopped fidgeting and became glued to the screen. Her father chuckled to the adult next to him, "That's the only way we'll get any peace!"'[1]

Another way of looking at this scene is to notice how parents have adapted to their culture by using its artefacts to create new ways of managing or regulating emotion. Instead of soothing the child with a game or a cuddle, or involving her in their conversation, they allow the child to be regulated by a story told by a machine. As Levin suggests, what is then missing from the child's experience is the warmth of inter-action with a living person, and the rewarding feeling of mutual relationship where each person has significance for the other.

When children are consistently offered products rather than relationship experiences, they are denied the opportunity to learn about people and, in particular, to recognise and value the needs and feelings of others. By the time that they enter the social arena by going to nursery school or school, such children often behave in ways that start to draw adult disap-proval. Their bad behaviour can then officially be recognised as a social problem. Teachers and officials arouse panic and anxiety when they describe the widespread evidence of poor socialisation in a growing number of very young children. This can make it very tempting to blame the parents.

The 'blame the parents' camp tends to target the parents' management of children's behaviour, and – like the liberal camp – ignores the experiences of infancy. When parents are criticised, it is often for their inadequate discipline regimes and for failing to exert sufficient authority to teach their chil-dren 'how to behave': from this perspective, the child in the restaurant should have been forced to comply with adult requirements. Parental loss of control is blamed on parents' ignorance, moral weakness or lack of responsibility – if only parents would behave appropriately too. But blaming and punishing people, whether parents or children, basically reproduces the problem; it doesn't attempt to understand why people behave the way they do. The same lack of reflective-ness characterises the blamers and the perpetrators.

The two camps come together in their shared support for trying to improve parenting 'skills'. Recent years have seen the rise of a burgeoning parenting education industry designed to help parents to understand their children's emotions better, as well as to manage their bad behaviour: parenting classes which teach parents how to talk to children about feelings, but also how to manage children using techniques such as putting them on the naughty step, or encouraging them into good behaviour with gold stars and treats. Of course, there is real value in giving parents strategies for coping with difficult behaviour, and more confidence in their own role as parents. Clearly, when parents start to act in a more parental fashion, protecting their children from over-stimulation, overseeing their children's choices, and enforcing consideration for others, children often feel safer and calmer.

However, the focus on 'good' or 'bad' behaviour is evi-dence of a culture that sees things primarily in terms of results, not of a thoughtful culture that attempts to understand the underlying process by which children come to behave in dif-ficult and anti-social ways. Most importantly, it is focused on the surface of things, the conscious accounts that children and parents have of their behaviour, and fails to recognise the much greater significance of what is unconscious and out of awareness. We need a deeper understanding of children – and of ourselves – one which goes beyond behaviourism to the underlying processes of emotional development, in particular very early development and how we treat babies.

## The baby maketh the man

But what, you might ask, does babyhood have to do with the selfish or unruly child who misbehaves in the restaurant or in primary school – let alone the greedy banker or brawling footballer? In fact, much of the behaviour that worries us in later childhood – such as aggression, hyperactivity, obesity or depression – has already been significantly shaped by these children's experiences in infancy. A whole range of unconscious assumptions, expectations and habits are put in place as early as the first year of life as the baby learns how he or she is expected to regulate and express feelings and to relate to other people. By the time adults are aware that a child has 'problem behaviour', the brain systems that regulate emotion have already been established and shaped by the infant's experiences with his parents. Yet until we understand how behaviour is driven by this early programming of the brain, and the way that we come to understand the social world during infancy, there is be a danger that we may continue to go round in circles, complaining about 'behaviour' and producing behaviourist responses to it.

I am not suggesting that our outward, observable behaviour is unimportant or superficial, only that defining it as 'acceptable' or 'unacceptable' is a very limited view of it. In some ways, such behaviour is more important than we think, because it conveys so much about our inner states. The psychologists and psychotherapists who make up the Boston Process of Change group – a group which uses the insights of child development to understand how psychological change occurs in adults – have helpfully made us much more aware of how it is in the nuances of interaction that relationships really happen and where meaning is created.[2] It's often the *way* things are done that expresses our relationship to the world, not just *what* we do. In particular, it's the way that our tone of voice, or sequence of facial expressions, body language, or the quality and timing of our speech convey rich layers of emotional meaning. This non-verbal level of relationship underlies all our more conscious, verbal communication. It is the foundation of how we interact with the world, and it starts in babyhood. If we want to understand how selfishness can be encouraged or discouraged by society, we will need to understand more about these developmental processes.

## How 'we' makes 'I'

A premature baby is the most vulnerable little scrap of humanity imaginable, hardly able to open his own eyes, yet such babies can show us that we are social animals from the very start of life, however tenuous that life might be. In a film about premature babies,[3] I watched a tiny newborn being held close to his father's bare chest. He was already taking part in a conversation with his father. As his father murmured to him soothingly, the baby responded in turn, squeaking in a fragile voice in the pauses after his father spoke. This touching image is now imprinted on my memory as an example of how every human being is born seeking an emotional connection, an attachment to a protective adult who will tune in to him and respond to him. Newborns not only show that they want to communicate by engaging in this basic dialogue of whimpers and coos and grunts, but are also programmed to search out faces. Watching a parent's facial expressions at close range, they will often copy them; it is perhaps most obvious when Mum sticks out her tongue and the baby imitates the gesture.

When they are separated from their protector, babies show their distress by crying. After all, their very existence depends on being loved and cherished. A landmark study conducted by Dr Rene Spitz in 1945, comparing the babies in two children's homes, showed how affection can be more critical to survival than food or shelter. In one orphanage, although they were kept clean and well fed, the babies had little or no emotional connection with their caregivers. The nurses were so obsessed with preventing the spread of germs that they hung sheets between the cots, making sure that the babies couldn't even see each other. Despite their good physical care, thirty-four out of ninety-one babies died before their second year. Yet when Spitz visited another institutional home based in a prison, where the convicted mothers were allowed to visit and cuddle their babies on a daily basis; he found that despite lower standards of hygiene, none of their babies died.[4]

Since babies can't survive on their own, from an infant's point of view the most effective survival technique is to stick close to the mother or dominant caregiving figure. Even though a new baby doesn't yet have sharp focus at a distance he can keep track of his caregiver's whereabouts, and can follow the shape of her hair and body. She is the centre of the baby's world, not only because she keeps him warm and fed, and protects him, but also because she helps him to understand and interpret the human social world around him, a crucial aspect of survival in human society. In fact, this is such a pressing need for us humans that learning about emotions and relatedness is one of the first tasks of early development. It's no accident that it's the right hemisphere of the brain which is most active in early infancy – this is the side of the brain which picks up non-verbal signals such as body posture, moods and facial expressions – the brain hemisphere which is most active in responding emotionally to other people, in bonding and in compassion for others.

## Early sense of self

Although we can see that babies are intensely focused on their caregivers in their early months, we have no way of knowing whether a baby has a sense of being a separate self from the start. We can only speculate about how it feels to be a very young baby. At first, without any personal memories or self-awareness as yet, the baby is likely to experience himself in many ways as an extension of the mother – his earliest sense of self is more likely to feel like a 'we' experience, a sense of 'me and mother', rather than a sense of being a separate organism. The baby is certainly not yet aware of himself as a centre of consciousness. He just reacts to what is around him, and lives very much in the present moment.

As a small human animal, he expresses his needs spontaneously. He cries loudly, seeks the breast and turns his head away when he has had enough. He acts out his emotions with his whole body and is easily overwhelmed by them. Although these behaviours seem to anticipate the possibility of a response, he isn't yet able to signal to his caregiver deliberately. He simply needs what he needs and expects those needs to be met in a magical way, beyond his comprehension. Probably

everyone can recall how it feels to be seriously unwell, that
state where you lie in bed with a fever, dimly aware of the distant sounds of activity or a radio playing in another room,
then a bowl of soup appears, you drink it and fall back into
a doze, without giving much thought to the effort of making
it, serving it or washing it up. Perhaps a baby experiences
something like this, assuming that his caregiver is just an
extension of himself; after all, he has no idea at this stage that
she could have a different state of mind or different needs
from himself. This is what makes some people think of babies
as rather egocentric.[5]

However, it wouldn't be fair to call him self-centred in the
sense of thinking he matters more than other people, since he
isn't yet aware that he is a separate self either. It takes time for
a baby to achieve that sort of awareness. First, he must build
up his own working knowledge of his bodily self and his
surroundings through his senses and create a mental map of
himself in his surroundings. He relies at first on the senses of
smell and touch to discriminate what is around him and
to guide him. Even newborn babies can distinguish their
mother's smell from that of other people and feel safest when
they are held in the arms of someone who smells familiar.

## Emotion evolves

Smells provide basic information about what is safe and
familiar, and what is not. The sense of smell is thought to be
the foundation of our mammalian emotional systems in the
brain. It is likely that our emotion systems evolved from an
olfactory bulb processing smells, which would alert us to
food, predators and potential mates or offspring. Evolution

then added on a slightly more complex detector, the amygdala, with which the olfactory bulb retains strong links. In fact, the amygdala can also detect smells – in particular, pheromones and other subliminal smells – but as it evolved, it amplified its social information-gathering by developing a more intense awareness of basic facial expressions, and learning to read their emotional messages, in a very fast, nonconscious way.

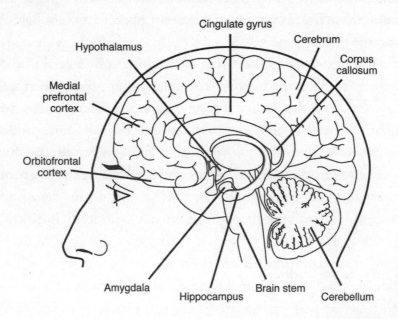

According to the neuroscientist Doug Watt, the reason why human emotions evolved from our more basic animal senses of smell and touch was to increase our ability to predict other people's reactions and thus make life more manageable. He suggests that one of the functions of emotional reactions is to 'supervise' our physiological self-management and to create 'routines' which are essentially a short cut to useful sequences of behaviour.[6] For example, when a 'fear routine' is triggered off, it helps us to run away from predators; when a 'bonding routine' goes into action, it invites nurture and protection. Many of these 'routines' or 'response packages' are still run by the more primitive parts of the brain, such as the amygdala and hypothalamus, which are responsible for the 'fight or flight' response.

This basic mammalian brain encodes experience in the form of neural pathways which are activated with more or less intensity. Many key areas of the brain, such as the amygdala, then respond to our perception of social events by triggering the release of biochemicals called neurotransmitters and hormones – biochemicals which the biochemist Candace Pert has referred to as the 'molecules of emotion'.[7] These molecules help cells to communicate with each other, and to transmit information through the brain down the neural pathways. This information can in turn activate the autonomic nervous system, affecting breathing, heart rate, sweating and so on, to help us to react appropriately to circumstances.

## Early regulation

During the first year or so of life this mammalian emotion system is still maturing, with the help of the baby's chief caregivers. Breastfeeding plays a vital, dual role in this development. Breast milk, with its essential fatty acids, nourishes the biochemical pathways of serotonin, dopamine and adrenaline early on (early stress and the stress hormone cortisol can damage them), while the act of breastfeeding also soothes the baby and turns off his stress system through the production of the hormone oxytocin. The instinctive cooing that proud parents do with their baby, or their devoted nightly pacing around to rock a baby back to sleep, also play an important part in keeping the baby's stress response stable during these early months.

During this period of intense dependency, the baby's ability to regulate himself or comfort himself is limited, so he is very vulnerable both to physiological and emotional stress. Even though very young babies are responsive to a range of people, they can feel anxious if left alone or with unsympathetic caregivers. If the baby doesn't feel safe, for whatever reason, it can feel as catastrophic as falling into oblivion; he may feel very uncertain about whether or not he will even survive. Then, once he has established who his familiar and safe caregivers are, within the first few months, it is the prolonged physical or mental separation from them which can be highly anxiety-provoking. Since the baby has no ongoing model of himself in his mind as yet, he may find it hard to feel he exists at all when an attachment figure isn't available and the 'we' sense of self goes missing.

Most adults are well aware that a baby can't change his own nappy or regulate his own basic bodily processes without help, but we are perhaps less clear about the fact that a baby can't soothe his own feelings or manage his own mind. Yet all of these basic regulatory processes are learned from others, from the way he is handled and the way his needs are met.

## Secure attachment

In a satisfactory attachment, the baby will be kept safe and protected from unmanageable distress. A responsive parent deals quickly with his physical or emotional discomfort, and gets him back to a comfortable state. As a result, his dependence on others will become a positive experience. The world will seem a benign place, in which other people are generally helpful and create pleasurable experiences with him – and so he will come to expect life to continue that way. His confidence in other people is mirrored by a confidence in himself, and the organisation of his brain reflects the good regulation he has received, since its systems function well and enable him to cope with stress. His biochemical stress response is less easily triggered, and he anticipates helpful support when needed.

The securely attached baby will also enjoy the social delights of being gently held and caressed, of being responded to, and of taking turns in imitating facial expressions and sounds – activities which are basically pleasurable, and are likely to generate the feel-good biochemicals. In particular, the hormone oxytocin may be the first bit of biochemical 'glue' to be applied, ensuring that the baby becomes attached to others. Oxytocin is released by pleasurable touch and positive social interaction, and helps us to feel relaxed and at peace. The developmental psychologist Seth Pollak has suggested that the baby who is well cared for actually gets hooked on oxytocin and will go on seeking out people to love him in the future so that he can reproduce these pleasurable feelings, whilst babies who are denied the pleasures of a loving embrace at the start of life may never acquire 'the addiction' to close relationships.[8] Currently, there are drug companies considering the possibility of manufacturing oxytocin sprays to enhance bonding. It has been found to increase trust between traders making investment deals.[9] However, it only enhances trust through face-to-face contact.[10]

## Emerging autonomy

When parents respond promptly to their baby he is, para-doxically, likely to become an independent self more quickly. This was something I learned from the childcare guru, psy-chologist Penelope Leach, when I first became a parent. She pointed out that when babies' needs are met promptly, instead of becoming 'spoiled' and demanding – as so many parents fear – they will be 'less work, less drudgery and less stress'. As she said in her unsurpassed guide to child-rearing, *Your Baby and Child*, 'your interests and his are identical': ignoring his needs only makes a baby more anxious and more difficult to comfort.[11] Although at the time I wasn't convinced that she was right, I tried out her approach (so different from the par-enting I had received) on my daughter and found it worked for us – and later, for my son.

When someone responds to his feelings, a baby is learning that those feelings are valid and have meaning. This is the beginning of a sense of self. But the baby is not only devel-oping confidence that his needs will be met, he is also discovering his own power and agency. When a baby realises he can bring his mother into the room with his cry, he begins to know that he has a will of his own and that he can make things happen. He can have an effect on other people – and be affected by them – and it feels good. In other words, he is discovering the pleasure of relationships.

This, however, is not every baby's experience. If a mother is depressed or withdrawn, her responses may fall short of what he needs. Even caring parents, following the current vogue for behaviour management of tiny babies through 'controlled crying', can give their babies a very different message: that their feelings don't matter and that they must subordinate their will to the more powerful people around them. Taught that comfort cannot be relied upon, and left to manage their distress alone, this can constitute an early but devastating life lesson.

## The pleasure of making things happen

The first sense of self, the 'core self' as the early relationship psychiatrist and psychotherapist Daniel Stern put it,[12] is the bodily self and its activity. The spontaneous baby loves it when he discovers – starting from about two months onwards – that he has the power to control his own movements. Babies get very excited when they realise that it's the movement of their own arm that makes the mobile spin round. Equally, some experiments have shown that babies can become frustrated and angry if their ability to control outcomes is taken away. In these early months, they are beginning to 'own' their own bodies and to discover what they can do. I have a vivid memory of my baby son lying on his back holding his own foot and examining it with rapt attention, then putting it in his mouth, as babies do at that age. All these activities build up an image of the baby's own body in the right parietal cortex, whilst the insula is also involved in awareness of causing an action, and tracks the bodily feeling of 'me' in social situations. As the baby becomes more able to manage organised sequences of behaviour, this sense of being an intentional agent increases.

Another crucial milestone is the discovery of the possibility of intentional communication. Whilst the baby's early communications were more reflexive, his piercing cries a survival mechanism, a way of ensuring that the social group doesn't forget to feed him, or leave him behind, he now begins to realise that communication can be deliberate. Sooner or later, if parents respond to their baby's distress with prompt soothing, the baby discovers that he doesn't need to scream loudly using all his body's energy to get a response; there are more pleasant and less exhausting ways of getting the parent's attention. He becomes aware that mother, father and siblings are purposefully signalling to each other with their voices and faces to change each other's behaviour, and that he can use eye contact himself to attract his caregiver's attention or to get help. Between about three and six months, he starts to understand that if he can give her the right sort of *look* or whimper, she will respond before the feelings get too strong and 'escalate into direct action'.

As he discovers how to signal with his face, the baby learns how to get control over his facial muscles, and uses them to smile or glare to signal his feelings – in much the same way as he learns to use his arm muscles to reach for what he wants. It would be hard to exaggerate the importance of this moment. It is such an important step towards entering the shared world of human culture, as the child starts the lifelong process of learning to communicate with other human beings through exchanging looks and glances and sounds. Many parents I have known show a palpable sense of relief when they feel that their baby is beginning to be able to choose to communicate with them; it can be a joyful transition, a feeling that now the real relationship begins. Instead of simply reacting in an intense, and often 'catastrophic', way, the baby's emotions have now been turned into interactive signals.[13] This is the beginning of a new aspect of agency – the social self.

Yet even so, this sense of agency is still dependent on the parent's willingness to respond. One rather unpleasant but important experiment carried out by the developmental psychologist Ed Tronick and his colleagues, based at Harvard Medical School, showed how babies as young as three months old have already come to rely on their mother's responsiveness to provide meaning and coherence to their lives. In this experiment, known as the 'still face' experiment,[14] the researchers instructed the parent to engage in a playful and smiley way with her baby for a few minutes, but then suddenly to freeze – and look at her baby with a totally blanked off facial expression for the next few minutes. Very quickly, the babies showed confusion and distress at this loss of contact and feedback from their mother, and tried frantically to get her to re-engage. For these young babies, only a few minutes of parental disengagement was highly disturbing. If this is most babies' reaction after only a few minutes, it's easy to imagine how difficult it is for babies of depressed mothers, who may get little response for protracted periods of time. The evidence suggests that eventually they become depressed too, and even end up avoiding face-to-face contact with other people, resorting to comforting themselves by touching their own bodies or sucking fingers.[15]

The danger is that babies in this situation will learn to withdraw from social engagement – or that they will not learn how to communicate their feelings with looks, but will continue to rely on direct action to convey how they feel. In other words, they become the children who grab things rather than ask for them, the teenagers who hit others rather than express their anger verbally. Lacking confidence in their ability to get their needs met co-operatively, they turn into those children and adults whose behaviour is labelled out of control, anti-social and destructive – not because they have not been 'disciplined' strictly enough, but because they have not learned to trust in the process of communication.

In the pre-verbal stage of life, tuning in to a baby's signals, as well as the baby tuning in to the caregiver, is a slow and mutual process which requires a deep immersion in each other's presence. This is not so easy to do on a part-time basis or when a succession of different caregivers are taking care of the child. The child development expert Stanley Greenspan and philosopher Stuart Shanker suggest: 'Many caregivers who do not spend sufficient time with their infants and toddlers in direct care may remain tense and anxious when their babies show strong affect'.[16] This can be a particular problem for fathers who are not with their babies all day. I have seen many fathers of small babies who are very tender and responsive when the baby is in a state of equilibrium, but who panic when the baby is gripped by a strong reaction which is hard to understand. One dad I worked with, called Rob, would become hostile to his crying baby and expressed a view that she 'ought' to take her bottle or 'ought' to stop crying once he had picked her up. He couldn't bear the uncertainty of not being able to read her signals and tried to blame her for it. This difficulty is also particularly likely to afflict parents of either gender who put their babies in daily day-care of various types. Simply through not being with their child for long enough periods of time, they can end up feeling less confident in being able to regulate and contain their baby's strong feelings – a difficulty that can translate into more insecure forms of attachment behaviour.

## Making sense of the world

Clearly, the more predictable, responsive parenting a baby gets early on, the easier it will be for him to organise his confusing new experiences of the world, and to start to make sense of them. This is a huge task, and the baby does it by gradually identifying chunks of experience, or 'schemata', which are a bit like a non-verbal vocabulary. By having a lot of repeated experiences – the same routine when a nappy is changed, the same bed or chair for breastfeeding, the same voice and face and way of doing things – he becomes more aware of the daily landmarks of his existence and can start to turn them into concepts.

In terms of social and emotional learning, faces are the major source of emotional information. They not only tell the baby about the parent's state of mind, they also give the baby the first feedback about who he is. The adult cannot help but resonate to the baby's body movements with her brain's 'mirror' neurons, which enable her to feel something of what the baby is feeling. For example, when the baby rubs his eyes, whimpering, she will instinctively know that he is tired and needs to sleep. Her own face might show a certain narrowing of the eyes, or a yawning mouth, or she might say in a slow voice, 'What a tired boy.' Or if the baby is crying in distress, her face may frown or look pained. The baby looking at these visual clues on her face, can see that he has had an effect on her. In turn, *his* mirror neurons resonate to her expressions and he has a new feeling in his body. These give him a slightly different version of his own feelings – a version which includes her view of his feelings. It is a mirror of a sort, although only a blurry, approximate sort of mirror which depends on how well the parent can 'read' the baby's states.

The feedback we get from other people, in this constant emotional interchange that goes on between everyone, is important to all of us as we try to negotiate social life. But for the baby, it's a new language and his first task in learning it is to realise when he is having a feeling and what that feeling means. This isn't something he can do on his own. It depends almost entirely on the adults around him teaching him the language of feelings.

Most parents are eager to get to know their baby and tend to attribute intentions to him from the start, long before his gestures have any symbolic meaning for the baby himself. 'He's going to be a footballer,' claims many a proud parent seeing her baby kicking vigorously. It's vital that parents do have a vision of the baby as a person, because his sense of self comes out of being seen by others as a self. However, what is most important is that his feelings should be recognised. For example, when parents notice the baby is physically tense and unsmiling, they might identify this state of mind as 'angry' or 'upset'. Their interpretations are essential in helping the baby to acquaint himself with his own states of mind.

It's the very act of directing the baby's attention to his own inner states which helps him to build a representation of himself and his feelings. According to the Hungarian developmental researcher Gyorgy Gergely's influential account of the construction of the social self, the way that parents first help babies to learn about their own emotional states is by 'marking' them out so that they are easy to identify.[17] The parent is a teacher, spelling out very slowly in an exaggerated way what is going on. As part of the process, parents arch their eyebrows or tilt their head or widen their eyes to indicate that this is about 'you' not me. Their body language conveys an exaggerated focus on the baby, and signals that the baby too should pay attention to himself at this moment. Gergely gives the example that a parent doesn't convey how to eat with a spoon just by eating with a spoon in front of her baby: she makes a dramatic production out it, flourishing the spoon, opening her mouth wide and raising her eyebrows. In other words, she gives a simplified and slowed down demonstration of the operation of 'eating with spoon'. The same teaching happens with emotions, using exaggerated facial movements to mark out the emotion and, in particular, to alert the baby to the fact that it is 'his', not the parent's, emotion. Thus cultural knowledge is transmitted, initially through gestures, and later through language.

When it comes to emotional learning, it is particularly crucial that the parent 'marks' emotional states in this way, because if they are unmarked – for example if the mother does not act in this parental and teacherly fashion, and simply responds to the baby's anger with her own anger, or to fear with her own fear – then the child's feelings are simply likely to escalate. The baby can then become overwhelmed and unregulated, and may have to resort to emergency measures to cope, such as dissociating from his own feelings altogether. 'Marking' makes it clear that the parent is aware of the baby's feelings, that they belong to the baby, and – most crucially – that the parent can tolerate them. They can not only be named and understood – but also regulated. Unfortunately, when parents have not had good care themselves as children, they may find it so hard to manage their own feelings that they are unable to 'contain' and regulate their baby's feelings.

They may not be able to help their baby to recognise his own feelings, and this can leave the baby in a state of arousal that he doesn't know how to manage or understand.

## Growing awareness of others

Whatever kind of parents they have, babies have no choice but to adapt to the parental figures they are given. Although a baby needs special help to manage himself and to become aware of himself as a 'self', he doesn't need the same kind of help to see that there is an 'other'. His awareness of the 'other' is already present in a growing database of non-verbal imagery based on his experiences with his mother or other attachment figures, stored largely in the right brain. Each baby needs to figure out what sort of caregiver he's got, what to expect from her, and how to keep her close – and to do so, must organise these images into a mental file.

The baby's repeated experiences with his parental figures builds up a sort of non-verbal vocabulary of feelings and images – what Bowlby described as 'Internal Working Models' – with their own particular associations based on the baby's unique social experiences. It's the patterns of interaction that are registered. For example, if the baby's anxiety is usually soothed by an adult, he might acquire an internal model that 'feeling anxious is followed by soothing'. If he is often on the receiving end of anger, he might build up an expectation of experiencing 'a disapproving face and a scared feeling inside', or the baby's own bodily feeling of joy might be remembered as a light feeling in his body together with a happy look on mum's face. In this way, emotions start to build up into a symbolic system.[18]

It takes a baby about five months to be able to identify other people's particular facial expressions and their emotions and to link these expressions with a matching tone of voice. For most babies, the first expression to be recognised is a happy face, but soon fear, anger and sadness can also be distinguished. These first basic emotions are interpreted at lightning quick speed by the amygdala from people's faces, body language and tone of voice. However, the amygdala soon starts to build up more complex forms of emotional meaning, storing whole 'emotional sentences' linked to sequences of behaviour. For example, it might make an association between the sight of a dog snapping at a child and a horrified face – and this can in turn become a personal cue which automatically triggers off conditioned emotional responses such as anxiety and fear whenever a dog comes into view.

Research shows that the amygdala is vulnerable during this early period. When its development is impaired in some way early on, the ability to recognise facial expressions can be affected, according to Michelle de Haan, of University College, London and her colleague Margriet Groen.[19] More specifically, Philip Shaw and his colleagues at King's College, London, discovered that it is very early damage which affects the ability to interpret emotional communications and read minds; later damage doesn't have this effect.[20] At the most extreme end of the scale, basic feeling responses can be impaired, as Adrian Raine's extensive research (now based at the University of Pennsylvania) has shown. His work with deliberately violent and sociopathic individuals has consistently demonstrated that they have poorly developed or dysfunctional amygdalas.[21]

By about ten months old, the baby can recognise a particular emotion as a whole distinct package of meaning. As the months go by, the baby adds layers of further associations and nuances of emotion to these first rough 'schematas'. For example, if he associates his mother with a relaxed breastfeed, and also associates her with a soothing baby massage, then his brain may register these links, enhancing his concept of 'mother' as someone who provides bodily pleasures. On the other hand, if his mother regularly walks away from the pram and leaves him to cry, and is also the person who feeds him at arm's length without cuddling in, then 'mother' will be associated with a painful feeling of distance and rejection. Or the links may be confusing and mixed. Although the baby develops a general idea of the role of 'mother' that will come to apply to all mothers, he will also have a more personal concept of mother richly imbued with his own emotions and associations. As he gathers more detailed and specific information about the world around him, the baby will be able to use it to guide his social behaviour in more and more complex ways.

## The social prefrontal brain develops

We might think of these emotional associations as our first form of thinking. From outside our awareness they guide us and help us to choose whether to approach an experience or to avoid it. To progress towards a more sophisticated participation in the human emotional and social world, the baby will need a wide vocabulary for such emotional nuances. And indeed, this is one function of the prefrontal cortex, which is the next evolutionary 'add-on' to the mammalian brain, and which has its most intense spurt of development in the period between six months and two years. This part of the brain acts as a sort of bridge between the reactive sub-cortical areas of the brain, such as the amygdala, and the more 'rational' and language-based areas of the brain, which are the last areas of the brain to develop fully.

These crucial prefrontal areas connect up when a baby has plenty of responsive early social contact. All those playful moments and active turn-taking social encounters generate good feelings and release the body's own natural opiates, which in turn trigger the release of a particular biochemical substance called dopamine which anticipates reward. As dopamine is released, it makes its way to the 'social' prefrontal brain, and activates other biochemical processes, all of which help to build connections in this area of the brain. In this sense, sensitive and responsive parenting plays a direct role in helping to build up connections in the social brain, which includes various early developing parts of the prefrontal cortex: the lower middle or 'ventromedial' part, including the orbitofrontal, as well as the nearby anterior cingulate.[22] These are also the areas of the brain that play the biggest part in moral cognition. Together, they create a sort of mental platform or overview in the brain from which the child can look at his own experiences. They represent the baby's growing sensitivity to his own experiences and emotions.

The ventromedial area stores our memories of our emotional responses to people and social situations. In more psychoanalytic terms, the ventromedial area of the brain has been described as an embodiment of 'the internalised mother' and the experiences we have had with her.[23] However, that presupposes that there has been enjoyable contact with the mother. When there is very little or no mothering bond at all, as in the orphanages documented by Spitz over half a century ago, or more recently in Romania, emotional learning can be severely affected, and connections in this area of the 'social brain' will be thin on the ground. In particular, the orbitofrontal region, which plays a key role in social behaviour, was seen as a 'black hole' in severely deprived orphans.[24]

The anterior cingulate has been described as a sort of 'warning system' which alerts us to problems in our social interactions. It is activated when our own bodily and emotional experiences come into focus. Its special role seems to be to sharpen awareness and to provide us with a running commentary on how social experiences *feel* – particularly when they are subjectively experienced as emotionally painful. This information helps us decide how to deal with social conflicts or mistakes and whether or not we should try to correct them. Early social deprivation may affect the development of this part of our brains too.

There is a basic alchemy at work in human relationships. The attention that parents give their baby is spun, not into gold, but into the baby's own capacity to pay attention to himself. Ultimately, all of this parental feedback and responsiveness will enlarge the baby's own self-awareness. This has a knock-on effect on the baby's relationships with others. The more aware he is of himself, the greater his capacity to become more aware of others' mental processes. On the other hand, the less self-aware he is, the more difficult he will find it to understand other people's experience or predict their intentions. Interestingly, the anterior cingulate is activated not only when we are aware of our own feelings, but also when we are thinking about other people's states of mind, showing how closely linked the two forms of awareness are.[25] This suggests that, in effect, *self*-awareness is the first building block of empathy and the moral feelings.

## Looking outwards

Our peculiarly developed social sense involves a constant interplay between self and other. There is always a dual process going on, looking inwards and identifying our own feelings, but also looking outwards and trying to understand others. Around the age of three to six months, the baby's own attempts to understand the world around him and to interpret the behaviour of his caregivers are boosted by improvements in his ability to see. Now the baby's vision has matured sufficiently to observe adults' body movements and behaviour more keenly, the wider scene starts to come into focus. Other people become more real.

Babies first learn to connect with other people's minds through their eyes. As he gazes into his mother's or father's eyes, the baby starts to recognise their feelings, and to build up his ability to read the body language of faces and movements. But the more aware he becomes of his mother's mental states, the more he begins to notice that she doesn't just revolve around him but also pays attention to other people and things. As he gradually develops more and more self-regulation, he becomes more able to tolerate this and to wait for attention.

Sometimes, when his gaze is locked on to his mother's, he starts to follow her gaze as she turns to something else, to see what she is looking at. Then the things around him, seen through her eyes, become more identifiable as distinct objects, including other people's distinctive faces. By about seven months, the baby can tell the difference between people, again using his ventromedial cortex.[26] But the more he is able to focus his attention on the particular things around him, the more he is also able to focus attention on himself as well. In this peculiar parallel process where self and other emerge together, the baby can also now start to recognise that he, too, can be an object for other people. This object is called 'me', which is, as the psychologist Kevin Ochsner has described it, a very particular sort of 'me', who recognises his own traits such as 'me boy' or 'me like chocolate', as well as being aware that he is a 'me' who has changing feelings like 'me angry' or 'me sad'.[27] Self-consciousness and 'other' consciousness develop together. Both are generated by the medial prefrontal cortex.

This greater awareness of self and other is also assisted by the expansion of the prefrontal cortex through the activation of its side areas – in particular the dorsolateral prefrontal cortex (again, assisted by dopamine). These areas develop more conscious layers of memory known as 'working memory'. With a growing store of memories, the baby can now begin to retrieve images of past events, and hold them in his mind for a few seconds, enabling him to compare past and present experience. This improved memory means that the most familiar people in his life start to exist in his mind even when they are not there and he can now consciously remember their particular characteristics, and how they are likely to behave. The baby can now move out of a more dreamlike sensory bodily state focused on the familiar smells and sounds and touch of his caregivers, towards attachment to specific individuals.

## Attachment patterns

In the second half of the first year, the baby begins to use his new powers of interpretation to adapt to his parents' way of doing things. He unconsciously works out how he can best influence his particular caregivers to meet his basic needs and how to get them to respond to him.

A lucky, secure baby has less adapting to do: he finds that his needs are met more or less promptly, and he does not have to strain to fit in with his parents; they are sensitive enough to his needs. However, if his parents are unhappy or distracted people preoccupied with other things, he may learn that he has to make more of an effort to get his needs attended to. One strategy is to keep crying loudly and often to remind them of his existence, even though he may resent them for it (the resistant attachment). Other children discover that crying makes their parent too angry or rough, so they learn to inhibit their cries and wait (the avoidant pattern). Worst of all, a baby with parents who are confusing and unpredictable, or frightening in some way, won't have a clue how to organise his behaviour to get the regulation and help he needs. He may swing between strategies, and never learn to regulate himself effectively (the disorganised pattern). These attachment strategies, a response to 'how things are done' or 'what works in this family' – ways of organising behaviour to make life more predictable – are well established as early as ten months old.

## Self-control

Whatever his particular experiences are, the baby gradually builds up his capacity to manage his own reactions in response to his caregivers and how they do things.

Using the neural pathways established by repeatedly having his emotional arousal managed by other people, by about eighteen months he will finally start to operate his own 'braking' and 'accelerating' responses to social situations. These are particularly based in the orbitofrontal part of the prefrontal cortex. Once he has got the hang of the 'braking' mechanism in particular, he can begin to control his own behaviour. This capacity gives him the benefit of a kind of 'pause button', as the American psychiatrist Daniel Siegel has called it, which gives him more time – even if only momentarily – to assess a social situation before acting.[28]

This very important human capacity to press a 'pause button', which makes it possible to reflect on one's own state or that of other people, is a central part of the socialising process. We need the orbitofrontal cortex to develop well, to moderate our impulsive, aggressive tendencies. A variety of personality disorders and impulsive anti-social behaviours are strongly associated with a reduced volume and activity of the orbitofrontal cortex.[29] In fact, there is a growing belief that some personality disorders, especially the borderline and narcissistic personality disorders, are rooted in a failure of care at this very early stage of development. Certainly, the behaviours that are associated with such diagnoses are strikingly similar to the responses of a young baby who has not had his early social needs met. For example, one common tendency for the borderline personality is a difficulty in managing emotional arousal and in controlling his own reactions; he often expects others to respond immediately to his needs, as a very young baby might. Lacking confidence in communicating his needs, or in his needs being met, he can be prone to 'act out' his strong feelings, for example slamming the phone down when he is upset, or shouting that he should be given what he wants; overwhelmed by the emotion of the moment, he has no 'pause button' to give him the chance to control his reactions. These are signs that something has gone wrong with his very early social learning and self-regulation. And indeed the 'borderline personality' condition, in particular, has been linked with having experienced abusive or inconsistent parenting.[30]

The orbitofrontal cortex develops in response to a particular form of attentive parenting that cannot be taken for granted. It is only highly involved, face-to-face parenting which helps to build up connections in these social areas of the prefrontal cortex, allowing us to regulate our social behaviour in a much more deliberate way than other mammals. Basically, the human social brain is the result of the human social process – in particular, the investment of parental time and attention in our offspring. Paying attention to a baby teaches him to pay the same kind of sensitive attention to himself and others, laying the groundwork for participation in a complicated social world.

## Emotional neglect

We are now beginning to recognise that more challenging early experiences leave scars, not only in the mind, but also in the brain itself. In particular, the physical abuse of children, with its obvious bruises and wounds, is taken very seriously in Western culture, and does indeed tend to create a brain which is less well developed in the limbic and social brain areas. The brain of a child who has had experiences of physical violence with his early caregivers often has a particular biochemical profile, with a tendency to low baseline cortisol and a flattened stress response. Children who have this profile are often those who are primed to interpret other people's faces and gestures as angry, and are also those who as adults strive for control and dominance in social situations.

It is less easy to identify emotional neglect or abuse, which is more common than physical abuse, but has equally damaging effects on the brain. Invariably in such cases, the mother has experienced early emotional deprivation of some kind herself – whether this is an early abandonment, adoption, rejection, humiliation or simply being ignored by her own mother. My client Millie was a typical example of emotional neglect. Her story was that when she was still a young baby, her mother had re-married; unfortunately, her new stepfather already had children and did not want Millie. Her mother was concerned about fitting in with her new family and lost interest in Millie. She failed to protect Millie, who ended up being scapegoated by the other children who treated her badly and left her feeling an outsider in her own home. Millie grew up with a great sense of inner deprivation and worthlessness. She became sexually active very young, still searching for the intense emotional connection she had lacked as an infant. While still a teenager, Millie became pregnant with an unplanned and unwanted baby. Although she considered having an abortion, she did not go through with it.

I met her after her baby Eva was born. In Eva's early months, Millie dutifully fed and washed and physically cared for her baby, as her mother had done for her – but she simply had no real maternal feelings for her. She could see her baby was lovely, but she said it was as if there was a 'glass wall' between herself and Eva. Millie described how empty she felt inside, and how little she had to give her baby. Without the social feedback and affirmation she had needed as a child from her mother, she was left with an undeveloped sense of herself, constantly searching for others who might help her to feel real. In our early sessions, she spent most of her time describing her attempts to find men to love her. Like her own mother, she was more preoccupied with potential partners than with her baby's emotional needs.

But what could Eva make of her situation? She became a very 'good' and compliant baby, trying not to make demands on a mother who clearly had so few emotional resources to offer. But having a mother who was emotionally so distant would, in time, make it very difficult for Eva herself to feel real, to have a sense of coherence and what the pioneering British paediatrician and psychoanalyst Donald Winnicott, writing in the 1950s, called 'going on being'.[31] Her sense of herself could be deeply affected, and indeed that appeared to be the case, as Eva, at the age of eight months, was already quite passive, not reaching out for toys, allowing Millie to take over her play whilst she looked warily or anxiously at her mother, yet smiling brightly when her mother expected her to smile. It seemed to me that she was on the way to becoming a 'false self' rather than someone deeply rooted in her own individual feelings and able to experience life fully and find meaning in it.

At this early stage, the effects of her mother's emotionally neglectful care on Eva were still largely invisible, but a large body of research indicates the lasting damage that a consistent experience of emotional deprivation – as well as more active forms of stress – can do to a baby's developing biological system during this critical period of growth. Early deprivations such as being separated from the attachment figure, being weaned early or being left alone too much, have all been shown to have major effects on the developing social brain. Stress can reduce the social bonding effect of oxytocin, and increase the stress hormone cortisol. These biochemical effects would be felt in Eva's emotion-processing systems such as her stress response itself, as well as in her other biochemical pathways. In turn, too much cortisol over a period of time can be toxic to the developing brain, particularly in key early developing areas of the emotional brain where there are many cortisol receptors[32], such as the amygdala, corpus callosum and cerebellar vermis. In these areas, cortisol can have an impact on the strength and speed of connections.[33] The biochemicals of stress can also affect other biochemical pathways such as the dopamine systems, which at this time are branching up into the prefrontal cortex, reaching their peak density at around seven to eight months old, helping to release glucose and to stimulate the growth of the prefrontal area.[34, 35] If Eva was unfortunate enough to experience these effects at the wrong time and to a relatively intense degree, they could potentially undermine the ability of her prefrontal cortex to manage stress and evaluate social situations accurately as an adult.

If Millie continued to relate to Eva in a distant and uninterested fashion, it would have further effects on Eva's developing brain. During the second half of the first year, as the prefrontal cortex becomes established, it can begin to make links with the quick-reacting amygdala and can even, importantly, modify its conditioned responses and re-appraise the triggers that set off fear or anxiety. The medial prefrontal cortex, in particular, can also suppress the activity of the stress response (also involving the amygdala). As these links strengthen, they help the child to regulate and tone down the emotions that are generated by the amygdala, and give her some capacity to calm herself. However, those connections are not made automatically. The neural pathways are based on having an *experience* of thoughtful, attentive and calming parenting. Without that experience, it would be difficult for Eva to make those connections, leaving her much less well equipped to handle her emotions in future.

Sadly, Eva's case is by no means unique. There are millions of children who grow up with poor abilities to regulate their emotions and a lack of understanding of how to get their emotional needs met successfully with other people. Collectively, when a particular society contains large numbers of people who are fearful of others like Eva, or aggressive like physically abused children, this can add up to a major cultural disaster. Such babies will bring their negative experiences of dependence on others into adulthood, in the form of their unconscious attitudes to the world, which will, in turn, affect their contribution to the culture.

## Emerging moral sense

As babies enter toddlerhood at the very end of the first year, and have more mobility and more control over their own behaviour, they acquire more responsibility for themselves. This is most obviously when a child starts to learn about 'right' and 'wrong', selfish and unselfish behaviour. But although it is true that morality is passed on from adult to child, this transfer of values takes place much more through the quality of the relationship rather than through conveying abstract principles. The young toddler is still running largely on the right hemisphere of his brain, dominated by his visceral feelings. He is very reliant on the adults around him to guide his behaviour, not by instruction so much as by their emotional responses: disapproving looks make him feel bad, approving looks feel good. Toddlers don't have much of an internal moral map as yet – they still need to look at adult faces to guide their own actions and check if the adult approves or disapproves of what they are about to do.

One of my favourite times when my children were very young was the toddler stage, and their enormous excitement as they took their first tottering steps across the room, looking to their parents for confirmation that they had achieved something spectacular: 'Look at me!' When a parent reflects back her own excitement and delight at such moments, this will generate pleasurable bodily sensations in the toddler too. Co-operation with parent figures is intrinsically rewarding. It stimulates the pleasurable internally generated opioids,[36] as well as triggering dopamine activation, which provides the child with the motivation and drive to continue the activity. Since there are a lot of dopamine receptors and opioid receptors in the orbitofrontal cortex, co-operation is also self-reinforcing as it is likely to activate and help to build the orbitofrontal cortex and future social skills.

However, social skills also depend on learning what is not acceptable. According to the American neuropsychoanalyst Allan Schore, the man who led the way in explaining the links between early experience and the brain, parental disapproval can also help to strengthen the neural pathways between the impulsive brain and the inhibitory orbitofrontal cortex, enabling the pause button to develop.[37] Both are necessary. We need to have confidence in approaching people and activities, but we also need to be able to avoid those experiences that are bad for us or for others by applying our internal 'brakes'.

Getting this right takes time. The toddler's ability to 'internalise' the parents' expectations and values, and to remember how they are likely to react, depends on brain pathways becoming established. In a relaxed situation, without too much stress, the prefrontal cortex will develop better, and with it increased memory capacity. This might take the form of an image of Dad's disapproving face popping into his mind as he reaches for the cat's tail – 'Oh no, Dad got upset when I did that before.' However, this depends on having internalised a picture, not only of Dad and his mental state, but also of an ongoing relationship between himself and Dad.

The human baby's moral and social development depends on ever expanding awareness and control of his body and emotions. In complex human societies, these capacities are so important that the whole of the baby's first year and beyond is taken up with learning how to identify emotions and regulate them with other people, and developing the beginnings of joint attention, self-awareness and self-control that underpin moral behaviour. However, this process takes time. A one-year-old still has a weakly developed orbitofrontal area and limited self-control. He doesn't yet feel responsible for his mistakes, perhaps because he does not yet have a strong sense of self or a clear understanding that he can cause things to happen. He remains impulsive, and has a limited awareness of how other people feel. Should we think of him as selfish?

# 3. THE SELFISH BABY

No child has ever been known since the earliest period
of the world, destitute of an evil disposition – however
sweet it appears.

*Theodore Dwight, 1834*

Using words such as 'selfish' or 'evil' seems an inappropriate
way to describe babies, who have not yet fully joined the
human social world of self and other. In my view, they
inhabit a 'land of beginnings', to use Ben Okri's phrase,[1] full
of many possibilities, ready to be part of life, whatever that
might turn out to be. In developmental terms, the baby is an
innately social, sensitive little creature who expects others to
meet his needs and in turn strives to adapt to their ways. But
he can't survive on his own, and is intimately bound to his
caregivers and dependent on their interpretation of the world.
As the psychoanalyst Donald Winnicott once famously put it,
'There is no such thing as a baby – only a baby and someone.'[2] That someone will pass on her attitudes to her baby,
but these in turn are heavily influenced by her own social
experiences and values. We might conclude that there is also
'no such thing' as a baby who is not part of a wider social

group which will pass on its own culture and unconscious beliefs.

In my consulting room – a room above a church, with thick walls and gothic windows looking over a car park, with a brightly coloured mat and boxes of toys – over many years, I have met a succession of young babies and their parents. There have been babies who looked wary or blank, passive, agitated or restless, babies who turned their heads away from eye contact with their parents, babies who gazed at them with adoration, babies who bawled fiercely and babies who made little contented sounds: sleepy or alert, relaxed or tense, sad or uncertain babies. It has never occurred to me that any of them was innately 'bad' – nor, for that matter, that their parents were.

At this early stage in life, it is hard to imagine what 'badness' or selfishness might look like. Of course, many parents are driven to the edge by a lack of sleep and come to resent their baby's needs and cries. They may not be able to understand why a baby needs to feed every two hours, or why he or she cannot sleep through the night. Their own distress can lead to a dislike of the baby, and even to thinking that other people have 'good' babies and they have a 'bad' one. The parents' difficulty in coping with a baby, practically or emotionally, can sometimes lead to blaming the baby rather than themselves or the way that the relationship is developing. Some parents feel very ill-equipped to respond to a baby's demands or have great difficulty in reading his signals, and their feeling of inadequacy can make them critical of their baby. One client of mine complained bitterly about her 'spoilt', 'whingey' toddler, Rowena, who followed her around and stuck to her 'like glue'. Distressingly, she said in front of her child that she 'couldn't wait to get rid of her' to day-care. This was a single mother who pushed her daughter away emotionally because she felt so unsure of herself, causing the child to respond by clinging on to her mother in desperation.

However, most parents are thrilled to have produced a baby, even if they have some ambivalent feelings about it. Through the ages, there seems to have been a universal delight in the arrival of a baby and in holding babies – much like, as anthropologist and historian Alan Macfarlane describes it, our pleasure in domestic pets.[3] From at least the sixteenth century onwards, they have been 'pretty things to play withal' or, in the nineteenth century, 'an object of general fondness', and enjoyed as mirrors of their parents. Two of the most talked about modern celebrities, Brad Pitt and Angelina Jolie, exemplified this attitude when describing their newborn twins in 2008. The actress told *Hello!* magazine that it was 'chaos', 'but we are managing it and having a wonderful time', whilst Pitt said that the babies were already showing traits of their parents: 'Viv is proving to resemble Ange in spirit, attitude and physicality . . . and Knox, he's a bit of me.'[4] In other words, most parents take a naturally narcissistic pleasure in their young babies, and instinctively want to cuddle them and play with them.

But when the resources are lacking to provide for a baby – either because the new baby is another mouth to feed in an already overly large family, or the baby was unexpected and unwanted, damaged in a traumatic birth, or because the parents simply can't find the inner emotional resources to care for their baby, due to the harshness and negativity they experienced in their own infancy[5] – the joy can be corroded by anxiety.[6] The baby may not be seen as a good thing, but as a potential problem. For example, one little boy I saw called Harry was probably what most adults would regard as a 'difficult' baby. His muscles were very tense so he was hard to hold, and he cried incredibly loudly and frequently, gobbled his feeds and then frequently sicked them up. However, it turned out that his frantic behaviour was at least in part a response to a mother who lacked confidence in her own body and her own instincts; she had difficulty believing that her pregnancy would survive, and after Harry's birth, she tried to cope with her anxieties about caring for him well enough by setting limits to his demands with rigid routines and depriving him of physical comfort. It turned out that she herself had been deprived of cuddles by a mother who 'didn't do physical affection' and had in turn seen her as 'difficult' as a baby.

Unfortunately, babies who are treated as if they are problems often become the thing their parents feared: those babies who are seen by their caregivers as 'difficult' or unlovable are likely to become more so. We live up to others' expectations. As teachers know, children fail at education if they are expected to fail. Even as adults, we are highly sensitive to others' expectations; if we are subliminally exposed to positive words like 'success' or 'achieve' we perform better – unconsciously primed to respond to these triggers. When I play tennis, my game is vulnerable to the influence of these triggers: if I make some bad shots, and my competitive opponent looks at me contemptuously, my confidence in the whole game is soon undermined. Some studies have found that even thinking about a particular person elicits the behaviour we associate with them: Marianne always talks about the news, so if I think about her in passing, I might be much more likely to pick up a newspaper.[7]

But parental attributions are the most powerful of all, and start even during pregnancy, making it crystal clear that these descriptions have little to do with the baby himself. Researchers have found that parental ideas of their unborn baby – whether positive or negative – tend to be consistently held after birth and into later infancy,[8] possibly even becoming self-fulfilling prophecies, whilst a parent's own attachment style – as revealed by tests during pregnancy – also tends to accurately predict her future, unborn baby's attachment style at one year old.[9] It is only too easy to project one's own expectations onto a baby – for example, if a parent fears that her unborn baby is going to demand too much of her, she is more likely to interpret his behaviour as 'greedy' when he eagerly sucks for milk. The baby may then come to believe that he is greedy and demanding and grow up easily shamed by his own needs.

While it may not be physical violence, attributing 'badness' or 'wickedness' to a small child is itself a 'hit' – the psychological equivalent of a body blow. It is an unreflective lashing out against something that threatens the parent or something the parent rejects rather than being the property of the baby himself – a defensive reaction, rather than an objective account of the baby. A child on the receiving end of these kinds of attribution has no way of organising his own sense of self. If parents say he is naughty or wicked, then he must be so. These harsh negative self images, accompanied by feelings of shame and self-hatred, then become the baby's own sense of 'reality', whilst his feelings of distress go unnamed and unregulated. This makes it difficult for the child to own his own feelings or to think about them. His ability to represent feelings may remain crude, polarised into basic categories of 'bad' or 'good': a dilemma characteristic of personality disordered individuals.

## Pain or pleasure?

The proportion of very young babies who are seen as 'selfish' today is probably relatively low. But in the past, when many babies were unwanted, and in large families might use up scarce resources and even threaten the survival of the existing children, there must have been many such 'bad' babies. The commonly accepted religious notion of 'original sin' only supported such beliefs, allowing parents to believe that they were morally justified in denigrating or punishing their children. The historian Lloyd de Mause's account of the history of child-rearing even goes so far as to suggest that most parents in the past were abusive; certainly, physical violence was ubiquitous up until comparatively recently, and it is likely that psychological violence was commonplace too.[10]

There are two routes to socialising a small child. One is to coerce him, and to compel him to act in the way you want through fear; the other is to build up a sufficiently warm bond between parent and child to motivate the child to make the adult's rules his own. Historically, the pain route has been preferred. This is hardly surprising if you consider our tendency to repeat our own experiences of parenting, particularly since parents' brains are also shaped by their early experiences with their own aggressive or neglectful parents. The wonder is not that humans have lost their capacity for empathy over the course of history, but that they ever managed to build it up at all.

## The medieval/toddler mentality

If we look back at our peasant ancestors, we can see how the subtle and precise communication of feelings is a cultural achievement as well as an individual one. Medieval culture was notable for a kind of psychologically primitive thinking, which modern psychoanalysts refer to as 'splitting': where complex social reality is crudely represented through polarisation into good and bad. In particular, the Church, which was the dominant form of culture as well as a major authority in medieval times, used such extreme ways of thinking to enforce its norms for good behaviour, threatening the populace with the prospect of dire punishments such as roasting in Hell if people failed to comply. The Church insisted that original sin was so deeply ingrained in human beings – as described in the story of Adam and Eve – that it could only be overcome through constant prayer and penance, and deference to religious authority.

In many ways, the medieval world view and the toddler world view had much in common. Like toddlers who also assume that their parents are infallible, and that the parental view of reality is 'true', peasant people often assumed that the authorities, particularly the Church, knew best, and accepted their harsh judgements. Young children assume that adults define what is real, and aren't yet aware that authority figures can hold 'false beliefs' and get things wrong. On the other hand, they sometimes assume that their own feelings are the only 'reality', often slipping from one polar extreme to the other. They cannot yet understand that actually there are a variety of points of view.

From about eighteen months to two years upwards, children tend to have an absolutist view of the world. However, they are starting to move on from a totally self-centred experience of reality, and are beginning to recognise that there are other perspectives. The first step in grasping how reality is defined by the social group is to notice that it has rules: some things are forbidden and some are allowed. Toddlers at this stage often interpret these rules in a very rigid way, seeing right and wrong as iron laws that cannot be broken. This is the age when toddlers often get upset when things are broken or messy or not how they 'should' be.

Peasant villagers in medieval Europe often reacted to rule-breaking in a similarly black-and-white fashion. They used coercive methods of ensuring compliance with expected behaviour against each other: they closely scrutinised each others' behaviour and often punished those who stepped out of line with physical violence or public humiliations, such as 'rough music', when they trooped round the village banging on saucepans and other random objects to draw attention to the wrongdoer. Punishment by shame was effective in a small community.

Pre-modern life could be brutal and was often violent. People drank alcohol every day to keep themselves warm and to dull their aches and pains. Men felt entitled to beat their wives. Parents also disciplined their children in much the same way. Force, rather than reason, was their instinctive response to unacceptable behaviour. As the moral psychologist Jonathan Haidt has pointed out, empathy for others was clearly not well developed in a society which used mutilation, torture and even disembowelling or burning alive to punish miscreants.[11]

Although children at a very early developmental level can show empathy at times, and can respond to others' distress, they often comfort others mainly to relieve their own discomfort with the feelings aroused in them by the other's distress. They don't yet have a strong generalised sense of compassion for others' weaknesses. In fact, the famous 'happy victimiser' literature[12] has shown that they don't yet feel too bad about hurting others, or breaking rules if it benefits them. Although young children are becoming aware of the social 'rules' – for example, that it's bad to steal – they don't yet *feel* bad about stealing a sweet from a friend, if they can get away with it. They feel pretty happy about getting what they want.

The psychologists William Arsenio and Anthony Lover explain this selfishness in terms of two things: the child's emotional experiences to date and the development of memory. They suggest that the young child is ruled by impulses, and taking what you want from someone else is responding to an impulse to grasp immediate pleasure. It doesn't involve thinking. Children this age are not unaware that having your sweet taken away from you will feel bad, but they don't yet mentally link their concern for the victim with their own satisfaction at getting the sweet. They can't yet integrate these two feelings nor can they yet curb their impulses for the sake of longer-term satisfactions, such as maintaining good relationships.

Arsenio and Lover suggest that the crucial developmental step of consideration for others really depends on building up a stock of accumulated goodwill within a relationship, and in particular on the child being able to hold a mental image of the relationship in mind, as something ongoing and valuable that he is aware he doesn't want to lose. They argue that this ability to prioritise longer-term moral values really depends on the consistent experience of strong emotional bonds with other people. It is likely that children who are insecurely attached will find it harder to develop consideration for others, since they will have worse relationships with their parents and their peers, and less investment in maintaining relationships that are unsatisfying. Although some insecure children will learn how to 'behave', their moral behaviour may not be deeply rooted in a sense of pleasurable emotional connection to others but remains an external sort of morality based on threats and fear.

In other words, the moral impulse to care about other people's needs and feelings is very dependent on having had your own needs and feelings cared about. Children need to experience warm, supportive relationships to develop *real* feeling and concern for others. When they don't experience such warmth, and in particular experience harsh punishment or lack of attention, they will have more tenuous connections to other people.

Harsh conditions of life can lead to more harsh and coercive relationships, particularly when the wider culture is punitive. And in the medieval past conditions were unimaginably harsh. Death was always just around the corner, and hunger was a regular occurrence. Physical and mental pain were part of everyday life. Living conditions were uncomfortable: 'This was a world of pedlars and local markets, of dirt tracks, wells, privies and fire or candlelight. Houses were damp, smelly and uncomfortable, sheltering animals alongside people.'[13] Perhaps this made a degree of insensitivity useful. People expressed themselves freely and robustly, without considering others' feelings overmuch. Even into the eighteenth century, many pursued their pleasures aggressively, catching them while they could: 'In social gatherings, people jested and capered, sang and shouted a lot; they threw themselves into the hurly-burly of fun-making, love-making, noise-making. They joined in rough sports, liked horse-play, and rode hard.'[14] This doesn't mean that they did not have affectionate relationships or strong bonds, simply that their style of relating was not particularly sensitive or empathic.

Our ancestors were at the mercy of forces beyond their control, like the weather and disease – they were the dependent children of an unpredictable universe. This feeling of helplessness led many to invest their love and trust principally in God rather than in people; other humans could not protect them from natural disasters, but they hoped that God would. But God as a symbolic father figure had two aspects: he was both a containing and soothing God who would give meaning to their suffering and a powerful, terrifying God who might punish them. With God as an almighty patriarch, ordinary people perhaps experienced themselves in a sibling type of relationship to one other: attached to each other, often playful and spontaneous with each other, but not particularly concerned with prizing, protecting or nurturing their fellow man in a society whose aim was basic survival, not progress.

Harsh conditions can also bring out the human potential for co-operation, however. According to the historian Robin Briggs, 'mutual aid was the norm', since 'the community was responsible for all its members, at least in theory; this was the principle on which the authorities tried to make vagrants return to their original parishes to be supported.'[15] In such a culture, dominated by the collective, individual feelings would have been relatively unimportant; it's unlikely that parents would have expressed great interest in their baby's personal development. Although babies enjoyed physical contact – for example, sharing a bed with others from infancy through most of their childhood – which would promote their sense of physical self, they were also often swaddled and hung on a peg to keep them safely out of the way, a practice which might have hindered their developing sense of agency.[16] There were emotional bonds, but they were not yet informed by an understanding of individual psychology.

In a small rural community, where the next generation was essential for survival, babies were chiefly valued as another pair of hands. Yet while they may not have had a great deal of one-on-one attention, and so perhaps lacked the emotional feedback which would furnish them with a fully developed sense of individuality as we might understand it, they were expected to derive a secure sense of self from fulfilling their allotted role in society, which was defined in advance by the class they were born into. Their role would provide them with a clear sense of who they were and how they were expected to behave.

## Collective cultures of child-rearing

The conditions of life in many undeveloped countries today are not so different. The economist Daniel Etounga-Manguelle describes the mindset of the majority of rural Africans today in similar terms. He says that they, too, manage their uncertainty about the future through their religious faith in nature and God. They take each day as it comes and have low expectations of themselves and others, living for their community and for the sociable experiences of dancing, singing, chatting and friend-ship, which take priority over working and earning money.

They are not concerned with bettering themselves and expect to remain in the place allocated to them by life. Power and responsibility is something you are born to, given by divine authority or magical powers, not something to which an individual might aspire. They, too, are rooted in their family and ancestry, and place little value on individualism. Etounga-Manguelle claims that 'African thought rejects any view of the individual as an autonomous and responsible being'.[17]

On the other hand, there is a collective sense of responsibility for babies and children. Child-rearing in African villages is tailored to the survival of the group. Babies are protected by being constantly carried and fed and responded to by their mother and one or two other women. They are never left alone or allowed to cry for long. In some communities, adults massage and oil babies' bodies, and encourage them to develop their muscle strength; they celebrate early motor competence, so that they can contribute to the family tasks as soon as possible. Beyond infancy, they are urged to participate and to take on chores, rather than being expected to play, like Western children. They pick up skills by observation and practice.

According to Etounga-Manguelle, the needs of the group come first. Although infancy is a protected time of development, ensuring a balanced stress response and a strong immune system, once the weaning stage is past many peasant communities, whether in Africa, the Middle East, or elsewhere, provide much less attention. At this stage, toddlers are expected to become part of the wider group of children and often to be looked after by older children.[18] This is likely to provide less optimal conditions for the development of those qualities of individual self-awareness, self-control and the capacity for long-term thinking which are emerging at this period of early childhood.

At the same time, some communities are physically punitive to children at this stage of development. This ensures that children learn to recognise the power structure. Children are generally expected to be obedient to their elders and are told stories of ghosts and witches (or the Evil Eye) to frighten them into compliance. They are taught to share what they have with each other and are rarely praised in case they become selfish. Individualism isn't particularly useful in a peasant village, since there is little chance for individual strivings to succeed in improving living conditions or to promote longer-term economic development.

Identity is very much group-based. As Christina Zarowsky has argued in her study of the experience of trauma in Ethiopia,[19] attacks against individuals tend to be seen less in terms of personal trauma than as an insult to the collective. She describes how she witnessed a casual shooting on the street. It was mid-morning and a young foreigner, a Somali man, had stolen some of the popular and addictive drug *khat* from some local Ethiopians, and had been punished with the loss of his life. Most of the Somalis whom she was with reacted to this as a political incident – they saw the severity of the punishment as an attempt to make their whole group feel afraid and silenced. Only one man showed sympathetic feelings of distress, saying he 'wanted to throw up' because he had heard the young man calling for his mother before he died. For most, personal feelings were minimised.

## Babies adapt

A baby born into this or any other culture has to negotiate the social niche in which he or she finds himself or herself, and

respond to it appropriately, tailoring his or her behaviour as
precisely as possible to his or her particular social group. A
baby born in a small-scale collective society might develop a
strong sense of physical self, practical skills and confidence in
the group's ability to support him. However, he may receive
less of the specific attention which promotes self-awareness
and verbal learning, meaning these will be less developed.

In our very different Western culture, there is more deliberate face-to-face interaction and emphasis on verbalising,
with encouragement to explore the environment and play
with toys at prescribed 'playtimes'. In the USA, individuality
and personal achievement are particularly prized. Children are
encouraged to think highly of themselves and to win 'smiley
faces, stickers, and gift-box rewards for every achievement,
however small'.[20] Relationships are primarily evaluated in
terms of how they meet one's personal needs, not in terms of
the needs of the social collective. There is a positive, 'can do'
mentality and an expectation that each individual will pursue
success and be a 'winner'. But where there are winners there
are also, inevitably, losers and in such an aggressively competitive society, it is taken for granted that this will cause
tensions and conflicts in interpersonal relationships.

In the West, independence, as a quality, is promoted virtually from birth. In the UK and the USA, babies are rarely
breastfed for long, are often walked around in outward-facing
buggies for hours without social feedback, are frequently
allowed to cry alone for some time as a way of teaching them
to settle to sleep without help, or are left on their own in cots
for long periods of time. These practices promote the ability to
manage painful feelings alone. In fact, in these countries there
is a terror of 'spoiling' babies by giving them too much

attention, and an almost religious commitment to babies sleeping alone. The task of separating from the baby at night is seen
as an urgent one, to re-establish the parents' individuality and
intimacy with a partner. As Meredith Small put it, 'The cultural
pressure to make the baby sleep alone is so strong in America
that even when parents do sleep with their babies, they are
reluctant to admit it, as if they were committing a crime.'[21]

From the perspective of more interdependent cultures, this
is close to abuse. The psychologist Barbara Rogoff reports that
Mayan parents responded 'with shock, disapproval, and pity'
on hearing that many middle-class US babies and toddlers are
put to sleep in a separate room. 'One mother asked, "But
there's someone else with them there, isn't there?" When told
that they are sometimes alone in the room, she gasped.
Another responded with shock and disbelief, asked whether
the babies do not mind, and said that it would be very painful
for her to have to do that.'[22] From an African perspective also,
such behaviour is unnatural, as is the Western approach to
comforting their babies. West African Nso women studied by
Heidi Keller and her colleagues were shown tapes of German
women looking after their babies. They thought it very
strange that the German mothers didn't comfort their crying
babies by breastfeeding them, and they commented, 'They
handle them as if they were not their babies, as if it belongs
to somebody else or as if they are a babysitter.'[23]

Japanese culture provides an unusual example of a collective
society in a highly organised, industrial context. In Japan, there
is a heavy emphasis on physical closeness between mothers and
babies. 'Babies are seen as being fundamentally good and co-
operative and a gift to their parents', according to anthropologist
Heather Montgomery.[24] But their early child-rearing is not

designed to promote individuality. It is focused on avoiding negative feelings and conflicts and on promoting conformity to group norms. For the Japanese the 'dominant goals of the self are to be like others' and do what is expected by the group. Children in schools are encouraged to practice *hansei* – self-reflection and self-criticism – at the end of each day, thinking about their shortcomings, 'so that they can look for ways to improve those in order to meet the group's standards'[25] and to preserve social harmony and peace.

Clearly, different cultures regulate emotion differently – 'each culture provides specific opportunities for emotion experiences' as the social psychologists Batja Mesquita and Dustin Albert put it.[26] All these different practices set the baby up either to think of himself as an individual who must look out for himself, or as a member of a group who shares and depends on others. Each baby starts to absorb these cultural expectations in his first few months, through the childcare he receives. Within a year or two he will already be an American child, or a Chinese child, or an African child.

At the same time, he will internalise a particular *version* of that culture, mediated through his own family's interpretation of it. Each baby rapidly learns how things are done in his or her particular family and culture – from the tone of voice people use, to the kind of food they like to eat, the noise they tolerate, the way they touch and smell. In modern society, some homes are quiet and anxious and supply bland food and surround themselves with neutral colours; others have the TV blaring out all day and smell spicy. A baby quickly 'sees' how things are and how people manage their feelings and he stores this information in his right brain, in an unconscious, image-based format.

However, what is most important of all is the emotional atmosphere of the baby's world. A baby who finds himself in a stressful home with unpredictable or punitive caregivers will develop differently from a baby who finds himself in a calm and supportive environment. Babies in harsh families who witness hitting and shouting are receiving powerful messages about their family's values, not only through their memories of such behaviour, but also because their nervous systems will become primed to respond in particular ways. Equally, 'civilised' modern families who leave their babies alone at night, are conveying messages about *their* family culture, such as the importance of their parents' intimate relationship, or the importance of becoming independent. In either case, babies are learning whether or not their needs will be responded to, and what they can expect from other people. A basic view of the social world as hostile or benign begins to form, which will affect the way they think of themselves and the way that they treat others.

## The stress of poverty

Babies join an established society, and a particular social group. However, in social groups or families that are struggling to survive with insufficient mental or financial resources, the baby's experience may be very different from those in families that feel well supported. Whilst social policy in the West has come to acknowledge the negative effect of material deprivation on children's development, and has promoted attempts to end child poverty, there is often a relative lack of awareness of the *emotional* impact of impoverishment on a child.

Aside from the priorities of securing adequate food and shelter, of meeting basic needs, poverty brings immense stress and damages people's chances of enjoying their lives and their relationships. An example is a client of mine, Pamela, who lived in a flat above a couple who were violent and abusive to each other; their screams, curses and blows could be heard through the thin ceiling. The couple downstairs were often aggressive to Pamela when she went to take out her rubbish, and routinely quarrelled with her about where the bins should be situated. Pamela had a baby and a toddler who were regularly woken in the night by the commotion downstairs. They were all tired and frightened. However, they had no resources to move to another flat, and their landlord, the local council, refused to take their complaints seriously and offer them another home. As a single parent on benefit, my client's poverty meant that she simply had to endure this situation. There was no way she could get the response she needed from either her landlords or her neighbours; in a sense, these relationships had failed. But without the power of money, she had no means to provide substitute care for herself and her family. Her autonomy was reduced by her lack of money.

Such powerlessness to get your needs met is highly stressful. But Pam's distress also seriously damaged her relationship with her babies, and her ability to respond to their needs. She was sometimes too depressed to respond to them, whilst at other times she would lose control and shout at them. When finally Pamela was offered a new home, after more than a year of stress, the change in her relationships was palpable. She slowly started to relax again. She and her children slept through the night. She ate better. She became less irritable

and more affectionate to her children. However, some harm
had already been done since the children remained wary of
their mother and uncertain of their security.

The effects of high levels of stress on babies ripple out into
society. When babies have a bad experience of depending on
others, it can leave a lasting cultural impact as it sets them up
to become adults who are fearful of others, or who anticipate
anger, or who strive for control and dominance in social situations. In other words, the baby's early experience of
dependence determines his unconscious attitudes to the
world, which will in turn affect his contribution to the culture. Neglected children may become withdrawn, depressed
adults with unfulfilled potential.

Children who are physically abused, in particular, are more
sensitive to anger. Although they are so familiar with intense
anger that they don't react as strongly to it as other children
do, they have much greater difficulty in recovering from an
outburst of anger. Even when it is over, they remain tense and
aroused and find it hard to relax and trust again; they are
primed for further threats, anticipating further danger and
ready to go on the attack.[27]

In these respects, we are little different from other social
animals with whom we share a basic mammalian brain structure designed to serve our social interactions. Jane Goodall,
who has spent her life observing chimpanzees in Gombe,
found that most of the chimpanzee communities she studied
were peaceful and cooperative, with 'frequent expressions of
caring, helping, compassion, altruism, and most definitely a
form of love'.[28] They were highly affectionate in a physical
way, and also sought physical contact when they were excited
or afraid, using grooming to calm each other down. She

noted that affectionate, tolerant and supportive mothering 'was likely to lead to self-reliance and independence in adulthood, while a disturbed early life might well result in an insecure adult'.

However, when social conditions are unpredictable, and food is hard to come by, the quality of mothering can deteriorate. Leonard Rosenblum's research on bonnet macaque monkeys has demonstrated that in these conditions, monkey mothers became more rejecting, and their infants more emotionally disturbed, more fearful and less able to learn and explore their environment.[29] Human parents are also affected by difficult circumstances. Public health researchers Sarah Stewart-Brown and Andrea Waylen recently studied longitudinal data on 8,000 children collected over a period of years in Bristol; they, too, found that when parents' financial circumstances and social supports got worse, their parenting got worse. Yet even when conditions got better, the effects of stressful experiences remained. The surprise finding of their research was that although the family finances had improved, their parenting hadn't.[30]

Jane Goodall tells a similar, painful story about one of her chimpanzees. Passion was a harsh mother, less caring and less playful than other mothers. When one of her daughters grew up, after a somewhat miserable childhood, these two mean and unhappy chimpanzees joined forces to viciously attack another chimp and her baby – a 'fun-loving', delightful mother called Gilka. Gilka seemed to represent the loving experience that Passion and her daughter had not had. Although there was no longer a food shortage, Passion and her daughter attacked and ate three of Gilka's infant chimps over a three-year period. They seemed to need an outlet for their anti-social feelings and Gilka, who had been disfigured and crippled by polio and so could not defend herself or her babies, was an easy target.

## Unmanageable distress

When an individual can't cope well with stress, and in particular can't manage feelings of envy and resentment, he can make use of the basic early defence mechanisms which psychoanalysts have called 'splitting' and 'projection'.

Splitting is a way of dealing with contradictory feelings. It can be a useful defence which helps us to set aside the things that are bothering us so we are not incapacitated. On a day-to-day level, it helps us to prioritise. We may be worried about a friend's hospital test tomorrow, but we have to set those feelings aside whilst we attend to the urgent letter we have to write, or go to enjoy the party of another friend. The 'higher' prefrontal brain may be able to override the 'lower' brain's anxiety. But this is a technique which can be used to extremes, as a way of denying feelings and pushing them out of awareness. In medieval times, the Church encouraged people to overlook the harshness of reality to focus on the rewards of the afterlife. At its worst, it can become a complete switching off from feelings known as dissociation. In response to trauma, in particular, there may be a 'freezing' response, and an inability to activate the higher brain, or a difficulty in integrating the different sides of the brain.

Alternatively we may use 'projection' to split feelings off by attributing them to other people. Like the mothers who label their children 'clingy', or 'difficult', this is a way of getting rid of painful feelings that we are unable to tolerate or don't want to own. We all use it to some extent to anaesthetise our own discomfort and deaden or reject an experience that is hard to manage. It may be an early form of defence that works by narrowing the brain's focus, switching from right brain to left brain or failing to integrate the two. However it works at the level of the brain, in practice it disowns the qualities of experience that are unmanageable and pins them onto other people. Other people then are no longer seen clearly for who they really are, as individuals, but only as human symbols of the reviled (or longed-for) qualities.

The urge to hit children is often driven by the urge to get rid of overwhelming feelings of humiliation or helplessness. When a small child shows her up by crying loudly in the supermarket, or repeatedly misbehaves in the kitchen when the mother is trying to make the dinner and juggling three other things besides, the impulse to discharge her own anger can seem unstoppable. At these moments, parents sometimes just want their child to feel as helpless and humiliated as they do. When the parent's own self-regulation collapses, it can become impossible to hold on to empathy for the child's experience.

Entire communities can make use of projection. Despite their protectiveness towards young babies, some African communities, such as one in Nigeria recently filmed for a television programme called *Saving Africa's Witch Children*,[31] can resort to extremely punitive behaviour towards children. When stressful events happen, such as an unexpected bereavement or terrible weather and bad harvests, the community may deal with it psychologically by projecting its distress onto one of the children in the community, calling him or her a 'witch'. The thinking seems to be that if something bad happens, someone must be blamed. Because they find it hard to tolerate their own helplessness, they turn it into anger. The village then freely vents its resentment and fury onto the scapegoat – in this case the children – burning them, beating them or excluding them from the village to purge the community of its own anxieties. This is redolent of medieval communities, who took similar 'retribution', usually targeting women who were vulnerable or disliked.

All these strategies are unconscious and primitive methods of managing unpleasant feelings. But parents also frequently pass on their own past distressing experiences in relationships to their small children by re-enacting them. This is how insecure patterns of attachment are recreated down the generations. For example, Darren had regularly been humiliated by his critical mother, who would roll her eyes whenever he got something wrong, as if he was quite pathetic and inadequate. Decades later, when Darren grew up and had a baby of his own, he played with his ten-month-old baby son in my consulting room. As baby Dean reached out for a toy animal on a string, Darren pulled it out of reach and laughed at him. Then he held it out to his baby, but just as Dean's hand was about to clasp it, he dropped it and laughed meanly at him again: 'Oops! You dropped it!' Dean was left feeling helpless and clumsy. The humiliation that Darren had experienced as a baby was now being passed on to Dean quite unconsciously. Like his father, Dean would store the whole experience in *his* unconscious memory systems. Outside his conscious awareness, he would have an internal model, not only of his own experience of being a victim, but also of his father's demonstration of how to feel more powerful by attacking others.

Forms of emotional regulation and attitudes to other people are passed on through such small events, particularly when they are repeated over time. The danger is that when parents fail to understand or tolerate their own negative feelings of distress, anxiety, anger and humiliation, they are much more likely to pass on such feelings to their children. Babies are then blamed for the feelings they evoke from parents' own infancy. Far from being original, 'sin' might turn out to be the recycled miseries of one generation being passed on to the next.

# 4. THE SELFISHNESS OF CAPITALISM

I have never seen a class . . . so incurably debased by
selfishness

*Friedrich Engels, 1845*

Sin has long been associated with eating the apple of knowledge and awareness, leaving humans suddenly self-conscious
and ashamed. Yet I find this ironic: in my view 'sin' has much
more to do with *lack* of awareness. When parents ignore their
young child's distress and leave him alone in a locked room so
that they can go out for a drink, when a small community
turns on its vulnerable members to vent its own anxieties, or
when a child grabs a toy from another child, the primary failure is surely their lack of sensitivity to the other's feelings.
Active, planned acts of cruelty are relatively rare.

Selfishness is often a symptom of a failure of human connection. We are much more likely to be aware of other people
and their feelings when there are close bonds between us. It
may seem to be stating the obvious, but when these bonds are
weak, people treat each other less well. Parents who have not
built up a sympathetic relationship with their child are more
likely to resort to threats and beatings, because they are at a

loss to know how else to get co-operation from him or how to motivate him to respond to their wishes. When they too feel uncertain about the attachment, they may also be less motivated to inhibit their own reactions. A similar process is at work when we deal with strangers – we often give less consideration to people who are not part of our own familiar social group. The common factor in most maltreatment is more likely to be a lack of thought and concern for others' feelings, which is influenced by the perpetrator's own developmental history and the state of his or her 'social brain'.

## The rise of the social brain

The social brain – a brain that develops, through the right kind of care in infancy, the social and emotional skills that make a person sensitive to others – is not just the responsibility of individual parents, however. Whole cultures, as well as families, can assist or undermine the development of a more empathic social brain. For while we might have the genetic make-up for, say, altruism, the brain is responsive to the circumstances it finds itself in, and most genes are expressed only when the environment requires them. The pioneering twentieth-century historian and sociologist Norbert Elias was the first to identify 'the civilising process'[1] as a historical process starting in the Middle Ages. In his view, there had been a gradual increase in self-control and more inhibited behaviour in Europe over a long period of time. Elias related this to changes in the way that societies are governed – arguing that self-restraint went with more stable, centralised power systems – first taking root in court society, then spreading to the general population as the bureaucratic state was established in Europe.[2]

Following on from this, it seems to me that modern neu-roscience gives us the opportunity to think about the ways in which the brain itself has been affected by the 'civilising process' over the last 500-odd years, and how the emotional skills and interpersonal sensitivity that depend on high levels of connection within the social brain have gradually become more developed as particular cultures have come to require these capacities. This has happened, not through some grand linear narrative of 'progress', but in a more uneven and patchy way as people responded to the demands placed upon them by their social situation. As societies became more focused and organised, so too did individual brains. I visualise it as a grad-ual pooling of increased awareness in particular small groupings of people, pools which eventually join up and form a river.

The spread of self-awareness is, I believe, key to the devel-opment of both individuals and societies. For hundreds of years, the unchanging nature of the feudal way of life meant there was little requirement for the more intense relatedness that develops the social brain. Peasant everyday life was hierarchical and socially stable and (apart from natural events like the weather or disease) relatively predictable, so there was little need for most people to have complex interpersonal skills, or to use conscious thought and planning – the higher executive aspects of the brain – to any great degree. In our shared medieval past, people's relationships were organised by the framework of Christian teachings, which helped to give a sense of meaning to what were mostly short and difficult lives. Christian ideas encouraged people to be stoical and dutiful, and to accept their lot in life – their social position, marriage partner, physical pain or emotional loss – without question, as God's will. Awareness of one's own feelings was not necessary.

What mattered was the survival of the whole social system, not individual personal fulfilment. Resignation to one's fate was more valuable than autonomy, especially self-regarding forms of autonomy such as ambition, money-making, and social mobility, all of which were seen as suspect and undesirable.[3, 4] Striving to be good, on the other hand, was encouraged because unselfishness and responsibility towards others sustained the social group – the rewards for the individual were not in this life but in the next.

The medieval brain was in some respects like that of a very young child who lives for the moment and who has not yet developed great self-control. Everyone knows how difficult it is for toddlers to resist distractions and sustain their attention – they wriggle in their seats and can't resist responding to the sights and sounds around them. We get better at self-control as the frontal cortex develops. It's as if the frontal area is a beam, a searchlight, which develops increased power as it focuses our experience and sustains our awareness at a higher, more conscious level. However, it takes a lot of energy to run the prefrontal cortex; more basic, unconscious habits run on the basal ganglia and don't use as much fuel. This energy can be generated by pleasurable, responsive relationships, which release the pleasurable natural opioids in the brain. In turn, these help to release glucose in the very same prefrontal areas which play a major role in focusing attention, suppressing unwanted thoughts, and prioritising tasks (the orbitofrontal cortex but also in its neighbour, the anterior cingulate).[5]

As history unfolded, social relationships changed. Human groups became larger and more complex in most regions of the world. Historians debate the precise timing of such events, but it is safe to say that by the fifteenth century, larger social networks were spreading. In these more complex social groups, new demands were made on the brain to manage a wider range of social experiences. Whilst in a small, feudal village, 'one could more or less tell from someone's social position, previous life, connections and temperament, how he would act', according to the historian Agnes Heller,[6] in towns and cities you could not possibly predict how people would behave. Strangers could deceive others to gain an advantage. They could even pretend to be someone they were not, a possibility that furnished Shakespeare with many of his plots, as Heller has noted. Shakespeare's Richard III described how people could be misled by facial expressions: 'Why, I can smile, and murder whiles I smile, And cry "Content!" to that which grieves my heart, And whet my cheeks with artificial tears, And frame my face to all occasions.'[7] In such conditions, humans needed to become more alert, potentially generating more of the biochemicals norepinephrine, for alertness, and dopamine, for mental drive. They needed to become more mentally flexible, encouraging a greater use of areas within the 'social' brain, such as the anterior cingulate, which is active when we deal with changing expectations or anticipating problems. People in more socially complex situations were likely to have developed the prefrontal area of the brain to support the greater self-control and planning they needed to achieve their goals in a more competitive environment.

## Early individualism and the discovery of agency

In individuals, the areas of the brain that support these more conscious thinking processes start to mature in late toddler-hood. In particular, conscious thinking is served by a region of the prefrontal cortex called the dorsolateral prefrontal cortex, which continues to develop through childhood. This brain area corresponds most closely to the Freudian sense of 'ego' – or 'I' (as opposed to the earlier sense of 'me' based in the medial prefrontal cortex).

As society emerged from the Middle Ages, the more individualistic 'I' became evident in various social strata. There was a greater sense of being able to make things happen, and individual talent and creativity were increasingly expressed by doing things and making things, a process which was so exhilarating that some Renaissance thinkers started to think that man 'possesses as it were almost the same genius as the Author of the heavens'.[8] Like the excited toddler who discovers with joy that he can move across the room under his own steam, this was a period when human society itself took a qualitative step forward as it developed a growing mastery over the natural world and exploration of the planet. Instead of experiencing themselves as an almost organic, unconscious part of a hierarchical whole determined by unseen, higher powers, people began to become more conscious of themselves and their own powers.

The traditional way of being was challenged by an eruption of creativity and self-awareness which spread through Europe between the sixteenth and eighteenth centuries. The historian Robin Briggs has described these changes as a 'profound shift in consciousness',[9] when increasing numbers of individuals made their own choices about how to live their lives – no longer automatically following in the well-worn grooves of their allotted role in society, but, to some extent, making their own luck in life. As Machiavelli had said, 'I think it may be true that fortune is the ruler of half our actions, but that she allows the other half or thereabouts to be governed by us.'[10] There was a sense of people waking up from their long medieval sleep, and starting to think for themselves. Craftsmen, farmers, merchants and others were discovering that by devoting more time and attention to their work they could develop their talents more fully.

The capacity to pay attention seems to be crucial to all forms of development, whether on an individual level or in terms of social innovation and improvement. It underpins thinking and problem solving. In this period, thinking became more valued. Adult literacy started to increase. It was aided by several important technological developments which triggered off a chain of events which changed human history. For example, the technology which led to the production of paper and the technique of printing made the Bible directly available to more people at this time, and in turn opened up the possibility that more people could learn to think for themselves without relying on priestly authorities. By the seventeeth century, Descartes and other Enlightenment philosophers were arguing that thought was the most precious human capacity, the one which made us different from animals. In particular, he believed that it was our self-awareness which distinguished us: 'Animals do not see as we do when we are aware that we see, but only as we do when our mind is elsewhere.'[11]

The increased awareness and attentiveness of this early modern period had practical consequences too. When farmers started to pay more attention to their own activities, they started to think about how to manage their land better. They began to experiment with new techniques such as fen drainage, crop rotation and the use of fertilisers to increase their crop yields. Ironically, given our sentimental vision of pastoral England, the huge changes which led to industrial capitalism probably began in the English countryside, with the discovery by farmers that they too could make things happen and could 'improve' the productivity of their land. As the Canadian political scientist Ellen Meiksins Wood has argued, this led to a major new phase in economic development, as those farmers who used their imagination and intelligence to find ways to make their land more productive were then able to pay higher rents to the landowner. Suddenly, there was competition for farm tenancies; and for the first time some less competent farmers found that they could no longer afford their leases and were squeezed out of farming altogether.[12]

These changes triggered off a process of thinking about the value of land differently. When landowners realised that improved land was worth more, they started to buy and sell land more frequently, and to enclose common lands – which ultimately pushed many people off the land and into the cities, looking for work. The static, unchanging, unconscious nature of peasant life was shaken by the cumulative changes brought about by increased consciousness and agency.

## The transition to capitalism – two examples

This human development on a mass scale was not one of smooth and unbroken progress towards the growth of a more socially advanced brain. The possibility of taking initiative and actively making things happen rather than passively submitting to fate was often done without much social awareness – without consideration for other people or a sense of duty to the social group. As an urban way of life increasingly became the norm, the tight control exerted by the parish church and the vigilance of neighbours over individual morality was loosened, and more selfish behaviour could result.

One example of this is given in Christopher Friedrichs' study of the weavers in a small town in Germany in the seventeenth century, and how the behaviour of one family, the Wörners, provides a glimpse of how the collective, village mentality gradually gave way to a competitive, individualist one.[13] Nordlingen, in Bavaria, was – and is – a picture postcard idyll of gingerbread houses with red roofs and white walls. Friedrichs tells the story of one of its inhabitants, Daniel Wörner, a determined and pushy textile merchant who ruthlessly pursued his own financial advantage to obtain a monopoly of the weaving trade in his area. Wörner used shady business practices such as not paying his taxes, passing off sub-standard, thinner yarns as the real thing, and charging unreasonably high interest on loans to other poorer weavers. This made it impossible for the more ethically behaved weavers to compete with him and make a profit. But Wörner was unconcerned about the effect on other weavers' livelihoods. On the contrary, he was unashamedly aggressive towards them in a very personal fashion. Various council documents reveal many complaints against the Wörner family, including allegations that they beat people up and made insulting remarks about the wool-weavers. The fact that people felt able to complain suggests that they did not regard this as normal or acceptable behaviour.

During this period, the town councillors – who were predominantly merchants themselves, but also included apothecaries, professionals, administrators, and publicans, with seats on the council also reserved for craftsmen – still saw it as their job to safeguard the quality of the local goods, support the small weavers and protect them from the thuggish Wörners. As Friedrichs put it, 'The medieval urban ideology, favoring communal and group needs over individual success, still dominated the thinking of Nordlingen's magistrates.' In 1698, the council even demonstrated their hostility to the ruthless capitalism that the Wörner family represented by insisting that the Wörners pay the weavers compensation.

However, in the century that followed, the attitudes of the council changed. Friedrichs tracked the Wörner family through various historical documents and discovered that by the early eighteenth century, the Wörners had become bankers – their principle activity had become lending money – making large capital loans to their fellow citizens. Soon, their ambitions turned to politics. David Wörner secured a place on the council by virtually bribing the council with a large donation, with the result that the Wörner family remained 'prominent in the public life of Nordlingen for the remainder of the eighteenth century'. The town council was gradually taken over by other rich men, and the seats reserved for craftsmen disappeared. The Wörners' success had been achieved by re-defining the relationships within their community, riding roughshod over others' needs or the needs of the community as a whole, unconcerned for their reputation or for any social bonds. The town magistrates, meanwhile, no longer saw themselves as protectors and regulators of all citizens in the community – they had instead become 'the agents of capitalist entrepreneurs'.

## The conscientious capitalist

The story of the Wörners reveals the power of money and force to overpower collective morality. The council was not a sufficiently solid social institution to withstand the economic pressures that the Wörners came to exemplify. The Wörners' bad behaviour, originally reviled, came to dominate and change the culture of their town. But the Wörners' smash and grab approach, while indicating a new social direction, was not necessarily the norm.

An alternative early capitalist narrative is provided by the example of Joseph Ryder, another cloth merchant, operating in the early eighteenth century. Ryder was different from the Wörners in being rooted in a tight-knit religious community of Protestant Nonconformists, a group of people who highly valued rationality and would have demanded high standards of social behaviour. Thoughtful and self-disciplined, Ryder built up his business by cultivating his relationship with the most competent weavers and supervising them closely, travelling on horseback to collect spun woollen yarn from their cottages dotted across the Yorkshire countryside.

Far from the Wörners' gloating delight in their power and shameless lack of concern for the opinion of God or man, Ryder's business success caused him much agonising over the clash of values between his religious sensibility and the entrepreneurial spirit needed for his work. In his diary, which he kept for over thirty years, Ryder acknowledged that it was the possibility of making a profit that was his 'greatest motive to industry', but on the other hand, he was terrified that becoming rich would provoke God's anger. Ryder was worried that he might become selfish and care too much about money, and be accused of 'covetous hoarding' or 'sinful greed'.[14]

He also had a sense of social responsibility. Although Ryder doesn't write very much in his diary about his relationship with his workforce, he does from time to time express concerns about their well-being and talks about helping the 'deserving' poor – those who couldn't help themselves, not those who were lazy and poorly organised.[15]

What do the stories of the Wörners and Joseph Ryder tell us about the development of the social brain? Ryder's diary was typical of a growing self-consciousness and introspection, often rooted in religious strivings, which became evident in this period as better education made people more interested in their own individuality. Even so, Ryder's diaries reveal little of any other aspects of his emotional life. Social historian Carol Stearns has suggested that at this time, diary writers were more likely to complain about their physical symptoms in their diaries than to talk about their emotions.[16] For example, they might notice and describe their own angry behaviour, but would not necessarily call it anger – they did not yet have that self-awareness.

## Modifying aggression

Although levels of brutality in the past would undoubtedly shock us today, it is striking that the Wörners' unprovoked aggression was in fact unacceptable in seventeenth-century Nordlingen. Yet, if you extend the toddler/medieval brain parallel, research has shown that even toddlers, who are not fully socialised, demonstrate pro-social acts far more frequently than aggressive ones.[17] The same is also true of our primate cousins, who spend far more time co-operating than fighting. According to the primatologists Paul Garber and

Robert Sussman, primates spend about 5–10 per cent of their time on affiliative social interactions, and only 1 per cent on aggressive interactions.[18] Interestingly, however, it appears that the larger the group becomes, the more difficult it is to manage. When primate groups get overloaded with too many members, aggression increases. In human society, the growth of cities and the increased competition for resources presumably put new stresses on our sociability.

The capacity for aggression is certainly part of our repertoire, an essential weapon in self-defence. However, although all very young children can react aggressively or with tantrums at times when they are frustrated, or afraid, we become concerned if it is their default behaviour. That starts to look like a failure of socialisation. Modern research confirms this common sense assumption that when children are particularly anti-social, they are likely to have poorly regulated parents. Those toddlers who are most likely to remain highly aggressive at the end of the third year are those whose parents have not enabled them to develop good self-regulation early on.[19] This could be because the mother is emotionally unavailable during the first year for some reason such as depression, or simply because the parent has not been able to model the behaviours of patience, self-distraction and self-control for the toddler to copy and build into his neural pathways. Good self-regulation, sharing and co-operating – rather than coercing and 'winning' – have to be learned by example and experience, and enforced by the social group. The Wörners had clearly not learned about sharing; they were notable for their unscrupulous and selfish behaviour. Friedrich's study, charting the Wörners across generations, shows their family culture to be an aggressive one, in which there was little example or incentive to inhibit their impulses.

Ryder's success, in contrast, came from establishing good relationships with his workforce, and from his own self-control: in other words, from his well-socialised brain.

## The new morality

This was a period when morality was in the melting pot. Although in the past it had always been taken for granted, from the Christian perspective, that virtue and morality consisted of putting the common good before personal interests, this ideal was challenged by the emergence of competitive individualism. Social values were no longer as clear as they had been in feudal times dominated by the Church. Both the Wörners and Ryder reorganised society in their way. The unsocialised Wörners' individualistic power grab disturbed the social order and made it increasingly difficult to sustain a collective, co-operative mentality. They no longer acted as if they depended on the community for anything – they had sufficient wealth and power to go it alone. Ryder's attitudes were in many ways typical of the new Protestant 'work ethic', which revered hard work – in stark contrast to the peasant tendency to work only as much as was necessary to live.

Diligent and conscientious men like Ryder, networking through their professional bodies, became the backbone of the new middle classes, gradually building up sufficient trust in each other for national and international trading, and ultimately empire building. This new social grouping eventually became the dominant force in society, shifted political power away from the landed aristocracy and organised society differently – with new legal and political norms built around individuals and their own productive work.

## Parenting for capitalism

As this more self-disciplined work ethic spread, it required the kind of developed social brain which would be assisted by new, more attentive forms of child-rearing. This is indeed what started to happen in the late seventeenth century as the emerging middle classes became increasingly interested in their children's education and development. According to Lloyd de Mause, the first child-rearing manuals had in fact appeared in the sixteenth century, marking a shift towards more conscious way of bringing up children.[20] But even if the existence of these early manuals spoke of a new willingness to think about what children needed to develop in the right way, their focus was on how to punish children to achieve their obedience. Now, inspired by the philosopher John Locke's theories of parental responsibility, the educated classes of the eighteenth century started to move away from parenting based on ideas of ineradicable original sin ('Break their wills that you may save their souls' as the preacher John Wesley advocated) towards a more optimistic belief that children could be taught moral virtues by their parents, in particular the virtue of deferred gratification. Locke hoped that children could be persuaded of the benefits of long-term satisfactions compared to immediate pleasures, since 'the Principle of all Vertue and Excellency lies in a power of denying ourselves the satisfaction of our own Desires, where Reason does not authorise them'. He also proposed using rational arguments to convince children of his moral viewpoint, rather than hitting them: 'I would have children very seldom beaten . . . a gentle persuasion and reasoning will most times do much better.'[21]

This argument has not yet been conclusively won even in the twenty-first century. It has proved a long drawn-out battle for parents to accept that they should follow Locke's advice, perhaps because it is difficult advice for those who have not fully mastered their own emotions. I believe hitting a child is often a sign of parental loss of control, a reaction which doesn't require any thought. In fact, it is a way of stopping the child's thoughts as well as actions, as I can testify from my own experience of being on the receiving end of physical punishment; my battle of wills with my father did not increase our understanding of each other. The goal of corporal punishment is for the child simply to obey, and for the child's behaviour to fall in line with the parent's wishes – not for the child to understand the parent's point of view. The entire transaction is stuck at the behavioural level, triggering powerful sub-cortical emotions of rage, resentment and fear – the activated amygdala – without involving a process of reflection.

Locke's approach, on the other hand, was based on the desire for the child to understand *why* he should obey the parent. It demonstrated a very new recognition that the child had a mind of his own, with his own thoughts and feelings. If you wished to influence the child with your own thinking, you would need to engage with his mind rather than hit him. Persuasion and discussion were beginning to be seen as the key to make a child become more aware of others' thoughts and feelings, no doubt engaging the prefrontal brain capacities rather than relying on 'acting out' feelings. Clearly, the more sophisticated and self-aware culture that was emerging required a much greater investment of time and attention in parenting than an impatient slap.

This process was assisted by a growing interest in personal feelings from the eighteenth century onwards, as the middle classes expanded. Unlike Ryder, whose diaries were stimulated by religious anxieties, personal diaries, along with the new art form of the novel, began to explore a wider range of individual experience. Those who had the leisure to notice their own feelings began to celebrate their sensitivity to the natural world and to their children. In certain sections of the middle classes, this became a vogue for 'sensibility'. As the French philosopher Jean-Jacques Rousseau passionately asserted, 'to exist is to feel'.[22] The Romantic movement, in which Rousseau played a central role, spawned poets, loose clothing and bohemian lifestyles. One of its successful campaigns was to stop upper-class mothers from using wet nurses and to encourage them to breastfeed their own children. Rousseau believed this would bring about a return of 'natural feeling' and 'a reform in morals'.[23]

Increasingly, middle-class writers and philosophers glamorised motherhood and dwelt on the tenderness of mothers and their empathy with their children. In some cases, this tendency went further than others. In some families, often the more wealthy and self-confident, parents could be positively indulgent to their children, adoring them and gratifying their every whim, as they did their own. Yet although freely expressing emotions, they perhaps spent little time reflecting on them. This could lead to inconsistency and spoiling.

The Edgeworths, a father and daughter who had written a book on child-rearing in 1798, urged a more balanced attitude towards children – neither over-indulgent nor punitive, an attitude that they called 'rational tenderness' because it allowed for sensitivity to a child's feelings whilst maintaining

a belief in reason.[24] Mary Wollstonecraft, a heroine of mine
and author of *Vindication of the Rights of Women*, had similar
concerns. She argued that mothers should not rely on the
'feelings of the moment', but should use their 'independence
of mind' to consider what was best for a child. Like others at
this time, Wollstonecraft recognised that early childhood
experiences were formative, but – a hundred years before
Freud – she described this not just as a disciplinary question,
but as a deeper shaping of the sense of self. She expressed her
view that the unconscious 'associations' of childhood had a
'determinate' effect on character which could 'seldom be dis-
entangled by reason' later on in adulthood.[25]

## Individualism and materialism

These different views of parenting mirrored the tensions
within society as a whole: the conflict between the increasing
power of individuals in the rising middle classes and more collective needs of the populace. By the eighteenth century,
people were poised between a collective mentality and an individualist one, and the question of public good versus individual
freedom was the big unresolved debate of the age. John Locke
was in the vanguard of the new individualism. He himself was
one of the first to take issue with a Nanny State which
assumed a shared collective morality. Locke did not want the
local state to shape his moral or religious choices, particularly
as the civic authorities were likely to be more ignorant than he
was. As an educated man, he did not want to have to submit
to a collective power which might be used to enforce communal priorities or religious views with which he disagreed.
In other words, he didn't trust the state. Instead, Locke argued

that the function of society, or government, should be limited to guaranteeing basic security and the protection of individual property, not to promote any sort of social goals.

This was not the only argument current during the phase of early capitalism that is echoed in our current debates. As it started to generate more wealth for the middle classes, questions were also raised about the validity of pursuing unlimited material goals. There were vocal critics of materialism from the mid-eighteenth century. The popular playwright and essayist John Brown, for example, conceded that commerce had succeeded in providing more people with the 'Necessities' of life, and had increased cultural production – from the arts to the sciences – but he worried that a more luxurious lifestyle could weaken moral fibre. He thought that it could lead to a preoccupation with the comforts of life, and 'a kind of regulated selfishness, which tends at once to the increase and preservation of Property', with a corresponding decline in the social virtues and public service.[26]

## The appeals of capitalism

Materialism, however, proved unstoppable. As the mechanisation of production took off, the entrepreneurs of the later eighteenth and early nineteenth centuries were able to supply more and more of the 'effeminate' pleasures, as John Brown called them, of carpets and crockery, linen and lace, sugar and tea to the general population. And slowly, as more people enjoyed them, possessions also came to represent status and express identity – in other words, to provide psychological benefits, as well as physical ones – for everyone, not just the very rich. As material prosperity became more widely available, it must have seemed to our ancestors that there might now be a real chance of an enjoyable life in the here and now. The satisfactions of being 'good' to gain rewards in the hereafter now had to compete with increased physical contentment in this lifetime.

But to get these material goodies, people had to work. They had to stop being idle – hanging around chatting, and taking many days off, as had been their practice – and work in a more consistent, disciplined fashion. This was a Faustian bargain, since work itself, particularly in the factories, was punishing: toiling at a monotonous task for long hours and poor pay. In practice, it also meant giving up the pleasures of sociable work and a varied pace of life. Some made these choices out of necessity, to survive, whilst others pursued the satisfaction of 'bettering' themselves materially and having furniture and decent food. And when people were focused on the practical goal of improving their living conditions, the loss of intangible benefits, such as everyday camaraderie or pleasing God, were easy to overlook.

## Selfish employers

Few employers had any idea of what they were asking of people, either. Many seemed to have a blind spot about their workers' lives. I have always wondered how the early factory owners could justify their exploitation of the poor who flooded into the cities to work in their factories. Part of the answer was supplied by the political scientist C. B. McPherson, who pointed out that these wage labourers were already of a very low status.[27] Most people in the countryside worked their own bit of land and provided for themselves with

a variety of activities; they saw wage labour as a rather humiliating last resort. Full-time wage labourers were regarded as
dependents, more like children than fully-fledged adults; even
the progressive Levellers didn't think they should have the vote.
But it was these agricultural labourers and farm servants who
were the first to work for a wage in the factories. Their factory employers respected them as little as the country folk had.
To the employers, they were just 'hands', not respectable artisans or family men. They felt comfortable about hiring these
least powerful members of society at a below subsistence
price – an attitude similar to the later colonialists, or even to
the current chief executives who have few qualms about using
cut-price labour in the Philippines or Bombay to make their
products cheaply (and of course we are happy to buy them
cheaply, too). After all, they should be glad to have work – at
any wage – goes the familiar argument then and now. All share
an assumption that those who are least powerful are also less
human.

In the relative anonymity of an urban setting, or at a distance across the globe, it is much easier to exploit other
people without conscience. Their humanity becomes relatively invisible and abstract. In early industrial capitalism, there
was a sense that an employee was already a degraded person,
so most employers did not concern themselves with his loss
of personal initiative and autonomy. Nor were they concerned
about the impact of the factory regime on his family life or on
the development of his very young children. To these
employers, the worker was simply someone who fulfilled a
function, not a fully realised person who might need support
when he was sick, rest when he was tired, education or stimulation to engage his mind.

## Factory conditions

The conditions of life for those drawn into the factory system were desperate; they had few choices and little possibility of caring adequately for their children, who were often drafted into the factories alongside them. There was not even the luxury of caring for their babies, who were mostly left with older children or frequently dosed with narcotics, such as laudanum, so the mother could go to the factory. It is heart-breaking to imagine the impact on their emotional and brain development. Children themselves were put to work from the age of seven or earlier, working a back-breaking twelve-hour day, which damaged their physical development as well as their mental development, to the point where girls started to marry as early as fifteen years old so that they could have chil-dren before their bodies were worn out by factory labour. As Karl Marx said in 1848: 'The bourgeois claptrap about the family and education, about the hallowed correlation of parent and child, becomes all the more disgusting, the more, by the action of modern industry, all family ties are torn asun-der and their children transformed into simple articles of commerce and instruments of labour.'[28] Society polarised: working-class family life was utterly smashed, whilst the middle class began to luxuriate in family life – or, at least, aspired to an idealised version of it.

Where once the feudal landlord might have regarded his tenants as under his care, the employer was absolved of respon-sibility. The employer/employee relationship was reduced to a contract which the job-seeker signed; the fact that the contract paid the worker so little that he had to live in an overcrowded, filthy house with barely enough to eat, and with little time for a relationship with his family, was not the employer's concern. He did not live alongside his workers in the squalid areas of town, and as factories got bigger, he would have had little face-to-face contact with his employees. The new social relations were impersonal, not personal. This was represented as 'progress' – being part of a great new 'political economy' that would produce more goods that everyone could enjoy.

The belief that every employer was responsible only for his own immediate profit and loss, and not for the social costs of his activities, was a manoeuvre which provided a great incentive to entrepreneurial action and profiteering, but which split off the damage to the social fabric, beyond conscious awareness. The same attitude survives in modern economic thinking, which has defined the environmental and social costs of production as 'externalities', extrinsic to the process and not the employer's responsibility. Once this attitude was established, it became the norm: other people trying to make a living in a competitive market had to adopt it too, or trade at a disadvantage. A new morality spread as the whole culture became infected by these values.

## Country versus city

Through the early phases of capitalism, most people in fact continued to live in the countryside, where almost everyone was part of a working group of some kind – whether family, village, guild or feudal estate – and was linked together by social bonds of various kinds. Although people lived in a hier-archical and unequal society, it was taken to be the natural order of things and there were often cordial relations between people of different social status. People still responded emotionally to each other and in many ways acted like a large extended family, which could tolerate and support all members of the community even when they were disliked or regarded as inferior. These social bonds might be tested or broken, but equally frequently, they would be repaired. For country folk, prosperity was still taken to include 'not only material comfort but good health, good temper, wisdom, usefulness, and the satisfaction of knowing you had earned the good opinion of others'.[29]

Meanwhile in the city, for the first time in human history, wage labourers had become lone individuals cut off from any stable community, neither boosted by its support nor dependent on its good opinion. Although this paved the way for greater autonomy, individualism and self-definition, it also made people more vulnerable. The price of becoming a freestanding human being with a mind of your own, rather than a functional part of a whole, was that there was no longer any safety net, no community and no care from other people that could be relied on. Traditional moral notions such as a sense of duty to others, of the strong protecting the weak, and of an imperative to prevent harm or pain being caused to others (except as deliberate punishment) likewise went off the map. Economic life became a sphere divorced from relationships, feelings, and morality.

### *Homo economicus*? **The emotional basis of morality**

The capitalist enterprise came to be defined as an impersonal force beyond human relationships. Its template for human beings was '*Homo economicus*', a cool, calculating man whose main goal in life was his own economic well-being. In this economic scheme of things, the heart of morality – understanding that other people's needs and claims are valid even if they contradict our own interests – no longer held any weight; others' claims were irrelevant and nothing mattered except profit. Rationality, objectivity and self-control were guiding principles, and emotions were devalued.

Whilst moral philosophers from Kant to Piaget to Kohlberg have believed that moral judgements are made using reasoning and reflection, recent developments in science have challenged these assumptions. The new evidence suggests that we make our moral judgements much more intuitively, with reasoning following on behind to justify our choices.[30] As the leading cognitive neuroscientist Jorge Moll puts it, 'Recent theoretical developments in moral psychology, which had been dominated by rationalistic theories for centuries, have emphasised the role of emotion in models of moral development and behaviour.'[31]

A much-used example of a moral dilemma is the 'Trolley' scenario. A railway trolley is hurtling towards five men working on the tracks and will soon crush them; but if you flick a switch, you will divert the trolley on to another track where there is only one workman. Most people choose to flick the switch and justify it logically, in terms of the good of the greatest number, an objective and somewhat abstract moral choice. Brain scans are now able to reveal that when we make decisions like this, we use the dorsolateral prefrontal cortex and inferior parietal areas of the brain, which develop slightly later in toddlerhood and early childhood than the more emotional areas of the brain, and which govern 'cool' thinking and working memory.

However, if you re-frame the dilemma, so that you are standing on the footbridge above the tracks, and the only way of stopping the trolley from killing five people is to push the very large man in front of you on to the tracks, very different parts of the brain are activated. Although the moral logic is the same, one person to save five, most people cannot bring themselves to resolve the problem in the same way. They find it hard to choose to kill another living person with whom they have a direct and personal relationship because he is physically present next to them on the footbridge. This sort of dilemma, the neuroscientists found, activates quite different areas of the brain – the more emotional areas of the brain, in particular the posterior cingulate cortex and medial pre-frontal cortex, as well as the amygdala and superior temporal sulcus. Killing someone when you can see their eyes, their expression, when you might resonate with their feelings, can't be done. It *feels* all wrong.[32]

So it seems that there are different sorts of moral judgements. Some do involve logic and 'cool' thinking: do we support euthanasia? What are the arguments for and against capital punishment? Is sex before marriage acceptable? And so on. These calculations – which include figuring out advantage or disadvantage to ourselves in the abstract – are made by the more conscious part of the brain. As a later developing brain tool, the function of the dorsolateral prefrontal cortex is to override the earlier, unconscious intuitive programming when it isn't able to deal with a situation. It can interrupt the automatic processes in order to enable new choices to be made. Relatively speaking, it's a very clunky, slow process.

In contrast, the emotional and intuitive areas act very rapidly and are in constant use. Whilst Kant thought that emotions could interfere with or 'corrupt' logical moral decisions, brain research shows us that it is more often the other way around. The conscious and logical mind is the one that interferes with the predominant forms of thought, which are emotionally driven. Most of the time, we simply automatically select the best option from our established repertoire of emotionally driven behaviours, like a lazy multiple choice question in an exam. Most decision-making is about what we sense is 'do-able' in the real world to survive,[33] and rarely uses the 'cool' forms of rationality so beloved of philosophers.

Logic and rationality have limited application. They help to generate fresh thinking when we're stuck, but mostly our moral judgements involve direct social relationships and are based on emotions and early programming. Much of our daily social life and quite a bit of our moral decision-making is, in fact, managed through the unconscious emotional responses that were set up in infancy and early childhood, based on our earliest interactions with other people. These automatic programmes help us to maintain our equilibrium without having to waste energy thinking about it. This is how it should be: the social brain makes social decisions, informed automatically by past experiences.

Emotions are *supposed* to guide our life as a social animal. Based on early learning in relationships, they become automatic processes which intuit whether or not someone is attractive to us, or if situations are good for us or not. Faced with an unexpected difficulty, our emotional reactions try to restore the status quo. For example, anger may be an attempt to maintain social status under threat, sadness a way of adapting to an unchangeable loss, and so on. It is only when this emotional repertoire fails to have a useful effect on the situation that the more conscious, dorsolateral, part of the brain is brought into play to try to come up with a new strategy.

People who aren't able to make moral decisions in this emotionally based way are regarded as abnormal. They have been compared to Mr Spock in *Star Trek*, the weirdly unemotional character who always thinks logically but can't respond emotionally. In real life, people who react like this – who are capable of logical responses but not emotional ones – are people who have brain tumours or aneurisms in the ventromedial area of the brain.[34, 35] Although their dorsolateral prefrontal cortex is still intact and able to function, they can no longer respond in a personal way to moral dilemmas. This changes their moral choices. They don't mind pushing the man off the footbridge.

## Counting the costs

When we moved from a feudal, rural way of life to an urban, capitalist way of life, working life privileged the calculating 'executive' brain which made plans and set goals. The new economy established purely instrumental relationships, not personal ones, and started to relate to other people as if they were pieces on a chess board – they were abstractions and could be dealt with by logic not by feeling. The links, the ties between people were cut or they were warped and distorted by the new structures that were set up and run by contracts and rights and laws, not by human responsiveness. The dorsolateral prefrontal cortex ruled.

Many commentators at the time of the industrial revolution noted that the new way of life undermined real emotional connections, and destroyed the village communities in which people responded to each other's needs. By the 1830s, it had become clear that this old inclusive society, in which the different strata mixed and related to each other, had more or less gone. This was also the time when it began to dawn on many that industrial capitalism was not a temporary money-making scam, like the plundering of the monasteries or the enclosures of land – it was here to stay.[36] As a result, the emotional costs began to be counted. One typical comment was from Thomas Carlyle, who wrote in 1843, 'We have sumptuous garnitures for our Life, but have forgotten to live in the middle of them . . . Many men eat finer cookery, drink dearer liquors . . . but in the heart of them . . . what increase of blessedness is there? Are they better, beautifuller, stronger, braver? Are they even what they call "happier"? Do they look with satisfaction on more things and human faces in this God's earth: do more things and human faces look with satisfaction on them? Not so.' Instead of mutual helpfulness, cash-payment has become 'the sole relation of human beings'.[37] Voices such as Carlyle's, however, were drowned out by the tremendous drive for material and scientific progress.

## The class divide

In the absence of a supportive community structure, the emotional connections between human beings, which Carlyle had taken to include the whole of society, now shrank to the limited sphere of the family (so much so, that even now we can only take for granted that we care about our families, not necessarily the wider world). And within those families a split occurred, dividing the way that middle-class families related to each other, and the way that working-class families operated. Child-rearing polarised and the experience of working-class children became radically different from that of middle-class children.

Once, within the cottage or hovel of the relatively self-sufficient peasant or artisan family, both parents had lived and worked alongside their children and were able to pass on their values and practical skills. Now, those forced into factory labour were cut off from their children and unable to pass on any of their social know-how. Women had always worked, but now that they worked in the factories they were inaccessible to their offspring for much of the day. On the other hand, as the new middle classes got richer and employed more servants, their women, increasingly confined to more spacious terraced houses and villas, were expected to devote their energies to family life alone. This enabled them to pay more attention to their children than ever before, and to supervise their children's moral and personal development closely, in particular their self-awareness and self-control, to build up their social capital. The new classist society was not only financially unequal, but held very different opportunities to invest in children's social and emotional development.

Although the professional and clerical middle classes may have experienced cool and instrumental relationships at work, they could find relief – and, it has been argued, a sense of identity as a class – in their enjoyment of domesticity and family life. In this sphere, feelings could be indulged. However, for the working classes, the vogue for tenderness and growing interest in children's psyches must have seemed remote from their concerns. Factory workers had little opportunity to attend to their children's emotions or moral training.

Nor did they or their children have much need for the social skills that were useful in pursuing a professional career. Their every move was controlled by their employer, and they had little chance of fulfilling personal ambitions. In such circumstances, it must have seemed to many that self-awareness and directed thinking were of little use. One response was to seek immediate pleasure in their lives. At the end of their long working days, many carried on the peasant tradition of living for the moment, which in the urban context included heavy gin drinking, smoking and sing-alongs in the public houses, treating themselves to oysters and lobsters, visiting brothels, and watching cockfights.

## Methodism

There were, however, other responses which did encourage the higher brain to engage. The early Methodist movement, in particular, promoted self-discipline. It had a strong appeal to many poor people, because it offered some hope for a better future – and preached that the poor had as much worth in the eyes of God as the rich. This sense of the value and worth of each individual started in childhood. Although Methodism had a puritanical hostility to the body and therefore to feelings, Methodist parenting did require a strong involvement in child-rearing, chiefly focused on their children's spiritual development. Methodists particularly promoted the development of individual qualities such as honesty, punctuality and diligence – qualities of self-control which required considerable parental investment in their offspring. It has been noted that those who took part in this well-organised movement often developed a strong capacity for self-organisation, which fed into other later working-class movements such as the trade unions. The strict, consistent parenting which they offered would have supported the brain's orbitofrontal 'braking' system, as well as the dorso-lateral's planning and thinking capabilities, but not necessarily the self-awareness and emotional capacity for empathy based on early loving interactions. Where these are missing, moral-ity is more likely to remain relatively external and rule-bound, rather than arising from the warmth of close nurturing relationships.

Many working-class people over the following two cen-turies looked for a way out of their miserable or impoverished conditions of life. Self-education was often seen as the key. One young man born at the end of the eighteenth century who followed this path was Francis Place. He had a rather neglected childhood roaming around London whilst his par-ents ran a pub, and became an apprentice tailor in the same casual way. When his father asked him what he would like to do, the young boy of fourteen said he would like to learn a trade. 'This was in the evening, and my father went immedi-ately into his parlour and offered me to any one who would take me.'[38] As a young man he lived and worked as a leather breech-maker in one room with his wife and children, and experienced a gruelling period of hunger and unemployment, as well as enduring the death of one of his children. He became fired with determination to escape poverty and to seize every opportunity that presented itself. He started to educate himself by reading voraciously, and at the age of twenty-four, he joined the London Corresponding Society, one of the many clubs and societies which sprang up to cater for this hunger for self-improvement and a better life. Its particular purpose was to achieve universal suffrage and annual parliaments, but its meetings primarily involved reading and discussion. As Place described it, 'The moral effects of the Society were considerable. It induced men to read books, instead of wasting their time in public houses, it taught them to respect themselves and to desire to educate their children. It elevated them in their own opinions. It taught them the great moral lesson "to bear and forbear".'[39]

Place hints at the possibility that education and mutual support could help people to develop self-control and self-awareness. Looking back at his youth, he remembered that 'drunkenness, dirtiness and depravity' had been the norm in his London life in the 1770s, even amongst the better sort of tradesmen and artisans. In his view, there had been a dramatic improvement in manners and morals over the subsequent fifty years of transition to industrial capitalism. Place partly put this down to better policing, increased wealth and more egalitarian attitudes since the French Revolution, but chiefly he considered the real source of change to be the spread of education. This had made a dramatic difference to his own behaviour and his own prospects, and he believed it was true for the public in general. His faith in education was demonstrated by the strenuous efforts he made to earn enough to give a good education to all his children (of whom he had fifteen, though many of them died young).

Place's autobiography does not give the same weight to the *emotional* development of his children. It does not comment on their infancies or childhoods, leaving all that to his wife as he concentrates on earning a living. It is not hard to understand how, for a man, being on the breadwinning side of the traditional division of labour would make it more difficult to realise the significance of babyhood and very early child-rearing in the improvements he had noticed. Yet Robert Owen, another 'working boy made good', bucks this trend.

Owen was Place's exact contemporary. The son of a humble ironmonger and saddler, he had used the machinery of capitalism to work his way up from running a basic cotton-spinning business with a friend to becoming the owner of a massive mill (and married the original mill owner's daughter in the process). Like Place, Owen saw education as a key to progress. His mills provided good living conditions and access to education at all ages.

Something in Owen's early development had provided a powerful incentive to promote caring values, and he applied these values, recognising that early emotional and moral education was as vital as literacy. He campaigned against child labour under the age of nine (interestingly, the age he was himself when he started work) and argued for restricting children's hours of work.[40] In particular, he saw the importance of providing good early development for babies and in 1816 set up at his mill an 'Institute for the Formation of Character', a kind of nursery school which catered for toddlers of one year old upwards. His values were expressed in his instructions to the teachers: 'They were on no account ever to beat any one of the children or to threaten them in any word or action or to use abusive terms; but were always to speak to them with a pleasant voice and kind manner. They should tell the infants and children . . . that they must on all occasions do all they could to make their playfellows happy'.[41]

By the start of the nineteenth century, child-rearing had become a major topic of conversation. During these years of industrialisation and increasing wealth, more parents were beginning to see Owen's point of view, and some were recognising that what was desirable was not obedience to external authority but the 'sublime power of self-government', as the American pastor and author Horace Bushnell put it in typically flowery Victorian language. In his compelling book of 1847, *Christian Nurture*, he argued against breaking the will of small children.[42] Bushnell – the childcare guru and Benjamin Spock of his day – was a loving father who had spent time with his own infants. He saw clearly that infancy was the most crucial time in moral development, a time when the baby's personality was a 'seed' ripening within the 'parent-stem', drawing nourishment from the parent's behaviour and presence, rather than from their verbal interactions. In fact, he suggested that a baby would not be able to understand the meaning of particular words until he had a lived experience of what they are referring to: 'The word love is unmeaning, to one who has not loved and received love.'[43]

During this period, more moderate and liberal Christians started to recognise that the extreme forms of discipline and punishment that were still espoused by evangelical forms of Protestantism were not necessarily the best way to achieve self-control. Although corporal punishment and bullying of children remained commonplace in many families and schools (such as those described in Charles Dickens' *Nicholas Nickleby* [1838] or Charlotte Brontë's *Jane Eyre* [1847]), there was a dawning recognition that kindness and self-acceptance could be a more effective route to moral behaviour. As Samuel Johnson had once put it: 'Love of ourselves becomes the foundation of our love of others.'[44]

The battle lines of two very different emotional cultures – coercion versus empathy – were now beginning to be drawn up. This was not a clash that ran on class lines, since different attitudes existed within the same socio-economic groups. Rather, it was a struggle between two different ideas of the moral self. There were still large sections of every social strata who had been brought up by severe authority figures, who would struggle to move towards a kinder culture. In fact, harshness in the middle classes could sometimes be disguised in new genteel forms. The Reverend Francis Wayland's 1831 diary reveals an odd mixture of sentimentality and severity in his attitude to his young toddler, after a very mild tantrum: '15m. old cries and throws bread. Put into room by himself, no food or drink, from 8 am. Visited every hour and offered the bread. He refused all day, would take nothing.' The diary describes how this treatment continued into the next day, when the boy cried but still refused to eat anything despite his father's kind entreaties. It was not until 3 p.m. the next day that the toddler finally gave in and 'Took Rev.'s hands, submissive, kissed father repeatedly, or whenever asked, "so full of love" and now preferred Rev. to any of the family. Since the event – easily subdued, happier and kinder.'[45]

This was a new form of 'breaking the will' of the child without beating, shouting or loss of control. It was a deliberate, sustained assertion of power on the part of the adult, to which the child eventually submits. Reverend Wayland clearly believes that it is for the child's own good, for his moral development. Yet his focus is entirely on obedience, and on enforcing desirable behaviour – not on empathising with the child's hunger and distress, or understanding the causes of his behaviour. Reverend Wayland does not ask why his child refused the bread in the first place; he simply assumes that this is a battle of wills.

But what would little baby Wayland have learned from his encounter with his father's will? Instead of learning to co-ordinate his own feelings with another person's, and to balance his self-regulation and self-agency with growing awareness of his father's feelings and perspective, little Wayland would have learned only that he was powerless. He would have learned that the only way to regulate and disperse his stress hormones was to give up his own agency to a higher power and he would have perhaps have tried to control his own behaviour in future by recalling the fear and distress of disobeying. He would have been highly likely to anticipate that future relationships would be organised through this same framework of dominance and submission.

Without any conscious intention on the parent's part, cultural values as well as individual ones are passed on. In hierarchical societies, where little value is given to the feelings and thoughts of individuals, punitive and unsympathetic child-rearing might be seen as a useful preparation for harsh reality. Those at the bottom of a power structure have to learn to submit to those who are more powerful; those at the top need to internalise the whole structure of dominance and submission. The writer George Orwell described his childhood as a preparation to be part of the ruling class in the early years of the twentieth century. In their boarding schools, the children of the upper classes practise 'being bigger, stronger, handsomer, richer, more pop-ular, more elegant, more unscrupulous than other people – in dominating them, bullying them, making them suffer pain, making them look foolish, getting the better of them in every way. Life was hierarchical and whatever happened was right.'[46]

However, people in the growing middle classes of society had other options. They were not destined to rule others or be ruled to the same degree. Instead, as a more democratic society emerged, the middle classes started to enjoy a small degree of influence, particularly in their working lives. They could make their views known to a limited extent through voting. They had sufficient wealth to exercise some personal choice in how they lived. Although they did not have real power, their wishes and feelings had some value and meaning. All this fed into their child-rearing practices. Many such families started to pay closer attention to their children and eventually to their children's feelings. Closer bonds more frequently developed between parents and children, potentially encouraging children's prefrontal brain development as well as their social capacities. A circular process was set in motion, where the more social recognition adults themselves had, the more some of them, at least, felt able to recognise their children's feelings – behaviour which could enhance the development of the child's sense of identity, as well as his or her ability to pay attention to others in turn. This was the start of a process which is still being worked through.

# 5. THE STRUGGLE FOR EMPATHY

From the conservative dark
Into the ethical life . . .

*W. H. Auden, from '1st September 1939'*

At the beginning of the twenty-first century, we are still poised between these two entirely different versions of morality, which have their roots in different forms of early child-rearing. Although I have described the first steps towards a more empathetic form of parenting, starting in the seventeenth century, hundreds of years later we have not yet conclusively established the culture of kindness and responsiveness — two qualities which are rooted in styles of baby-rearing — that is essential to develop an unselfish society.

In a recent British television series called *Bringing Up Baby*,[1] various baby-rearing ideologies were pitted against each other: the disciplinarian approach of Truby King, the unstructured, empathetic approach of Benjamin Spock, and the physically close (but not necessarily mentally close) 'continuum concept' inspired by Jean Liedloff. The programme generated huge public reaction, a petition to the British Prime Minister, and columns of press coverage and internet chat. In the USA, the

parenting clash is at its most intense between fundamentalist
Christians and progressives, or as the novelist Lionel Shriver
caricatured it, the 'stand-off between the strait-laced, self-
righteous, toe-the-line types who wear hats to church, and the
grubby, licentious long-hairs brandishing peace signs.'[2] George
Lakoff, a professor of cognitive linguistics at Berkeley, and by
this reckoning a natural 'long hair' (he in fact has a beard but
not long hair), has referred to the intense feelings and mutual
hostility that opposing parenting styles evoke as nothing short
of a culture war.

## Strict parenting

Lakoff's pioneering work *Moral Politics* attempted to give an
impartial account of the different positions in this culture war,
for the first time linking parenting styles with political attitudes.[3] He suggests that there are two principle models of the
family – the Strict Father and the Nurturant Parent – which
give rise to different moral systems and different 'unconscious
cognitive concepts'. He argues that these are the basic concepts that we use to organise and categorise our experience,
including our political life. Strict parents have a conservative
view of politics, whilst Nurturant parents are drawn to
liberalism.

Lakoff identifies the underlying deep structures of thought
in both types of upbringing. Nurturant parents have a democratic model of family life, in which parents communicate
openly with their children and explain their decisions. Their
child-rearing is designed to help children develop through
positive relationships and to become fulfilled and happy.
Discipline is achieved through 'love and respect for parents,

not out of the fear of punishment'. Their moral and political concepts are based on ideas of nurturance and empathy.

Reading Lakoff's book, it soon becomes clear that he is much more interested in understanding the unconscious concepts underlying Strict parenting, which have proved so difficult for liberals to grasp. Lakoff describes the traditional set-up favoured by Strict parents. They run a family in which the father is in charge. His role is to provide for and protect his own family, whilst the mother takes care of the home and children. Children receive 'tough love' and are punished for their own good, because the unconscious assumption of Strict parents is that the world is a harsh place and that 'life is difficult'. Their parenting is designed to develop 'character' to cope with the competitive struggle for survival in a hierarchical power structure that lies ahead.

Although Lakoff acknowledges the insights of attachment theory, he rarely talks specifically about infancy. As a cognitive linguist, he is interested in words and in the ideologies that are revealed through words, an emphasis that keeps him focused on later child-rearing. However, he reveals in his acknowledgements an interesting conversation that he had with a friend, the late Paul Baum. He describes how his book was triggered by a conversation with Baum, who suggested that the litmus test for detecting liberal or conservative attitudes was to ask someone, 'If your baby cries at night, do you pick him up?' In other words, what really matters is the parent's attitude to the child's dependency needs. I would agree with Paul Baum that the unconscious frameworks which Lakoff discusses are actually established in infancy, and are passed on long before language.

Strict parents do not believe that they should meet their baby's needs at all times. Often, they experience their baby's cries as devious and manipulative and the baby is seen as a little tyrant out to control the parent, much as we saw with the Rev. Wayland in the nineteenth century; the parent's duty is to teach the child how to behave. The relationship between parent and baby is experienced as a battle of wills. In the TV programme *Bringing Up Baby*, the strict 'expert' advises parents on how to 'train' their baby into complying with the parents' schedules. The parents are told to leave their baby to cry alone for several hours at a time, and to withhold milk from the baby until the scheduled feeding time, even if she seems hungry. This is so she can be overfed at the 'correct' time, and sleep through the adult night.

One possible source for this belief that the baby must fit in with their own convenience is that the parent herself had to do so as a child. If her own needs were not met as a dependent infant, she may become an adult who feels resentful or overwhelmed when expected to meet someone else's needs too. However, by failing to offer prompt regulation to her baby, a co-operative relationship between them can be much more difficult to establish. Instead, she will be more likely to prepare the way for compliance or rebellion.

Strict parents believe that their child would behave badly if they didn't threaten and manipulate him or her into good behaviour. This approach fits in well with the 'veneer' theory of morality, which understands morality as something external to human beings, which has to be plastered over the festering sore of our innate badness and imposed by force. Indeed, strict parenting itself does tend to produce moral behaviour which is merely compliant or generated by fear. In a relationship lacking in mutual trust and confidence, the child does not learn to identify with the parent's perspective, or to feel spontaneous concern for others. In the absence of an empathic response to others, morality *can* only be imposed from the outside, rather than coming from the inside.

So far, so bad. However, Lakoff takes great pains to try to empathise with the conservative outlook, and he argues that this is not an ethos of 'selfishness', but a positive moral outlook based on real values such as self-reliance, hard work and individual freedom to achieve. Certainly, babies who have to learn to cope with isolation and stress may learn these values. Those who are manipulated into compliance will, most likely, grow up to do as they are told and to insist that others do likewise. And those whose emotional needs are not met by warm and responsive parenting, will turn to other sources of gratification.

The Strict parenting outlook makes a certain sense when the conditions of life are difficult and the only things between you and starvation are hard work and luck. In the past, the majority of our ancestors lived in such conditions, so it was natural that they should pass on their values down the generations. Even within the twentieth century, there was still a fine line between the 'respectable' working class and the imprudent, irresponsible working class, and it was hard work which kept you on the right side of that line.

I believe that my grandmother was typical of a 'respectable' working-class view, even though her family were not typically proletarian. She was the daughter of a small-scale tenant farmer in East Anglia, with a wide extended family living in the neighbouring villages. Her great-grandfather had been the local blacksmith in the same village in which she grew up. Financial survival was a struggle for such families, just as it was for urban factory workers. Their insecure physical conditions led to a certain harshness in relation to others. Like the working-class women in Lancashire who talked to historian Elizabeth Roberts about their upbringing by their late nineteenth-century mothers,[4] my grandmother was intolerant of human foibles and her attitudes were focused on not sinking to a lower position in life. Like them, she extolled the virtues of hard work at all times, and saw those who didn't work as 'good for nothings'. Children were expected to 'behave themselves' and 'keep out of trouble', and to do what they were told without questioning (enforced with physical penalties). Good manners, eating what you were given and helping with household tasks were important.

The Lancashire women had low expectations of the marital relationship, as did my grandmother: for them, a man was a good husband if he kept the family out of debt, didn't drink and was kind to his family if they were ill. Men were often fed the largest helpings of food, and they were fed first, because they did more hard physical labour than the women (a practice my grandmother carried on into the 1970s with my father who sat at a desk all day!) The attachment between parents and children, or husband and wife, was taken for granted as a background phenomenon, but little sentiment or physical affection was ever expressed.

My grandmother enforced certain standards of behaviour, overtly passing on her materialistic values and her puritan sense of self-discipline and hard work, rather than a desire to enjoy life or the company of others. My sister and I had a running joke about her attitude to our love lives. Whenever either of us acquired a new boyfriend, Granny could be safely predicted to ask 'What kind of car has he got?' As someone who had grown up in precarious material conditions, she saw security in terms of material goals not emotional ones.

'Materialistic values increase when environmental circumstances fail to support needs for security and safety', as the psychologist Tim Kasser says.[5] Under such conditions, people will try to improve their fortunes and aim for material goals; people from poor families or neighbourhoods are more likely to be materialistic. However, emotional insecurity too can drive materialism. The hope is similar – that material goods may make you feel more emotionally secure. Materialistic individuals are often driven by the hope of approval or the fear of disapproval, and compulsive buying may become a way to relieve anxiety or internal pressures rather than providing any lasting satisfaction. There is some evidence emerging that materialistic values are highest in those who have had harder, less nurturing or less secure childhoods,[6] and that more materialistic young people are the most insecure. In one unusual piece of research, Tim Kasser and his wife Virginia studied the most memorable dreams of a group of students. They found that a high proportion of the more materialistic students remembered dreams to do with death or with falling. Those who were less materialistic rarely mentioned such themes, but when they did, their disturbing dreams had a narrative in which they managed to *overcome* some fearful experience.[7]

Unconsciously, my siblings and I learned from Granny's example how to relate to other people: keep a distance, make few emotional demands and try not to depend on others. Despite becoming a single parent of three young children at the relatively young age of thirty-two, when my grandfather died during the war, Granny never remarried, living for over seventy more years without any partner. She retained the attitudes which had survival value in the rural world in which she grew up: after all, farmers who lacked self-discipline would not have flourishing farms, and marriages based on overly high expectations would be in danger of floundering in small communities where there was little choice of partner.

Recent research confirms that Strict parenting is most entrenched in the lower social and economic classes. It coincides with a style of parenting first identified by Diana Baumrind (a psychologist also based at the University of Berkeley, California) as 'authoritarian'.[8] This is characterised as parenting which is high on demands and low on responsiveness. The child must learn to obey authority, and the parent will use power and physical punishment to get the child to comply with the adult. Adults should not respond to children's demands. Although she did not link this style of parenting with social class, more recent work has done so. Erica Hoff and her colleagues found that authoritarian parenting is consistently associated with the lower classes.[9] Whilst the educated middle classes are more likely to be 'authoritative' parents, the lower classes seek more control over their children. It is their babies who are pushed to say 'thank you' and to be toilet trained at the earliest possible age. Later on, they are the parents who tend to dictate their children's behaviour in minute detail, insisting that they should not put their elbows on the table or must wear clothes in a certain fashion, taking these matters as seriously as moral issues. Instead of getting involved in the child's own activities or attempting to understand the child, authoritarian parenting is much more about asserting the parent's dominance and getting the child to submit.

Many currently popular childcare gurus such as Richard Ferber in the US[10] or Gina Ford in the UK,[11] also come from the Strict parenting stable. Their mission seems to be to adapt Strict parenting to the middle-class working mother's lifestyle. They use techniques such as 'controlled crying' primarily to train the baby to fit in with parents' busy work schedules. As the psychologist Oliver James once put it, Ford's bestselling *Contented Little Baby Book* could equally be re-named the *Contented Little Parent Book*. The parents who followed the Truby King approach in the programme *Bringing Up Baby* had a similar goal of getting the baby to adapt to the parents' pre-baby lifestyle. They were determined to 'get their life back' only weeks after the birth of their twins, and were shown throwing a party downstairs whilst their babies obligingly slept through the noise upstairs. As their adviser, Claire Verity, put it: 'At the end of the day, the routine is all about getting the baby to fit in with your way of life. And if you want to have a party, great, have a party. Those babies won't wake up, they'll be fed and put into bed at seven o'clock as normal and you can party all night. So it's all very much about the baby fitting into your way of life. Don't let it stop you having fun.'

The idea that babies just need to be trained well and will be happy with a fixed routine is seductive. But the baby's psychological reality is not quite as convenient. When babies are managed through controlled crying, what they are really learning is that it is hopeless to expect the comfort of physical contact from a responsive adult, so they might as well give up crying for it and go to sleep, needs for comfort unmet. Children brought up like this are discovering that their feelings can be ignored and that their own feelings are perhaps not of great significance compared to their parents' wishes.

Often, work is the great god of the household, and they must learn to subordinate their needs to it.

This may be a message that some parents are happy to convey. Emotional strategies, after all, do have to adapt to a changing world if they are to stay useful. Some that may once have had survival value, no longer do so as circumstances change. Just as mothers who experienced starvation during pregnancy pass on a genetic loading to their children to lay down fat whenever possible, which is no longer adaptive in a world of plentiful high-calorie food, so too our unconscious repetition of old emotional strategies can be maladaptive. In the late twentieth century, Granny's method of saving one's way to prosperity did not fit in a world devoted to spending. And whilst her tendency to emotional distance may not have been a problem in the small interconnected communities where my family has lived for generations, it has not proved the most successful emotional strategy for some of her descendants, at least, in pursuing the closer personal relationships we seek in the twenty-first century.

The Strict parenting regime, however, has proved widely malleable to the demands of a consumer society. Indeed, separating babies from their mothers at night, a lynchpin of Western baby-rearing in the twentieth century, could even be said to promote a materialistic attitude. As Barbara Rogoff says, this is 'an unusual practice when viewed from a world-wide and historical perspective'.[12] The effect of this practice is to encourage babies 'to depend not on people for comfort and company, but on objects – bottles, pacifiers, blankets, and other "lovies".' Sooner or later, the developing child learns that things are more reliable than parents. Things do not let you down when you need comfort: they are there to hold and cuddle, they can be controlled or purchased, they provide security and a sense of meaning and identity. This attachment to things, and acquiring more things, has now become so powerful that it supercedes other values.

Interestingly, by the 1990s and 2000s, many parents in the lowest social and economic classes were no longer 'strict' in the sense of placing realistic and tough limits on their children's material aspirations, although some might still be strict in the sense of demanding that the child obeys their wishes. Encouraged in this period to indulge in debt, new attitudes emerged in child-rearing too. Many more parents switched into a materially indulgent mode, both for themselves and their children, and tried to live up to the advertisers' fantasy world, believing that they ought to fulfil their child's every wish on Christmases or birthdays.

This has muddied the waters of Strict parenting. When both parents are working long hours in paid employment, or in the growing number of single-parent households struggling to cope, it is often easier to say yes – just let them do what they want. Over-control can become under-control, or even neglect. Both are sides of the same coin, since both are designed to fit the child in with the parent's needs. Neither, however, is based on an assessment of what the child requires to develop and mature well.

## Permissive parenting

George Lakoff describes only two types of parenting: Strict and Nurturant. However, Baumrind's original typology offered a wider range of possibilities. In particular, Permissive parenting was a significant type. Baumrind defined it as warm, tolerant parenting which does not make demands of the child, but lets the child decide. Her research found it correlated with high social and economic status. But this is a form of parenting which Strict parents detest, much as Permissive parents detest Strict parenting. Although it has existed in some form at least since the eighteenth century, it gained adherents in the last few decades of the twentieth century as one strand of the 'hippie' culture that was emerging in the 1960s and 1970s, accompanying the radical politics of the time. Those of us who participated in these movements believed that we were anti-materialistic and anti-authoritarian, yet such attitudes proved surprisingly easy to co-opt into an expanding consumer society which relied on the idea that you deserve to have what you want, and why should anyone (particularly authority figures) stop you?

As the consumer society took off in the 1960s, parenting practices began to shift towards a more relaxed, less authoritarian stance in all groups of society, moving away from Strict parenting. Writing in 1963, psychologists John and Elizabeth Newson recorded a change in attitude which they suggest had taken place in all classes. They quoted a 'driver's wife' in Nottingham, who thought 'there's a much closer relationship between parent and child . . . they can talk to me a lot easier than ever I could with my mother – even though she was a real good mother, I mean she was a wonderful person really, but you just couldn't get through to them in those days,' and a 'labourer's wife' who said, 'When they get big they're very difficult, aren't they? They seem to be more full of life than we was, I don't know if it's the war that's done it or what. They seem to like their own way a lot more . . .'[13] There was a certain sense of bewilderment amongst the parents in their sample about the egotism and rowdiness of children in the modern era. Children were no longer deferential, but were starting to regard their parents as 'pals'. They were more self-confident and, interestingly, 'greedy'.

The idea that parents should be 'pals' with their children was a rejection of authoritarianism and a desire for a more democratic style of parenting. However, it might also be a way for adults who had felt unloved as children of Strict parents to heal their own hurts by overindulging their children.

The dangers of this sort of parenting were identified by the social scientist Christine Everingham, in her 1994 ethnographic study of three playgroups in New South Wales.[14] Each group of mothers and children that she studied was characterised by a different mothering sub-culture. The 'sub-urban' group was mostly of working or lower middle-class mothers who were employed part-time; the 'kinship' group mainly consisted of women previously in low status jobs who were on benefits (almost all were authoritarian parents); and the 'alternative' group consisted of educated middle-class women with counter-cultural ideals, some of whom lived in communal households. It was this latter group that Everingham depicted as the Permissive parents.

Everingham clearly conveyed her irritation with the middle-class hippie mothers. She described how they organised their lives around their child, putting their child's needs before their own. In particular, they breastfed for a long period and, in her view, constantly offered the breast instead of trying to understand the child's problems. They were desperate to be 'nice' and to avoid confrontation with their children, a stance that Everingham particularly seemed to despise, although she offered the insight that their reluctance to express anger may have been based in their lack of self-confidence. Research carried out around the same time by the developmental psychologist Judith Smetana confirmed that Permissive parents were often ineffective in passing on moral messages to their children; although they might talk about what other people might feel, they could undermine the lesson by failing to enforce moral behaviour in practice.[15]

Christine Everingham portrayed Permissive parents as horribly indulgent – not in a material sense, like the sickeningly doting parents in Roald Dahl's *Charlie and the Chocolate Factory* who try to give their self-centred daughter Veruca everything she desires – but giving in to their children in other ways. Everingham felt that this would hinder the developing autonomy of the child and would promote narcissistic self-centredness.

In practice, their behaviour in the playgroup sounds surprisingly ordinary. Everingham described how the 'Alternative' mothers would settle their child down as they arrived at the playgroup. At first, the child stayed close to mother, then gradually moved away to explore, and then came back to the watching mother. They got on well with other children. On the surface, that sounds to me like classically secure attachment behaviour, in which a child can safely explore his world and become autonomous because he has so much confidence that the parent will be available when needed. But the feminist in Everingham was frustrated that the mother was so 'tied down' whilst the child was free to come and go. She was more comfortable with the working mothers who settled their child in, then moved away to talk to other mothers and only reluctantly responded if the child tried to 'tug them away' from other mothers to watch them play. These working, lower middle-class mothers had a dash of the Strict parent about them – they expected their children to be independent at an early age, and demanded obedience and good behaviour from their children, presumably because they would need to fit into the working world. However, Everingham's take on it was that these were well-balanced parents, who were also willing to negotiate with their children and to try to understand the child when distressed.

It is impossible to judge parenting practices without knowing what their impact is on the child. If a Strict mother expressed so much irritation with her child when he wanted her attention that he felt it was best to give up making too many demands, or if an indulgent mother was inconsistently attentive and made her child feel unsure what mood she would be in today, then insecurity might be the result in either case. And certainly insecure attachments can be the result of under-confident, overly permissive parenting, as much as from overly strict and unresponsive parenting. Insecurity is basically fuelled by inadequate understanding of the child's emotional needs. Both can feed into materialism.

Today, an increasingly common and worrying manifestation of parenting is the combination of material indulgence with emotional neglect. This is found in a range of social strata. I have met some parents who are devoted to their baby, and take great pride in their baby's appearance – whether they express it through a fondness for 'bling' such as gold chains and bracelets, or whether they lavish money on high-end designer clothes – yet who fail to recognise their babies' need for personal attention. Their babies and toddlers may be left in front of the television for hours at a time, or kept in their buggies for long stretches whilst their parents carry on their social life. For these parents, love is more easily expressed through buying things rather than by giving children their time. It seems to me that this is neither Strict nor Permissive parenting, but a growing phenomenon of emotional neglect in the midst of material plenty. But if the generation of children raised in a Permissive style has indeed grown up narcissistic, what will these children become?

## Parenting for empathy

Since John Bowlby first drew attention to the impact of very early parenting on children's long-term development, there has been increasing awareness of the difficulties that so many parents can experience. My work as a parent-infant psychotherapist brings me into frequent contact with those parents who are not confident or happy about being parents. This can make it easy for me to overestimate the number of parents in difficulties. But it is important to remember that the majority of parents – around 60 per cent according to well-established data in attachment research – are in secure attachment relationships with their children.

Although the categories that Bowlby and his colleague Mary Ainsworth developed to describe styles of parent/child relationship were resisted at first, the sheer volume of confirmatory research that has followed over the last few decades has made it difficult not to accept the power of the attachment paradigm. Nowadays few experts would dare to question whether secure attachment is a good thing. The psychologists have come to dominate public debate about such matters, and have achieved a consensus about what is desirable. Their ideal form of parenting is close to Lakoff's Nurturant parent, but also to what Diana Baumrind first identified as 'Authoritative' parenting. This label describes parents who hold firm to their rules and boundaries, yet can be flexible when necessary. They respond to the child, but expect the child to respond to them too. This model of parenting produces children who are individualistic, self-directed and high in educational aspirations. Perhaps unsurprisingly, it is more often found in the higher social and economic classes who anticipate a working life of self-directed professionalism (like the psychology professors themselves). In other words, it may be a predominantly middle-class ideal – although not necessarily achieved by all middle-class parents by any means.

Despite Lakoff's efforts to give due respect to Strict parenting, he too cannot help conveying his sense that Nurturant parenting is the ideal. He describes it in somewhat glowing terms as a system where children become responsible, self-disciplined individuals through being cared for, supported and respected. Parental authority is based on parental empathy, wisdom and willingness to engage in rational discussion – not on an assertion of power. Children raised by Nurturant parents will model themselves on their parents' behaviour and try to meet their expectations. Babies of Nurturant parents enjoy their relationship with their parents and want to maintain it. Although these children may be motivated to achieve their own goals, these are rarely so compelling that they ignore what their parent wants and feels.

The picture of 'authoritative' and 'nurturant' parenting painted by Lakoff and Baumrind is backed up by decades of psychological research, which confirms that if we want to create a society peopled by individuals with a strong capacity for empathy, this is the kind of parenting we will need, particularly in the early years. I have already described how the foundations of empathy are laid in the first year of life, when babies learn how to identify and regulate their feelings with the help of others, and form a view of whether the social universe is supportive or hostile. However, in the second year of life, the child begins to create a more complex moral world based on the way that people behave to each other. The child of Nurturant parents is more likely to build on an early foundation of self-awareness, to look outwards and to become more aware of other people's feelings. Toddlerhood is a crucial moment in moral development because the child is already attached to those who have cared for him, and usually identifies with his parents, yet his growing sense of self and of physical agency is expanding rapidly, offering exciting new possibilities for pursuing his own goals. A difficult balance has to be struck between his increased ability to do what he wants and increased awareness of what others want him to do. It is a moment when the growing awareness of 'me' runs up against the growing sense that other people are also 'me's.[16]

## Learning how to feel for others

The development of empathy is a slow process. Although it's a central strand of morality, it's a relatively advanced stance, which is made possible through various tracks of development. However, they all depend on having an experience with a parent figure, and then using that experience in other relationships.

Right from the start, we are all responsive to other human beings. Even newborn babies have a basic capacity to imitate others and to resonate with other people's feelings through their brain's mirror neurons. Very young babies will copy their parent's strange activity of sticking out a tongue, or yawning. Through copying other people's facial expressions, in particular, their own bodies come to know something of what it feels like to be them. If you copy a smile, you often feel happier, and if you copy a yawn, you are likely to feel more tired. These mirror neurons fire whenever we observe someone else doing something in a purposeful way. They give us a watered-down simulation in our own bodies of what they are experiencing. When someone falls over and bangs their head, we go 'ouch!' and wince momentarily, experiencing a flicker of pain. We need this ability to be social creatures. Without it, it would be difficult for us to judge what other people are feeling or to learn from others.

But the process of learning that others have experiences like ours is also tangled up with discovering ourselves, and identifying what we are feeling: 'the self and the other are just two sides of the same coin', says Marco Iacoboni, one of the neuroscientists who first identified mirror neurons. 'To understand myself, I must recognise myself in other people.'[17] To the brain, self and other are part of the same process. In fact, it's the same area of the brain – the right frontal insula, in particular – which lights up whether we are being aware of our own body states or other people's. It's also the anterior cingulate that is activated not only when our own bodies feel pain, but also when we observe other people in pain.

This identification of my experience and yours continues into the second year, when toddlers still assume that other people feel and think the same as them. It isn't yet clear to them that feelings may *not* be shared. Although they realise that other people are physically separate beings, they aren't yet aware that other people have 'independent inner states'.[18] It seems very cute to adults when a toddler responds to another upset child by bringing his own 'cuddly' or comforting object for him. However, this is generally considered to be an egocentric stage of empathy, because the toddler is largely motivated by the distress he himself is feeling. The other child's cries have evoked feelings in him through the involuntary activity of his mirror neurons. At this stage, the toddler isn't really aware that the other child has an inner world with his or her own history, and might be comforted by different things from himself.

Many toddlers in fact find it hard to respond to others because they become overwhelmed by their feelings. The ability to respond to others' feelings does rely on the child having achieved a certain degree of self-regulation, which in turn depends on how well he has been regulated by adults in his first year of life. When a child has plenty of experience of having been soothed, he's more likely to be sensitive to his own states and able to manage them. Having learned how to calm and distract himself, he becomes more poised and more able to respond to other people's distress.

All this expands the orbitofrontal part of the prefrontal cortex, which, as I have already described, is a central area of the social brain involved in reading the emotional significance of social situations. It starts to develop rapidly from about six months old, as the baby becomes more aware of the social world. By about eighteen months, it is fully functional and able to make social judgements about people and situations. The 'pause button' it provides also gives the toddler time to reflect and to be more aware of himself and others. And at this time of orbitofrontal maturation, there is indeed a turning point in social awareness. This is when the toddler starts to realise that he is a separate person and can now recognise himself in the mirror. This is also when he makes the momentous discovery that other people can feel differently to himself, as well as the same. One well-known experiment by the psychologists Betty Repacholi and Alison Gopnik found that eighteen months is the age when a toddler realises that even though he personally hates broccoli, it is possible that someone else actually likes it.[19]

Without the self-control provided by developing the orbitofrontal cortex, it's not easy for a child to focus on what another person is feeling and needing. Extensive research over nearly twenty years by the psychologist Grazyna Kochanska has shown how important this *early* self-regulation and self-control is to moral development. She found that the degree of what she calls 'effortful control' a child has at twenty-two months predicts his self-control at three or four years old. Even though self-control increases between the ages of two and six years old, as the connections in the orbitofrontal cortex are established, her research has shown that the more effortful control a child has learned early on, the better all his social and moral capacities will be: the less anger he will show at frustrating situations, the more empathy he will have, and the more moral conscience.[20]

Self-control is also assisted by the development of another part of the prefrontal cortex – the dorsolateral prefrontal cortex – which develops slightly later in toddlerhood. This helps by holding information 'on-line' in memory, so that it can be considered at greater length. It enables the child to have more conscious thoughts about how to behave and how to solve problems. Although he needs the emotional regulation of the orbitofrontal cortex to hold back impulses and inhibit aggression, without the more focused attention and problem-solving of the dorsolateral prefrontal cortex, he won't be good at distracting himself or thinking through how to manage situations.

All these early aspects of brain development enable the child to manage more complex forms of empathy, building on the more instinctive responses of his mirror neurons. Neuroscientists have found that empathy particularly activates the early developing, right side of the brain – in particular the ventromedial prefrontal cortex, which includes the orbitofrontal cortex, the medial prefrontal cortex, right inferior parietal and amygdala. These areas of the brain also seem to be where the child stores bodily memories of his own particular experiences, and then links them with other emotional associations and memories. (This is the part of the brain which is also involved in mind reading, irony, faux pas, reading others' affects, realising deception – all forms of inference of other people's intentions.) It's not until a child has built up a store of mental imagery of his own personal experiences that it becomes possible for him to draw on this library of images to intentionally imagine what others might be feeling. He can now use his own past experiences to simulate what they are feeling in his own mind and mentally pretend he is in their situation.

But these abilities very much depend on having had enough attentive and responsive parenting. Babies and toddlers of more authoritarian parents who are ignored, left to cry or actively punished may learn to comply with authority figures, and to 'behave' in the ways that they demand, but will not necessarily learn to empathise with others. Without parental encouragement, the mental processes which support self-awareness and empathy for themselves may develop more slowly.

## Mind-mindedness and mentalisation

I described in an earlier chapter how the parent figures in the first year already start to help a baby to identify and label particular emotional states, and to become aware of himself as a 'self'. Current researchers are very interested in this dimension of parental empathy which they call 'mind-mindedness', a concept which has been defined as the adult's willingness to 'treat her infant as an individual with a mind, rather than merely as a creature with needs that must be satisfied'.[21]

Elizabeth Meins, a psychologist from Durham University, has shown that identifying feelings and talking about the child's own feelings plays an important role in babies coming to understand that other people have minds or 'individual inner states'.[22] She found that it is only by being treated as an individual with a mind, that the child comes to understand that people have mental agency as well as physical agency. Surprisingly, Meins' research revealed that this mattered even in very early infancy, before a child had any verbal capacity. Those mothers in her study who talked to their five-month-old baby about his feelings, compared to mothers who didn't, had more psychologically aware four-year-olds, who were better able to grasp that others thought differently from them. In other words, children learn to recognise that other people have a separate existence with minds of their own only when their own minds are acknowledged first. Having a 'mind-reading' parent from the start of life helps them to grasp that feelings can be organised and categorised, and have meaning. However, when babies are simply fed and changed without conversation from their parents, or when toddlers are sat for long periods in front of television cartoons, they miss out on the opportunity to develop their mentalising skills.

Meins' work suggests that providing a secure attachment, while pivotal to self-regulation, is not the only thing that matters. Although mind-mindedness was strongly linked to attachment security and parenting that responds to the baby's needs, and Meins found some overlap between the two, 'mind-mindedness' depends on a different kind of parental input. The specific process of making 'mind-related comments' at six months old is what makes the difference to later awareness of others' minds.[23]

However, according to the psychologist and psychoanalyst Peter Fonagy and his colleagues, it is also vital for a child to learn how to 'mentalise'. Again, this is a very similar concept to mind-mindedness and overlaps with it in some ways. It too includes the awareness that all individuals have minds and feelings. However, mentalisation is a slightly more dynamic concept which emphasises the way that our inner states motivate our *behaviour*. For example, a parent who takes a mentalising approach with her child would say something like: 'He threw a tantrum in the supermarket because he was tired and hungry and I'd been dragging him around all day and he was sick of it . . . I tried to pick him up but he didn't want to be picked up because he was in the middle of being angry and I interrupted him. It was me who needed to pick him up to make him feel better so I put him back down.'[24] On many levels, this parent was demonstrating a high level of emotional awareness, both of the links between her child's inner state and his behaviour, but also of how that connected with her *own* inner states and behaviour. Interestingly, mentalising does activate the same part of the brain that is active in self-awareness – the ventromedial prefrontal cortex.

Mentalising is dynamic in another sense too, though. As well as thinking about mental states, it also involves the capacity to *experience* feelings and emotions fully – both one's own and other people's – without defensively shutting down.[25] In this sense, it's impossible to mentalise if you can't regulate your emotions; the parent in the supermarket would find it very difficult to stay open to her child's emotional experience if she were unable to maintain her equilibrium under stress. But although mentalising does involve being able to stay in touch with your own feelings, its main function seems to be *to understand* people and feelings, and predict how they will behave. This distinguishes it from empathy, which is more about *sharing* the emotional experience of the other person. Moral behaviour may require both.

Research has shown that children learn more about morality from emotional understanding than from learning social rules. While we often talk about 'teaching' a child to behave, various studies have shown that talking about rules, or highlighting the consequences of actions, don't play much part in promoting the development of conscience. Although John Locke was ahead of his time when he advocated reasoning with children, current research suggests that it isn't as crucial to moral development as was once thought. The most vital element in socialising children is for parents to talk about the child's emotions and help the child to think about what other people might be feeling.[26] In fact, parents best promote their children's moral development when they resolve conflict with their two-and-a-half-year-old children by discussing the *emotional* impact of the conflict.[27] This fits well with Meins' research, which has shown that if the mother talks about her child's own feelings, there is more chance that her child will develop a sense of conscience. This ability to identify and recognise emotions is linked to later empathic and pro-social behaviour.[28]

It seems likely that co-operative social behaviour will depend on all of these early-developing capacities of emotional self-regulation, self-control, empathy and mentalising. It turns out that they are the key component parts of the bigger engine of morality, not the attempt to make children comply with rules. Once again, modern research implicitly questions the old assumptions of Strict parenting. Moral character is better developed by focusing on the meaning of behaviour – understanding why people behave the way they do – than by punishing children for behaving inappropriately. In fact, when harsh parents make demands on their children to conform to good behaviour in the absence of emotional understanding, morality inevitably becomes merely a 'veneer'. On the other hand, when parents acknowledge and accept their child's feelings and help him to become aware of them and to think about why he feels what he feels, the child is more likely to become interested in how other people feel too.

## Dealing with the negative

Of course, other people often feel things we don't want them to feel, and understand things differently from ourselves. What we call morality is to a great extent the way that people resolve their conflicting interests – how we negotiate and reconcile differences between others' feelings and wishes and our own. A very important stage of moral development is about how a child learns to regulate his social interactions with people who think or feel differently from him.

Inevitably, conflicts produce uncomfortable feelings of threat and anxiety. Social bonds are threatened, however slightly. When a child is already emotionally insecure, this may be overwhelming. Children whose caregivers treat them with punishment and criticism quickly feel threatened and become defensive. In this state of arousal, they are so focused on protecting themselves from their attacker that they are unable to think about others. They are afraid of the negative and unsympathetic parent, who is so disappointed and angry with them. According to tests carried out by the developmental psychologist Ross Thompson, such children have lower scores on moral cognition.[29]

A child who has been taught how to 'mind-read' or 'mentalise' has a great advantage in situations of conflict with others. Mentalising is particularly helpful because it expands the child's repertoire of self-regulation techniques. It adds the possibility of thinking about experiences in a way that can give the child a helpful distance from painful experiences. For example, a 'mentalising' child who is being criticised is more able to say to himself, 'I wonder why she is behaving like that?' and to keep different answers going in his mind, rather than feeling compelled to accept a negative view of himself. However, children cannot develop these capacities without appropriate adult support in the first place.

## Disordered personalities

Without mentalising abilities, the child is at the mercy of adult feedback and projections. The child may then end up taking on board all sorts of 'alien' self-images – ideas about himself as mean, stupid, bad-tempered, weak or whatever the parents throw at him when they cannot manage their own anger or distress, or cannot face their own deficiencies. Just like his parents before him, he is likely to find these self-images so painful that he tries not to recognise them. Instead, a common defensive strategy in childhood is for the child to disconnect from his own feelings so that he does not have to identify with such hateful self-images. What can then happen is that on the outside, the child learns to fake normality and fit in with other people's expectations, but a gap opens up between the outward 'persona' and the inner self with its painful feelings.

Children who have been abused or maltreated by others often have no way of escaping from their damaging relationships; they cannot throw back the negative treatment they are receiving from the powerful adults in their life, and they do not yet have an established sense of a 'good' self to restore their own well-being internally. Yet escaping inwards and resorting to the technique of dissociating from unpleasant experiences is a risky strategy. When children switch off from their feelings, it can make them even less in touch with themselves and their inner worlds, which in turn makes it more difficult for them to understand other people's emotions. It undermines social connections and learning to relate to others. Maltreated children are not good at reading facial expressions[30] or describing inner states in words[31] and sometimes find themselves unable to respond to others in distress. Presumably because they themselves weren't comforted when they were distressed, some maltreated children behave in a rather shocking way to other children who are in distress;

instead of comforting them, they react with anger or fear.[32] The more negative the mother–child relationship, the less able the child is to respond to others with concern.

As these children grow up, they may end up living their life in compartments – for example, when they treat someone badly, they find it difficult to 'own' their actions. Instead they mentally seal them off, denying the shameful parts of their own experience to themselves and others in an effort to ensure that the 'badly behaved self' never comes into contact with the 'well-behaved self'.

Part of the reason why experiences have to be dealt with in this way in the mind is because families which are intolerant of bad behaviour and are not good at repairing relationships offer no way to integrate them. This capacity is absolutely crucial to mental health. If conflicts between people can't be repaired, and every mis-step counts against you for ever, then it becomes very difficult to admit mistakes. A child who is labelled as 'bad' will fear he is beyond redemption, and will be left in the grip of overwhelming shame with no means of making himself feel better. So instead, the child behaves defensively and claims that he never makes mistakes, never hurts anyone, and tries to seal off his inevitable errors in a separate mental compartment which he tries not to think about. Alternatively, he may try to get rid of his badness by blaming others and making them the 'bad' ones. It is a strategy that can all too easily be carried into adulthood; we have all seen divorcing adults behaving like this.

These defensive states of mind are linked to a range of personality disorders, from the narcissistically self-absorbed to the borderline personality who is most liable to manage his feelings by splitting, projecting and compartmentalising. At the furthest extreme of this spectrum are the sociopaths, who seem almost numb to other people's feelings. Because they themselves lack feelings of concern for others, they can't quite believe that other people have them – they imagine that others are 'dishonestly play-acting something mythical called "conscience"'[33] whilst they are more honest.

Many insecure children are unsure what to do with their negative emotions, particularly anger. They may have had little experience of constructive conflicts involving discussion, persuasion, argument and resolution. When adults don't help them to recover equilibrium and restore the relationship, they may be left in a painful state of negative arousal, with little means of feeling better. Although they may have learned to hold in their anger out of fear – to protect themselves – they haven't learned to do so to protect others. Instead, they may have learned from their caregivers that it is acceptable to hurt others physically or psychologically, and that aggressive behaviour is an effective way of forcing others to do what you want. They have learned that there are 'winners' and 'losers'. This, I believe, is how Strict parents pass on attitudes that ultimately promote selfishness.

Children of Nurturant parents, on the other hand, are more comfortable with negative emotions. Their parents have conveyed the message that their negative feelings are just as valid as their positive feelings. They don't have to 'make happy' when they are distressed, or take care of a parent's feelings rather than attending to their own. When they experience conflict with a parent, they know that their feelings are valid – the adult doesn't tell them they are 'rubbish' or stupid, but respects both parties' right to express their feelings. This means that, for them, relationships aren't threatened by conflict. Even if they are highly agitated, they are able to keep thinking and understanding others' feelings too.

In these secure attachments, empathy and co-operation are more likely outcomes than in insecure relationships. Grazyna Kochanska's research into the development of conscience in childhood suggests that an affectionate relationship between primary caregiver and child – in particular, a mutually responsive relationship – is the best predictor of good moral development.[34] Children in happily mutual relationships have a strong investment in paying attention to their parent's wishes, because they want to preserve the relationship. As a result, they have been found to be much more co-operative without being asked, and more likely to follow the parent's rules even when she is not there. They trust her judgement and listen to what she says.

Basically, good behaviour comes out of internalised experience in relationships. Whilst Lakoff pays his dues to Strict parents and points out that they will help others in their community who are victims of natural disasters, and will protect their children from the dangers of the modern world if they can, they tend to call upon willpower and duty as motivators rather than empathy. Yet one study of gentiles who rescued Jews in World War Two found that they had not acted courageously to help others out of a sense of duty or because it was expected of them. On the contrary, coming from empathic rather than strict families, their most notable characteristic was their ability to trust their own emotions and not worry about what others would think. Magda Trocme, a French Protestant who put herself at risk to help Jews during the Nazi occupation of France, described her motivation in a casual fashion as nothing special: 'I do not hunt around to find people to help.

But I never close my door, never refuse to help somebody who comes to me and asks for something. This I think is my kind of religion. You see, it is a way of handling myself.'[35] 'Handling herself' implies something habitual and ingrained from childhood – her basic moral position, her stance on life, her assumption that others had value and it was natural to respond helpfully to others – an attitude that she did not question, a response that she trusted.

It is not reasoning which overcomes selfish impulses, nor strict moral guidance that guarantees children's moral development. All the evidence points instead towards the importance of love and affection, good self-regulation and self-awareness, as the true precursors of morality. Yet a relatively high number of families are still not able to pass on the habits of attentiveness and care that produce secure bonds. In fact, attachment research consistently reveals that around 40 per cent of families relate in insecure ways. Although this is a minority of parents, it is a minority which is large enough to have a significant impact on society. Their authoritarian, neglectful or permissive strands of parenting continue to be passed on down the generations. Although many of these parents sincerely believe they are doing the best they can for their children, the evidence is that their styles of parenting do not enable empathy to flourish.

## Finding time for empathy

Giving attention and building affectionate relationships with children takes up time. In many homes of the past, parents were preoccupied with physical survival. Domestic labour was arduous and time-consuming, and their priority was to keep their children alive by feeding and clothing them, and caring for them when sick. Harsh discipline was a shortcut to obedience, and Strict parenting was the most common form of parenting. It is still relatively common amongst parents who have little time and attention to give their children – whether they are ambitious and driven middle-class parents or lower-class parents working shifts and struggling to survive.

The development of more empathic forms of parenting depends on being able to give time and attention to children's feelings. It has paralleled the rise of the middle class and the peculiar division of labour that was established during the industrial revolution, which for the first time gave some middle-class women the time and leisure to focus attention on their children and think about child-rearing. However, people who themselves had been raised by harsh parents did not always know how to achieve empathy. Even in the middle classes, Strict parenting did not die out.

Now, more than two hundred years later, many children still grow up in insecure relationships lacking in empathy. While there is potentially time available for all parents in the industrialised countries to pay attention to their babies and small children, since we now have many labour-saving devices and a high standard of living, the inner battle for empathy has not yet been won. Although we have conquered the material sphere and provided ourselves with comfortable, well-fed lives, we have not conquered the emotional poverty within, rooted in forms of emotional attachment that get passed on down the generations. In fact, the revolution in women's lives over the last few decades has thrown new challenges in the path of developing an empathic society.

# 6. FAMILY FORTUNES

There was a child went forth every day;
And the first object he look'd upon, that object he
  became;
. . . His own parents,
He that had father'd him, and she that had conceiv'd him
  in her womb, and birth'd him,
They gave this child more of themselves than that;
They gave him afterward every day – they became part
  of him.
The mother at home, quietly placing the dishes on the
  supper-table;
The mother with mild words – clean her cap and gown,
  a wholesome odor falling off her person and clothes
  as she walks by;
The father, strong, self-sufficient, manly, mean, anger'd,
  unjust;
The blow, the quick loud word, the tight bargain, the
  crafty lure,
The family usages, the language, the company, the furniture – the yearning and swelling heart,
Affection that will not be gainsay'd – the sense of what
  is real.

*Walt Whitman, from 'There Was a Child Went Forth'*[1]

Family life and child-rearing are always taking new forms and subtly adapting to different social conditions. The family, whether it has a primarily economic function, or is a sentimental haven from the stress of the working world, remains the first social group, and passes on its own 'social capital' in the form of attitudes and habits, as well as its own unique internal 'love culture'. But what is happening to the family in our current phase of history? Is our current mode of family life moving us closer to an empathetic culture?

We have come a long way since the era conjured up in Whitman's poem. Its sense of traditional teamwork between husband and wife belongs to an earlier age when the family was a productive economic unit. For centuries, a practical partnership of husband and wife would work their small-holding or follow a trade or craft, sharing a daily life with each other and their young children, until this way of life was broken up by the industrial revolution. Whatever the frustrations and limitations of such a life, Whitman conveys the deep sense of belonging experienced by living a life with predictable roles and familiar people. The poem suggests that it is the family members' very lack of choice which enables them to accept each other's idiosyncrasies and even to feel as if they are a part of each other.

After the industrial revolution, the family was no longer a working group. Instead, each member of the family had to seek employment and often saw little of the other family members, as they worked long hours to survive. People came to think of themselves as individuals pursuing their own goals, although many still interpreted their wages as a means of supporting their family. Today, this individualism has reached its zenith: more and more people regard their incomes as personal, and experience domestic life almost entirely as individuals, eating fast food alone, watching separate televisions or using computers in different rooms. Within the domestic sphere, people can be marooned in a comfortable isolation since relating to other family members is no longer necessary for survival. Although women still assume much of the responsibility for the physical and emotional care that is needed to sustain family life, few women are available in the way that they once were.

The old division of labour that has been through so many permutations is currently being re-shaped by the new social and economic conditions we find ourselves in. Much of this happens unconsciously, just as it did when conditions changed in the past. During the industrial revolution, huge changes happened to the family, without any particular conscious intent. Women's lives diverged: some had to work long and hard in paid employment to feed their families, whilst others were restricted to the home and were obliged *not* to work. Both ways of life were highly oppressive to women. Gradually, as prosperity increased, women's lives converged again and well before the middle of the twentieth century most women were living similar lives – although it was still a restricted life, since women from every kind of background tended to be poorly educated, had limited professional opportunities and after marriage had little choice but to devote their lives to their husband's and children's needs. They stayed in the background, enabling men to pursue their goals.

But in the later twentieth century, various significant changes came together to move things on once again, and to extend individualism to women. The advent of the Pill meant women were no longer at the mercy of their reproductive systems and could choose how many children to have and when to have them. From the 1960s, more women found it possible to carry on working even after they got married, often in part-time jobs. Although the majority still stayed at home while their children were young, there was a new trend for mothers to go to work when their children were still under school age. It's a trend which has gathered momentum, sweeping up more and more mothers into paid employment. This has challenged the whole nature of the family as women have absorbed themselves in the working world, leaving the domestic sphere behind. Today, there is often no one in the home during the working week, maintaining the home, managing the children or preparing nourishing meals, no one with the time and energy to take on the 'emotion work' of soothing others as they return from their labours. Women have become better paid and in many cases no longer need men to provide for them economically. The family's economic functions have shrunk and its emotional functions are uncertain.

Many of these changes were led by the economy. The decline in industrial production in the second half of the twentieth century meant that the economy switched from relying on the production of heavy goods, work which often depended on workers' physical strength, to an increasingly high-tech and service-based workplace, which didn't need 'masculine' strength to the same extent but which did require a more educated population. These changes opened up the workplace to women.

Higher education became available to more people, women among them. Although female graduates still made up only a small minority, their education gave these women the confidence to be vocal and demanding, and triggered off a new movement for women's rights – particularly the right to work and to participate in public life on equal terms with men. My mother left school at sixteen just after the Second World War, too early for her to benefit from these social changes; she was always frustrated by her lack of education. My luck was different, and I found myself in the midst of these exciting changes, campaigning at university for more places for women, and taking part in the Women's Movement of the early 1970s. The vocal young feminists of my generation were aggrieved that women's domestic activities had been taken for granted for so long and were given so little economic or social value. In my kitchen, I still have one of the posters we produced at the time, a screen-print of an assembly line, showing women's nurturing activities at home as part of the process of production. Its slogan was: 'Capitalism depends on domestic labour.'

Ironically, it was the very success of industrial capitalism and the spread of affluence and technological innovation that fuelled the growing dissatisfaction that women felt. The prosperity of the twentieth century, which enabled people to live in better, more spacious houses rather than crowding whole families into a few rooms; the twentieth-century technology which enabled women to take control of their fertility and restrict the number of children they had; the twentieth-century legislation that ensured that children went to school well into their teenage years – these changes, which appeared to be (and were) so beneficial, had unintended consequences. Together, they meant that – for the first time in history – increasing numbers of women were bringing up their young children in relative isolation. Whilst child-rearing had been a group activity for most of human history, it now became a private activity within the four walls of your own house. Mothers no longer had company, and someone to pass the baby to, whilst they got on with other tasks: older children were unable to help because they were at school; other mothers were in their own homes with their own labour-saving washing machines and vacuum cleaners. This left women who looked after a baby at home socially isolated and socially powerless. Many women found it intolerable, and after less than fifty years of this way of living, they started to protest – led by Betty Friedan in the USA, who in the 1960s gave voice to 'the problem that has no name'.[2]

The Women's Movement that followed was highly successful in establishing women's right to work and to equal pay, and in opening up opportunities for women to participate in the public sphere. Women suddenly found their voice. But many women did not feel comfortable moving out of their old roles, and expressed their sense that they had been oppressed not only materially but also psychologically. As the feminist Lee Comer put it: 'We have had our mental and emotional feet bound for thousands of years.'[3] It took a massive effort by many women to overcome the internal conditioning that prevented them from enjoying their new power and realising their own potential. Consciousness-raising groups were central to this process, providing the support for women to change their own behaviour – to speak up when men ignored their contributions, to challenge their own sexist child-rearing practices, and to learn how to overcome their own tendency to treat boy children differently from girls. The intensity of this psychological work, alongside the more conventional forms of political intervention that women made, was probably a major factor in enabling a decisive shift to occur over the relatively short space of about thirty years.

During this particular period of rapid change, women were highly focused on their own dilemmas and needs. It took a great deal of energy and determination to transform not only the way women were regarded by men, but also the way women regarded themselves. An essential part of the process was to insist that women should refuse their previous roles of caring for babies and children and husbands, making meals and cleaning houses. The fear of falling back into the old roles led many women into extreme positions of hostility to traditional family life. A more nuanced position felt like treachery – anyone who suggested women belonged with their small children was an oppressor forcing them back into the home. John Bowlby, the pioneer of attachment theory, suffered this fate when he argued that early attachments were crucial to children's well-being. His timing was unfortunate.

But the division of labour was so entrenched that it was hard to imagine a new one that would involve men re-thinking the way they lived too; men were seen by many women as adversaries and as unlikely allies in creative re-thinking. Instead, women made demands for the state to take over women's domestic duties. At the time, these demands were fairly extreme attempts to socialise women's role, including demands for 24-hour nurseries and communal canteens. This was so unrealistic that it made it easy for both state and employers to continue to ignore the claims of domestic life. In the end, it meant that women simply attempted to enter the labour market on the same terms as men.

The working pattern women came to adopt was based on the existing division of labour between men and women. Instead of challenging the prevailing norms of working life, ambitious women challenged themselves. They strained to be heroines, attempting to compete with men at work without a supportive 'wife' at home; struggling with the impossible task of performing the shopping, cooking, cleaning and child-care on top of a long day in paid employment. They were afraid of being seen as inadequate or incapable, so they tried not to let their domestic commitments, their premenstrual tension or their children get in the way of matching the performance of men. It became popular to talk of 'superwomen' and to believe that women could 'have it all'. Special pleading was seen as dangerous because it might return women to second-class status.

Capitalism happily adjusted to the presence of women who joined the workplace on men's terms: it came up with ready meals, microwave ovens and − eventually − nurseries, to enable women to work. Women's demands for equal pay and opportunity have been slowly addressed, although not yet fully met. But as the new situation became established, women defined themselves more and more as workers and less and less as mothers, to such an extent that the old slogan of women's 'right to work' has now become an *obligation* to be paid employees. We have turned 180 degrees from our previously limited traditional identity as only wives and mothers to an equally limited modern identity of primarily being workers. The current consensus is that everyone ought to be economically self-sufficient at all times. Even the feminists' dream of 24-hour nurseries is not far off as government talks of 'wrap-around childcare'. Increasingly, even mothers of

young babies are expected to work and this is seen as
normal – and confirmed by government policies which make
financial support for working parents much more forthcoming than financial support for those who stay at home with a
baby.

Michelle and Barack Obama are typical of modern,
middle-class, post-feminist families in their assumption that
both parents would work after having children. In the USA,
maternity leave (unpaid) is available only for three months,
and professional women are expected to return to work
quickly. It's not clear whether Michelle felt under pressure to
do so, or whether it was simply her personal wish to continue
with her successful career, but she did return to part-time
work when their first baby was three months old. Barack
Obama endorses the view that both parents of babies need to
work, since it is a financial necessity to pay for the inflated
mortgages that have become necessary to live in middle-class
neighbourhoods and attend the better public schools.
Certainly, Barack and Michelle were well-off enough to hire
an 'in-home babysitter', as well as a cleaner, to ease the difficulties of the transition. For those less fortunate, Obama
advocates more 'high-quality daycare'. He rather patronisingly
acknowledges that some parents will want to stay at home and
bring up their own baby, but implies that this slightly wacky
choice will incur penalties – it will involve doing without
'certain material comforts' or moving house 'to a community
where the cost of living is lower'.[4] In other words, whilst he
is happy for the state to fund better daycare options for working parents, he sees stay-at-home parenting as a personal
eccentricity. These attitudes have become the norm in the
middle classes.

In recent years I have observed a similar shift in attitudes amongst many of the families with whom I work, at either end of the social scale. Although poorer women often live in social housing or cheaper neighbourhoods and are not always struggling with massive mortgage debt, nonetheless they increasingly share the social expectation that mothers will carry on working. For women on a lower income, it is not always about financial necessity, as the work available to them is invariably poorly paid and does not necessarily improve their standard of living greatly. Sometimes it is just about making life more interesting – it can be about a positive renewal of self – a chance to get some 'Me-time', as one of my clients called it. Very often, such mothers are able to balance this desire with their children's needs by looking for part-time work that fits around their children.

Professional women, who feel that they 'ought' to return to work, sometimes even full-time, to keep their careers going or to pay their mortgages, can have a more pressurised experience. For these mothers, whose pre-birth lives have centred on their working identities, there is sometimes a real dread of losing their sense of self if they become a stay-at-home mother – it can be seen as a sort of social death, as well as almost inevitably damaging their career prospects. However, even when they feel they *have* to go back to full-time work, professional women are often conflicted and experience great anxiety about how their working will affect their babies. This makes it very hard for them to hear any evidence that suggests that their young child might indeed be suffering from their unavailability.

My client Sally-Ann would probably be described as falling between these two groups. She had a clerical job that bored her. Although she expected to go back to work part-time when her baby was ready, she was very concerned to be a good mother and saw this as just as big a part of her identity. However, the social pressures on Sally-Ann were such that she ended up returning to work before she had intended to. Her story shows how complex this process can be, as the cultural expectations about working motherhood played into Sally-Ann's own emotional difficulties.

Sally-Ann grew up with parents who weren't able to give much support to her developing sense of self. Her father was highly critical of her as a child and would shout at her when displeased, whilst her mother was a manic-depressive who drank too much and who was preoccupied with herself. Neither gave her much attention. When Sally-Ann's baby was born, she felt depressed and angry. She had great difficulty in adjusting to motherhood, and frequently felt like 'being self-ish' and going to bed for a rest, leaving the baby to his own devices. She had little faith that her baby would love her and found it hard to look him in the eyes, fearing that he would see what an inadequate person she was and would judge her as her father had done.

When I started seeing them together about three months after Frank's birth, Sally-Ann kept him at a distance. In our sessions, she kept him turned away from her on her lap, or put him down on the mat and largely ignored him. As our therapeutic relationship developed, Sally-Ann gradually found her protective feelings for Frank. With encouragement not to take his crying personally, she discovered that she could calm him. Through my demonstrations of 'mind-mindedness' with Frank, she started to see him as a person in his own right. She grew more confident in her mothering. Frank started to relax and smile at her more, and together they started to enjoy their relationship.

Just as the relationship was taking off, when he was around five months old, she came to her session with a bright, excited air. She told me that she had been back to work for a day to discuss arrangements for her return to work, which she expected to do when Frank was ten months old. Her boss had seen her and made it clear he wanted her back as soon as possible. In fact, he wanted her to return to do a four-day week, not their agreed arrangement of three days a week. He was offering her a new, restructured job with potential career opportunities. She immediately agreed to return within the next few weeks, when Frank would be seven months old. She didn't mention Frank's needs.

My heart sank, as the relationship between her and Frank was still fragile and Sally-Ann still had many moments of feeling unlovable and lost as a mother, whilst Frank could be fretful and unsmiling. I asked her more about what it had been like going in to work. She said that as she had gone up the stairs to the office, her spirits had lifted. Although she now loved her baby, it was wonderful to be back in her old life for a day. I asked what that feeling was about. She said she knew who she was in the office; she knew what to do and how to get approval. She felt in control. At home, she couldn't predict how Frank would react. She would often feel unappreciated if he didn't enjoy what she had planned for him or if he wasn't quickly soothed. For Sally-Ann, looking after Frank was a more demanding job than being employed, because it was so much to do with reading his emotions, something that had not been done well for her as a child.

Our work-centred culture seems unable to factor in the needs of babies. Instead of supporting Sally-Ann through her uncertainties about her mothering ability, and helping her to establish a good emotional foundation for Frank's future well-being, this culture pushes young mothers to downgrade emotional needs – whether their own or their babies'. Feelings are so messy and complicated compared to the certainties of work and money.

## Becoming a mother

In this changed climate of opinion where women have adapted to the masculine work culture, it has become increasingly difficult to express a different view of womanhood, to value motherhood as an *expression* of female individuality, not as a denial of it. As women define themselves more and more in terms of their work, they can lose touch with a specifically female identity. In our current work-dominated culture, it is seen as quite provocative to express the view that a mother's bond with her baby is unique and precious. When I have done so in talks and lectures, for example, I have discovered that those in the audience who share some of my views don't find it easy to respond in public, but sometimes come up to me afterwards to thank me for saying what they were thinking but dared not express.

Whilst in some cultures of the past, the biological dimension of the female experience – the physicality of being pregnant, giving birth and breastfeeding a baby – and the pain and joy that these experiences generate were venerated and celebrated, in modern society there is a tendency to downplay or even erase such experiences. Natural birth is being replaced by a huge increase in unnecessary Caesarian sections, breast-feeding is regarded by many as repulsive and does not last long for most babies. Women's biological femaleness seems to be something to avoid or get past as quickly as possible. And now babies are increasingly hurried off to substitute carers too, as if spending time with a baby is an unnecessary indulgence at best, or a waste of time.

The downplaying of women's biological role has, on the other hand, opened up an opportunity for men to get more involved with their young children. Now that women no longer monopolise the job of child-rearing, it is much more common to see men out and about pushing buggies and taking an active part in bringing up their families, which is a hugely positive change. However, it is interesting to note, as Oliver James pointed out to me, that fathers rarely look after their own *babies* for any length of time. Even in Sweden and Denmark, where they have the option of doing so, few fathers take their paternal leave whilst their children are babies. In Sweden it is rare for fathers to take leave when their babies are younger than eleven to fifteen months, whilst in Denmark, most paternal leave is taken in the three to five year age group.[5] It seems as if men instinctively respect the biological connection between mothers and their babies – a connection based on breastfeeding, hormones and bodily closeness as the baby makes the transition from the body that gave him life to a separate existence.

The birth of a child is still a major *female* event – mother and baby are after all connected through their bodies, and are involved in biologically regulating each other from the start. For many modern women who are now used to living lives largely unfettered by their biology, this confrontation with their bodily reality can be a challenge. Sue Miller's novel *The Senator's Wife* expresses this sense of shock and revulsion via the protagonist Meri:

> *Corruption*, that was the word for what was happening to her. She'd entered the biological procession, the one that ends in total corruption. She'd been claimed, by time. By birth and death. She'd been changed. But this was what happened. This was what women *did*. She thought of the mothers she'd known. Her own. Nathan's. Lou. Delia. Several of her friends. They'd all had to give up some sense of themselves as inviolably who they were, physically. They'd all had to learn to watch their bodies change in ways they had no control over. To learn to share their bodies with the stranger taking shape inside them. Why should she be any different?[6]

At the same time, participation in this unchanging biological event can be deeply satisfying and moving. In her book *Of Woman Born*, Adrienne Rich describes her own sense of wonder at the process of giving birth, and how mother and baby are connected 'in a way she can be connected with no one else except in the deep past of her infant connection with her own mother'.[7]

When people talk about 'childcare' for babies, it doesn't convey this intense emotional bond. 'Childcare' is a word which conveys physical and educational care, not a powerful relationship which carries so much human and spiritual meaning. Nor does it convey what is really going on in infancy, a major process of *unconscious* learning of how to be human and how to relate to other people, which comes about largely through the parent's sensitivity and attunement to her baby. As I have described in earlier chapters, the quality of attention that a baby experiences really matters, and ultimately helps the baby's brain to develop a balanced stress response and a capacity for self-control and empathy for others. One of the benefits of breastfeeding is that it encourages mothers to spend long stretches of time focusing their attention on their baby, rewarding them with a raised level of the hormones oxytocin (which is also the hormone released after sexual intercourse, providing a feeling of gratification and lack of motivation to go anywhere or do anything) and prolactin. These hormones also make mothers more responsive to their baby's cries. Of course, bottle-feeding mothers, fathers and adoptive parents are all perfectly capable of giving sensitive attention to their babies too, and enjoying it, but it is interesting to note how nature has set us up to receive these very specific physiological rewards.

For a mother, infancy is a unique period of time with her baby, yet after the first few months, more and more parents are handing their still very young babies over to the care of other people. This is a relatively new development. For example, in 1980, when I had my first baby, around three-quarters of eligible working mothers were at home with their babies for the first year. Today, it is more like a quarter. In fact only 3 per cent of mothers took off more than a year's maternity leave, according to one study carried out by the UK government in 2007.[8] This is a dramatic change in our child-rearing practice, and is particularly extreme in the USA. In one substantial study of American mothers in Minnesota, 50 per cent had returned to work eleven weeks after the birth of their baby[9]. Tiny babies, as young as six weeks old, are now put into group-based day-care nurseries as if they were already 'children' who need to socialize and learn. Increasingly, both in the UK and USA, performance-driven values permeate early childcare, with a focus on the physical milestones such as sleeping through the night, eating what you are given, walking and talking. There seems to be an urgency about growing up fast – so as to be as little trouble to your carers as possible. The drive for everyone to be *economically* self-sufficient has pushed us into an expectation that everyone should be *emotionally* self-sufficient – even babies.

The pressure on parents to conform to these new expectations has been mounting. There is little social support for the parental couple to share early childcare. Even egalitarian, well-off couples find it difficult to resolve these problems by re-shaping their working hours, when employers do not understand the need for them to do so – after all, isn't that what nurseries are for? Instead, more and more middle-class parents are attempting to maintain their demanding work schedules relatively soon after childbirth, by farming out the childcare to other – poorer, less well-educated – women. Although many do use childminders and grandparents, there is currently a vogue for day-care where many parents believe babies will be 'stimulated' by spending time with professionals trained to look after children. Actually this a far cry from the reality, which is that most nursery staff have had little training. In the UK, although half the staff of a nursery must have a qualification, this is more likely to be a one-year, on-the-job National Vocational Qualification (NVQ) than a substantial training or degree of any kind. Yet the myth of training persists. In her book *Because of Her Sex*, the journalist Kate Figes quotes Nicky Padfield, an academic lawyer and mother of three children, who declares: 'It's good for babies to be with professional carers. Professional mums are not necessarily as good. To be stuck at home with Mum all day can be the least stimulating thing, particularly if it's me and I'm reading the newspaper.' Figes endorses this view.[10]

This misreading of babies' needs may be a necessary part of some mothers' denial of their own sadness at not being with their babies. Instead of recognising their baby's need for intimate and personal cherishing, parents may prefer to think of their baby as a developmentally more advanced older child who needs 'company', and mental 'stimulation' rather than the ordinary loving attentions of his own family.

Figes suggests that the solution to many childcare dilemmas is for workplace hours to be more moderate so that parents can 'go home at a reasonable hour and see their children', but she is horrified at the prospect of forcing 'capable, qualified women back to full-time motherhood' which she sees as 'punishment'. Clearly, the incapable, unqualified women will just have to look after the babies instead. Indeed, this is what happens; it is often the poorest and least educated women who are given the task of caring for babies, as if looking after babies was an unimportant task which anyone could do – no more than the drudgery of changing nappies and feeding.

However, what these substitute caregivers in nurseries sometimes have in common with the parents who employ them is a focus on physical care or cognitive stimulation, rather than the emotional care of babies. It seems to be easier to view nursery care as a form of education, and to think of it in terms of measurable tasks which can be performed without emotional commitment by anyone. What is more difficult to believe is that temporary, poorly paid caregivers could provide an adequate substitute for loving and responsive parenting. The low pay inevitably attracts young and inexperienced staff. Few nursery workers are themselves mothers or fathers, yet they are given very little training in understanding a baby's feelings. This can lead to a pragmatic approach focused on feeding and changing, not on the meaning of the baby's squawks and cries, and moods: 'He's just been fed so he can't be hungry.' Without individual bonds between caregiver and child, interactions can get stuck at the level of 'small talk' – like adults at a party whose conversation soon fizzles out – instead of forming deeper relationships based on mutual regulation and mutual understanding.[11] Although the UK government now provides nursery workers with basic guidance on early emotional development, together with examples of good practice, without extensive training this is no more effective than giving someone a recipe book and expecting them to be a great cook. Similarly, despite great progress in moving towards the provision of a 'key-worker' for each child, this is still no guarantee that a particular member of staff will be present every day, nor that she will stay in her post for any length of time – a state of affairs which makes it difficult for a baby to form a secure attachment to anyone.

There are many nursery workers who genuinely enjoy relating to babies. But there are also caregivers who display a harshness and a lack of recognition of the uniqueness of each baby. I heard of an incident in one nursery where several young nursery staff were in a room with a small child who had just been told off for something she had done wrong. The toddler was crying desperately in a corner. The administrator then came into the room and asked if any of them were going to talk to the child or comfort her. Their collective response was: 'I'm not her key-worker' – therefore they would not respond to her feelings. Something similar was observed by a young TV reporter for the BBC 'Whistleblower' series.[12] As she watched another young and inexperienced member of the nursery team caring for a baby who was crying on her lap, the nursery worker referred to the baby by saying, 'The noise in my ear is doing my head in.' Although anecdotal, it is hard to see how children in such situations could be learning about trust and empathy, or developing good self-regulation.

## Social engineering through nurseries

Government policy on children has been driven by the twin objectives of creating a well-educated labour force and reducing child poverty (which also is linked to low educational outcomes). To this end, it has stated its intention to get more lower-income parents into work, by increasing the number of places available for their children in registered forms of childcare, including nurseries.[13] As Penelope Leach put it, 'In the English-speaking countries, child care is primarily about parental work and only secondarily about child well-being . . . a benefit for the adult world rather than a service to children'.[14] To a cynic, it might look as if day-care is also being used as a tool of social engineering, particularly to bypass the perceived inadequacies of lower-class parents, rather than as a valuable experience in itself. This attitude has been around for a long time. Denise Riley described how, in post-war England, one 'Hygiene Committee' advocated the nursery school as ' the only agency capable of cutting the slum mind off at its root'.[15]

Dispiritingly, the values of workaholics continue to be applied to babies. Despite evidence that policy-makers are much more aware of children's emotional needs than ever before, still they have encouraged parents to share their perspective that educational achievement is the primary objective of even the earliest childcare. In its national 'curriculum' for babies, the UK government even views young babies' reaching and grasping for toys as preparation for their future handwriting skills.[16] The early years curriculum uses the same skills framework for babies – including a category for 'problem solving, reasoning and numeracy'– as for older children, for whom pre-school education is genuinely valuable.[17] However, there is no consistent evidence that the nursery-based approach works for babies. Whilst some research has shown that high-quality group care does enhance their cognitive and linguistic performance, at least in the short term, there is other evidence that when babies receive care from changing caregivers, language development is often less good.[18] Since most day-care has a very high turnover of staff (nearly 40 per cent), this isn't a very convincing basis for social policy.

Today, the political classes are also determined to get the poorest families off welfare benefits and into work, for their own 'self-esteem' as well as for finding a way out of poverty – a view which has some validity – and supporting childcare so they can work is a part of that. However, as a means of breaking the intergenerational cycles of *emotional* poverty, it leaves something to be desired. The most up-to-date evidence from a huge and long-term American study by the National Institute of Child Health and Development (NICHD) confirms that the earlier babies are put into day-care, and the more hours they are in non-maternal care over their first few years, the more disobedient, boastful, argumentative and all-round aggressive they are likely to be when they start school.[19] These negative social and emotional consequences seem to me to outweigh any potential cognitive benefits.

Furthermore, even those cognitive benefits are uncertain. Whilst babies who are cognitively stimulated by their caregivers, whether at home or in high-quality nurseries, may well develop a wider vocabulary early on, the educational gains at this early stage of life are also quite likely to be ephemeral. They don't have lasting effects on academic performance in later childhood.[20] On the contrary, new research implies that if we want babies to 'achieve', we would do better to ensure that they have positive early relationships with sensitive caregivers. Developmental psychologist Clancy Blair and his team at Pennsylvania State University have found that what underpins the emergence of all-round academic achievement in the first years of school is the capacity for self-regulation.[21] This means that it is the quality of emotional care that babies receive which has the most impact on their eventual ability to make use of learning opportunities at school and beyond.

## Parenting policies

On top of trying to meet demanding financial expectations, to hang on to their work identities or to be weaned off welfare benefits, there are other new pressures for modern mothers coming from government – a pressure to perform as a parent, to deliver a 'product' which is literate and numerate and not emotionally damaged. These demands have been building as governments have intervened more and more in parenting, to the point of endorsing parenting classes and now even a parenting 'academy' in the UK.

Although these new parenting policies are probably ultimately driven by economic concerns – about the soaring costs of obesity, deliquency and poor mental health, in particular – they do at least benefit from following the latest scientific research. There are now clear guidelines in place that urge the appropriate authorities to promote sensitive and attuned parenting in the early years in order to prevent social ills such as anti-social behaviour and depression, and to protect babies' neurological development.[22] For example, it makes sense both in health and in social terms to encourage breastfeeding for at least six months. Breastfed babies get more of the nutrients they need for the brain to develop in an optimum way. Compared to bottle-fed babies, they have been found to be more emotionally resilient and better able to cope with stress.[23] Reading government documents such as the Child Health Promotion Programme of 2008, you would think that the arguments that I and many other people in the infant mental health world have been making for years about the importance of babyhood as the foundation for mental health have really been taken on board at last.

Yet the problem remains – how *can* parents meet the emotional needs of their children if they're working long hours? How can mothers breastfeed their babies if they are at work, and how can either parent be sensitive and attuned to a baby – or an older child for that matter – if they only see them at the end of a long, busy day? If governments are confused, so are the parents, who are equally torn between the pull of their financial needs and the pull of their baby's emotional needs. There is no clear and unambivalent support for parents (either mothers or fathers) to stay with their own babies, no serious financial back-up which would send the message that this is a valued and essential job. Although we have extravagantly high aspirations for emotional well-being, and are beginning to be aware of the role that babyhood plays in achieving it, we are not giving parents the support they need to enable that process.

## Unacceptable dependence

One problem is that our culture dislikes dependence of any kind – whether that is the baby's dependence on his parents, or the primary caregiver's dependence on other people's financial and emotional support whilst caring for a baby. This used to be an attitude that was more common amongst conservatives or Strict parents – who loathed people who saw themselves as victims, and dreaded boys turning into effeminate homosexuals instead of 'strong' men. But now the fear of dependence seems to have spread more widely into the culture, as women's attitudes have changed and adapted to the masculine workplace.

In the 1980s, during the period when women started to achieve full participation in the working world, stay-at-home mothering was increasingly mocked by other women. Feminist academics Valerie Walkerdine and Helen Lucey characterised them as wimpy middle-class mothers who spent their time in thrall to their children – baking cookies, answering their children's questions, and chauffeuring their little darlings to ballet lessons. They painted a picture of an ineffectual mother who would respond to her children's rudeness by saying, 'It's not very nice to say things like that,' or 'You're being silly'[24] – a despised woman who could not assert herself and conveyed little authority.

The working mother, on the other hand, was approved of, because she fitted in mothering around the 'real' world of employment. Career women often justified their devotion to their careers in terms of their own fulfilment; a common argument at the time was that a happy mother makes for happy children: 'I feel much more able to give emotionally to the children since I started working full-time,' said one mother, Cathy Johns, in an interview in the *Independent*. Although this may still be true for some working mothers, it is a rather one-sided account. This particular mother was a little frustrated with her child's inability to see that this was all for the best: 'All she sees is that Mummy's not there in the day. She doesn't understand that I enjoy my work and we can afford a nice holiday. She just feels that something is missing.'[25]

Sociologists Peter and Brigitte Berger called the modern search for individual identity the 'brutal assertion of self against the claims of others'.[26] Like Christopher Lasch, they saw it as narcissistic to look at the family as a way of 'getting my needs met', rather than thinking of it as a social institution which concerns itself with others' needs or which demands things of us. As they put it, in our narcissistic world, each person is preoccupied with his or her own biography: choosing his next piece of clothing, his next house and his next relationship; his primary concern is what he needs, not what others need from him. This is a bleak view of modern life, given that most individuals still remain personally supportive of friends and family, and in many cases show concern for others by giving generously to charities. However, the trend they describe is unmistakably towards individual fulfilment and away from a sense of responsibility for others. Perhaps the economic developments that were spearheaded by families like the Wörners, which pushed us towards selfishness and away from mutual support, have made it more difficult for us to think about the needs of the group or society as a whole. But now that individualism has penetrated into mothering itself, it is challenging the whole nature of the family and raising new questions about child-rearing.

In this more narcissistic world view, it is difficult to find a place for dependence. However, in babyhood dependence is necessary and even enjoyable. Babies are not preparing for school, they are learning about their bodies and their emotions – through the very physical and intimate love relationship with their parents. Although it seems counter-intuitive to many in our culture, it is a good experience of dependence early on that enables children to grow up feeling emotionally confident and truly autonomous – not pushing them into independence before they are ready for it. Of course, everyone must grow up and become responsible for himself or herself, but the first priority for any human baby is to know they are loved and safe. *Someone* must provide sensitive and responsive parenting for every baby if we want to have an empathic society.

So does this mean that women must return to economic dependence on men, and give up their complex identities as participants in the working world when they become mothers? When feminists argued against the 1950s image of Apple Pie Mom, and rejected what they saw as the idealised 'sensitive' mother beloved of attachment theory, they were identifying something important. Of course mothers do not want to be enslaved to their biology, nor to their children's needs, and to be expected to think of nothing else. Women

are rightly terrified of their motherhood becoming, as
Adrienne Rich put it, 'an identity for all time', and of losing
their autonomy. Feminists have struggled so hard to establish
women's right to equal opportunities to fulfil themselves, the
prospect of letting women sink back into an unpaid, unsupported role without status or respect is unthinkable and is a
prospect that women should not have to tolerate.

However, I would argue that there are other solutions, to
which I will turn in my final chapter. These must involve
finding a way of paying attention to the evidence about early
childcare, and valuing motherhood, whilst at the same time
avoiding the conservative trap of advising a return to a traditional division of labour.

## The conservative view

Conservatives often reject the current freedom people have to
make their own living arrangements – 'living apart together,
same sex couples, commuting couples, patchwork families,
long distance relationships, trans-national families'[27] – because
they are seen as unstable and unsuitable for child-rearing.
They place a strong emphasis on two-parent families and on
lasting marriage and often argue that the 'broken society' is
the result of the rise of single parenthood. However, they
sometimes lack historical awareness. Their ideal family, in
which mothers cared for children at home whilst men were
the breadwinners, was a particular historical phenomenon, a
nineteenth-century invention, a middle-class way of coping
with the brutality of capitalism. By the time that most of the
population could afford this solution, capitalism was already
beginning to move on to its next phase: high consumption,

a service-based economy and increased job mobility, in which the traditional family is not as useful. This is when the middle-class ideal family began to fragment.

But rather than understanding the current breakdown of this ideal family in terms of its broader context, conservatives tend to pin the blame solely on feminists. Clearly, there are grounds for doing so: feminists have threatened the traditional patriarchal set-up by claiming their own sexual freedom and rejecting financial dependence on a husband. Since women claimed the right to work, single parenthood has massively increased; it has leapt up to over a quarter of all families in both the UK and the US, after 150 years of stability at a much lower figure – 7 per cent in 1845 and 8 per cent in 1970.

Conservatives tend to ignore other causes of family change and family fragility, such as the demands of the globalised economy for flexibility and deregulation. Increasingly, employees are expected to be geographically mobile, and to work long hours in various complex formulas. This makes it very difficult to sustain relationships, to find time together to be as emotionally close and intimate as many people would like to be. Jobs are no longer plentiful or secure, but frequently involve short-term contracts and unpredictable changes of circumstance. As the social scientist Elizabeth Beck-Gernsheim put it, material conditions are increasingly 'precarious' and as she asks: 'How is one supposed to found a family on such meagre and shaky grounds?'[28]

'Founding a family' sounds like just the kind of weighty enterprise, requiring commitment and a strong bank balance, that conservatives might be expected to espouse. Their desire to create a secure and unshakable family life is understandable. Yet just as their economic policies fail to recognise the impact of job insecurity on family life, the attempt to achieve family stability through a policy such as special tax breaks for married couples lacks understanding of what really makes people secure. It tries to prop up the outward form of traditional relationships, and their financial stability, rather than the quality of relationships themselves. And as Kate Stanley – Head of Social Policy at the Institute for Public Policy Research – has pointed out, 'the introduction of tax breaks for married couples in the 1970s famously coincided with the sharpest increase in divorce seen in the UK'.[29]

This tendency to imagine that the structure is more important than the content of relationships is at odds with the fact that, at other times, conservative thinkers show a more intuitive grasp of the emotional power of family life. They are often more comfortable than those on the left in asserting the need for love. Even as an economist, Jennifer Roback Morse is willing to defend the view that love is the foundation of society, and that people take care of babies because they love them: 'Babies come to know that they matter and they come to allow other people to matter to them. They come to know that human contact is the great good upon which their very survival depends,' she writes.[30] Yet although her book *Love and Economics* demonstrates much wisdom and thoughtfulness, and carefully talks about 'parents' rather than 'mothers', ultimately it falls back on an assumption that mothers will be financially dependent on their husbands, and that a father's role is to be an authority figure who enforces rules.

Laurence Thomas, another interesting conservative – a philosopher and political scientist based at Syracuse University – also acknowledges the power of family feeling, yet couches it in the severe language of 'self-sacrifice'. He suggests that what is central to parenting is that adults put themselves out to meet their child's needs, that they are devoted to their child's flourishing, and they 'accord that person's life weight in one's own life that is independent of one's wants'.[31] His hymn to parental love suggests that it is a unique relationship with the power to create and affirm a child's sense of self and worth. Parental love shows that 'a life can have value independent of appearances and performances, and that a life can have value in the eyes of another without being given over to satisfying that person's wishes.'

This is a version of parenthood that we can recognise as an ideal, but I doubt whether many families live up to it – certainly not my own, where my parents' main mode of relating to their children was very much through approving or disapproving of our 'appearances and performances'. When I myself became a parent in my twenties, even though I was besotted with both my babies, I experienced it as a hugely demanding challenge to put my 'wants' aside: to wake in the night when I certainly did not feel like it, to overcome irritation with the baby's persistent cries or to struggle with boredom as I helped build that tower of bricks for the sixth time. It was a completely new mindset to make choices that gave priority to someone else's needs and to give up some of my own goals and wishes for the sake of my children – and not one I was always able to sustain. Sacrificing one's own interests is not easy, particularly when we are brought up to expect self-fulfilment. And in our self-centred culture, this is rarely the spirit in which modern women are encouraged to talk about motherhood; look at any magazine, and you will find articles about how much time to take off work, how mothers can get their figures back quickly, and whether or not to have babies on their own if the biological alarm clock rings. The idea that starting a family may require self-sacrifices of various kinds is not part of our current popular media discourse.

The conflict that women experience between the pull of biological ties – our mammalian instincts – and our modern opportunities for individuation, is still unresolved. But in recent decades, the balance has increasingly tipped in the direction of women working even whilst their babies are in the pre-verbal stage of bonding and learning about emotions. Instead of holding onto the importance of love for babies, and thinking about how to improve the conditions of early parenting to ensure that these needs are met by men, women and society in general, I am concerned that women have simply adopted the existing masculine culture of work based on a division of labour where 'someone else' thinks about feelings. This work culture is not interested in sacrifices on behalf of children, only sacrifices for the benefit of the employer. My fear is that women are being sucked into this culture and are ending up, like men, unable to spend much time with their children. Women are choosing to return to work earlier and earlier, often forced to base their childcare solutions on what is convenient or affordable rather than what form of care is best for their baby.

Something important has been lost, as well as gained. The values of love and care which women 'held' as best they could on behalf of society, through the turbulent period of industrialisation, are in danger of going AWOL altogether in the post-feminist era. Whilst we can be grateful that the 'Angel in the House' is no longer an ideal, and happy that the feminist revolution has brought women back into the public sphere, nevertheless, handing over the care of babies to people who have no long-term emotional investment in them, at the very time when the foundations of emotional regulation, morality and relationship are being laid, is a very dangerous development. It exposes babies to the risk of being chronically stressed and emotionally underdeveloped. In these circumstances, it would not be surprising if the rates of personality disorder, anti-social behaviour and depression continue to rise. This particular social trend could potentially threaten the spread of empathy and co-operation despite the increased public interest in emotions and what some have called the rise of the 'therapeutic state'.

# PART III

Emotional Development in the Public Sphere

# 7. 'No More Heroes Any More'

It's time for our business and political leaders to help re-define morality beyond sex, drugs, and rock and roll to include lying, hypocrisy and callous indifference to those in need.

*Arianna Huffington, 2003*

As women have taken up their place in public life, there has been a sea change in our culture. One of the most positive aspects of this change is that it has kicked off a process of mending the psychological divisions between women and men which were exacerbated by the industrial revolution. To put it simplistically, women have reclaimed their 'masculine' qualities (demonstrating their capacity for ambition and self-expression), whilst men have been recovering their emotional and domestic (and therefore traditionally 'feminine') qualities.

As the old boundaries break down, the emotional life that was once managed by women and confined to the private sphere of the family has spilled back into public space. Family life is no longer as private and inaccessible as it once was; we are more aware of what goes on behind closed doors, how unstable many families are, and what effect this has on children. Some people now hold their family arguments on daytime television shows. Many behave in public as if they were in their own living rooms. Through the internet, we are privy to all sorts of personal information about others. Partly as a result of this greater awareness, we have begun to take more collective responsibility for many parental functions. When children come to school without having eaten break-fast, some schools will now provide it. Since many parents don't manage to educate their children emotionally, schools are stepping in. We are starting to see that emotions can't be sealed off in a separate box called 'family'.

Yet the current attitude towards emotional life is a strange hybrid: on the one hand, we have a 'therapy culture', where feelings are more freely discussed than ever, while on the other hand there is still a relentless focus on economic pro-ductivity which excludes emotional needs. In parenting, we seem to be in a period of transition which swings between the 'Strict' and 'Permissive' tendencies, and in cultural life we stumble from the liberal attitudes of the 1960s and 1970s to the 'power-dressed' tendencies of the 1980s and 1990s and back again.

The leaders we have reflect this uneasy state of affairs: they are no longer required to be patriarchal, authoritarian 'fathers of the nation', but are now expected to present a combination of pragmatic toughness and emotional openness. This is a dif-ficult balance for them to strike: Tony Blair's tears at the death of Princess Diana were to many a welcome sign of sensitiv-ity, while others were turned off by his childlike eagerness to please George W. Bush.

One positive benefit of our increased emotional awareness is that we are more able to recognise that politicians and other leaders are driven by their own emotional histories, and we are increasingly reluctant to idealise politicians as all-knowing father figures. Although political leadership is still often the preserve of privileged upper-class men, dignity and authority are no longer regarded as mandatory in a leader. The style of politics itself has become more informal. People no longer want to feel subordinate to their leaders. In the USA, in particular, the electorate has in recent years tended to show a warmer response to candidates who seem approachable and even flawed. George W. Bush's garbled talk and alcoholic past seemed to have made him more rather than less acceptable, whilst both Al Gore and John Kerry, with their more aloof and intellectual personae, struggled to win hearts and minds.

This has infuriated some liberals, whose guiding faith is in rationality and science as a means of improving and controlling the world. As one American liberal, Susan Jacoby, commented: 'A president may be described as stubborn, or as impatient, or as a sexual libertine – even, on rare occasions, as a liar – but it would be unthinkable for "objective" reporters, in print or on television, to bluntly raise the question, "Is this man smart enough to be in charge of the country?"'[1] She went further still, exclaiming somewhat contemptuously that 'the relationship between incompetence and sheer stupidity is almost never discussed'. But the Democratic party has in the past put forward candidates from the intellectual elite at their peril. Until the recent election of Barack Obama, in the last thirty years the only Democrats to succeed at the Presidency were Jimmy Carter and Bill Clinton, who both came from less privileged family backgrounds, and whose 'smartness' was cloaked with the persona of Southern charm and their emotional ability to relate to other people – a trait shared by Obama.

What seems to be most crucial in choosing a candidate is the voter's emotional sense of identification with him or her. As the psychologist Drew Westen's work has shown, there is evidence that we vote largely in the grip of emotion rather than reason: 'People's positive and negative associations to a candidate were better predictors of their voting preferences than even their judgements about his personality and competence.'[2] The parts of our brains which light up when we make political judgements, he found, were not the areas of 'cold' verbal reasoning, but the emotional and image-based areas of the brain. In other words, it is our *feelings* about political figures which guide our choices as much as – or more than – our thoughts. Liberals tend to identify with and look up to highly educated people; the mass of middle Americans appears to feel a stronger identification with war heroes, film stars or rich business executives whose lives they might aspire to. Party loyalties also play a large part in voting, since once attached to a particular party people rarely change allegiance: in the USA, Southern white men and Evangelicals are loyal to the Republican candidate, black people to the Democrats, and so on.

These emotionally driven choices are determined by the same kinds of responses we have to the people in our everyday life. When National Election Studies researchers looked back at the 2004 US election and asked a large sample of voters what had *really* determined their choices, and why they had selected George Bush over John Kerry, they learned that it was in large part because voters saw Kerry as indecisive, and Bush as more trustworthy.[3] Similarly, personal loyalties can influence our judgements on the morally dubious behaviour of politicians. Many Democrats reacted to Bill Clinton's sexual antics and lies as if he were a relative or friend who had no doubt behaved badly, but was still held in high esteem. Amongst Republicans, there was an equally high degree of tolerance for Sarah Palin's manipulative behaviour in office, when she used her political power to pursue a spiteful personal vendetta against her ex-brother-in-law. As long as she was perceived as 'one of us'– as 'hockey mom' or 'working mom' – all would be forgiven.

Whilst policy debates may have always relied less on logic than on emotional rhetoric, body language and image-making, the dominance of visual media in our current culture pushes us further towards such emotional responses. As we watch our political figures on television, we tune in to their feeling states as much as their reasoning. During the unfolding events of 9/11, the TV footage of George W. Bush sitting in a children's school library looking blank and frozen did as much to help the viewing public evaluate his emotional response as anything he later said or did. In recent presidential debates, McCain's physical stiffness and Obama's fluidity of movement around the studio seemed to communicate as much as their words.

The valuable non-verbal information we pick up from other people is processed outside of awareness. Words and symbols then give us the means to fine-tune our gut responses and think more objectively about them. Is McCain's physical posture telling us something about his mental inflexibility, or about his dignified coping with war wounds? What does Obama's calmness mean to us? For some, his poise is reassuring and soothing, for others it may feel too smooth. Those gut feelings we have about our political leaders are shaped by the associations we have about them and are highly conditioned by our own past experiences in the family.

## Family politics

I have already described George Lakoff's typology of 'Strict' and 'Nurturant' parenting in relation to child-rearing practices, but he also describes how these different styles of upbringing generate different unconscious 'frames' through which we understand politics. Lakoff suggests that each type of parenting generates different models of politics: 'Strict' families believe that politics is about absolute right and wrong; they value the individual drive to work hard, compete and acquire property to support their family. 'Nurturant' families, on the other hand, see politics as about human rights and social responsibility, and place more emphasis on the values of helping the poor or less fortunate.[4]

The conservative economist Thomas Sowell's analysis of traditionalists and liberals chimes with Lakoff's descriptions. In *A Conflict of Visions*, he sketched out his version of the two camps in the culture war.[5] Traditional families, like Strict parents, are those who rely on habits, experience and pragmatism – not intellect. They have low expectations of human beings, expecting them to be selfish and motivated by self-interest. They themselves rely on loyalty to their in-group and their local neighbourhood to help them survive and have little interest in climate change or international affairs. Since the world as they see it is unfair and uncontrollable, perfect justice and rationality and attempts to improve the world are mirages. The market is as good as it gets.

Sowell's view is that liberals – who share some features with Nurturant parents – rely on intellect. They believe that rationality and scientific knowledge can make the world a better place and can eliminate poverty and inequality (which they see as immoral). They rely heavily on education, believing that when everyone is better educated they will make better choices and challenge old ways of doing things. Their expectation is that when people are fully rational, they will not harm others and will spread empathy for the human race.

These 'competing moral visions are at the heart of today's culture wars', as the sociologist James Davison Hunter put it when, in 1991, he first introduced the concept of a 'war' between differing sub-cultures.[6] Yet, however useful it is to identify the different strands in society, it is a highly polarised description. My own inclinations are on the liberal side of this culture war, yet I can appreciate that the conservative view has the merits of adaptability and realism in the face of limitations – qualities which are crucial in harsh environments. Perhaps the reality is that we all exist on a continuum and, in practice, many people can be pragmatic, as well as being optimistic about progress through increased knowledge and understanding.

Nonetheless, Lakoff has identified something important in linking styles of child-rearing with political attitudes. The way we are treated as children inevitably sets up particular expectations of the world around us and the best way to survive in it. To my mind, a limitation of Lakoff's 'frames' is that they are primarily describing the *cognitive* unconscious, the *thoughts* and beliefs that go with particular experiences of family life. It is relevant and instructive to apply this to political life, but we can go back even further than this, to the early emotional development and brain structures that influence the way we respond to other people. In earlier chapters I have described the way in which early relationships do not just influence our *thoughts*, but actually shape our *emotional* responses and the

architecture of our brains. Early family experiences play a particularly key role in setting up these unconscious patterns of
relationship and emotional self-regulation.

I believe that the differences described by Lakoff largely
centre on each family type's attitudes to dependence, and the
way early experiences of dependence generate confidence or
a lack of confidence in the availability of care from other
people. What strikes me most forcibly about the characteri-
sations of Strict families is that they abhor dependence; they
view the world as hostile, and urge their children towards self-
reliance to protect themselves and make a good life for
themselves. Like the medieval family, they use intimidation
and punishment to ensure compliance. Nurturant families, on
the other hand, seem more comfortable with dependence.
They assume that they are in a relatively benign world, put
great faith in reasoning with children and tend to believe that
they can generally get their needs met by others. Yet Lakoff's
picture, while dualistic, does make it clear that most people
can draw on both Nurturant and Strict models. For example,
Hillary Clinton, according to her biographer, had a Nurturant
mother and an authoritarian father, and has at times shown
both facets in her character.[7] In many ways, we can think of
these different tendencies as simply the necessary twin poles
of the human psyche – approach or avoid, love or hate, bonding with others or defending ourselves against others. They
are potentials which are expressed in particular individuals and
families in response to their situation – the wider environment
as well as the family history.

When early development does not go well, whether because
of inadequate parenting or outright maltreatment of the child,
individual psychopathology can be the result. In recent years,

we have begun to consider the impact of early development on people who are labelled as deviant or mentally ill in some way: the 'depressed', the 'personality disordered', the 'anti-social' and 'conduct disordered' – those who make demands of society either in the form of care and medication or for legal processing and incarceration, all of whom cost taxpayers a great deal of money.

But to a greater and lesser degree, poor emotional development in individuals plays itself out in many other arenas of adult life, including politics, where it may have an even more far-reaching effect. Political leaders are emotionally shaped in the family like everyone else and bring their psychological make-up to bear on our social institutions. However intellectually astute they may be, it is their ability to manage human relationships which is most crucial in politics. Their weaknesses, writ large through the state, can harm many human lives or even end lives as a consequence of war.

## The rise of narcissistic politics

From the 1970s onwards, a variety of commentators observed the growing narcissism of the electorate. This coincided with new patterns of consumption and production. During this period sexual mores were liberalised, and individuals gained more freedom and choice in their personal lives. People became less willing to tolerate the restrictions of lifelong marriage, as well as other financial and sexual restraints. And as a culture of instant gratification spread, these changed attitudes affected political life. Politicians no longer dared put forward policies that would promote the long-term well-being of society if they were likely to upset people in the short-term.

The electorate has an implicit power to demand what they want when they want it by threatening to withdraw their support for politicians who do not supply it. In this sense, the cumulative moral and emotional development of the mass of people clearly makes a difference to the quality of a society; it can help or hinder long-term thoughtfulness and care for others.

In Britain the development, in the post-war period, of a more informal and egalitarian culture expressed itself in the selection of leaders who were more like the electorate rather than the distant authority figures that had seen Britain through two world wars. Leaders with a liberal, paternalistic outlook, who had invariably been to Eton and Oxford, or who had led men in the Army, and exuded the authority of the upper classes, were increasingly superceded by clever, ambitious men and women from lower middle-class families.

The new leaders were less interested in pursuing the type of social reforms promoted by past leaders such as house-building (Macmillan), prisons (Churchill), pensions (Lloyd George, Asquith) or health (Attlee) than in expanding and sustaining the capitalist economy. Often lacking the financial and social privileges of their more patrician predecessors, leaders from the 1960s onwards were in tune with the upwardly mobile values of the era. Margaret Thatcher was the iconic figure in this new era. Her vision was a middle-class dream of a better material life for the next generation – to go on holidays abroad, to own a video recorder, deep freeze, shares, and their own home: 'Our aim is to spread these good things.'[8]

Politics itself was commercialised. The electorate was gradually turned into consumers and 'customers' instead of citizens. As politics became increasingly dominated by the medium of television, it 'sold' the personalities of politicians rather than their policies. Leaders responded by becoming more concerned with their image and with 'spin'. New Labour, in particular, courted popularity by socialising with the rich and the famous. Increasingly, they conveyed their policies through 'sound-bites' rather than considered debates. All these developments pushed politics away from a parental role, however patronising that might have been in the previous class-dominated society, towards a more competitive 'sibling society'. In this role it was difficult for the political class to encourage the population to face the limitations of reality or to subordinate some of their own wishes to the greater good. Instead of pursuing the goal of moral leadership, politicians became key figures in a culture which idolised the glamour of the wealthy, inexorably leading to the irresponsible financial behaviour of the last decades.

## Bush 'n' Blair

George W. Bush and Tony Blair both came to power in the same period of the late 1990s and early 2000s. Although their era is now over, they represented the new narcissism in politics which remains the predominant trend today. Psychologically both had a strong drive for recognition, which they played out on the world stage. This drive is common in individuals who have missed out on attention or emotional validation in their early lives. One response to growing up with authoritarian or emotionally unavailable parents is to seek positions of power to reclaim a sense of self-esteem.

Bush had grown up with a mother who was described by a childhood friend as a strict disciplinarian who 'instilled fear' into her children with her verbal aggression and criticism. According to Oliver James, she was described by her closest intimates as prone to 'withering stares' and 'sharply crystalline' retorts.[9] Her son Jeb Bush described her as an 'outspoken person who vents very well – she'll let rip if she's got something on her mind' and referred to her as 'our drill sergeant'.[10] According to their uncle, this 'letting rip' often included slaps and hits.[11]

For much of his early adult life, George W. struggled against his parents' demanding standards. He was something of a party animal, abused alcohol, crashed a car and failed to live up to their ideals. However, a turning point came after one particularly serious incident, which involved crashing a plane. At this point, he seemed to give up rebelling against his parents and trying to establish his own individuality; instead of being the victim of their strict attitude, he seems to have decided to adopt it himself and to become a sober, self-disciplined politician like his father – a phenomenon known by psychoanalysts as 'identifying with the aggressor'.

As a young man, Tony Blair was also described by some who knew him at the time as an uncertain, restless personality. Despite his academic success, his enjoyment of playing in a rock band and his active social life, apparently he never felt he 'belonged' anywhere.[12] His own father had been the illegitimate child of an upper-class family, but had grown up with working-class foster parents, perhaps never quite belonging either, but in hot pursuit of social status. When Blair was ten years old, these difficulties were heightened when his father had a stroke and transferred his ambitions onto his children. This must have been quite a burden for a young child. As Blair said, 'It imposed a certain discipline. I felt I couldn't let him down.'[13] It also suggests that Blair was pushed into living up to someone else's standards rather than being accepted as he was. In the eyes of fellow MP Leo Abse, Blair was someone who was prone to seeking others' approval. Abse described how Blair used an 'over-ready winsome little-boy smile' to placate others and deflect hostility.[14] It's easy to recognise this as a common defensive behaviour in people who have grown up not feeling sufficiently accepted and emotionally secure. In tune with the modern zeitgeist, Blair's later behaviour also suggested that he may have believed that power and money would satisfy his need for recognition and self-worth.

Power and money are likely to be particularly attractive to people who, for whatever reason, lacked an emotionally secure childhood. Both power and money offer a direct route to recovering a sense of agency that individuals may have lacked as children, or redressing the wrongs they experienced. This makes politics one of the arenas of public life that exerts a magnetic pull for the personality disordered.

Power certainly focuses our attention on an individual. Under the magnifying glass of public attention, he or she can come to seem 'larger than life' with both his talents and his deficiencies that much more visible. It also means that he can enact psychodramas on behalf of large numbers of people. For example, as the cultural studies academic Heather Nunn has pointed out, when Britain's economy was weakening in the 1970s and 1980s, Margaret Thatcher projected herself as a strong leader who would make Britain strong again, defeating the ferocious Argentinians and the burly miners, as well as the 'trendy teachers' and 'loony lefties' who were weakening British society.[15] These enactments of inner psychic states play a considerable part in political life, but their psychological dimension tends to remain unacknowledged.

The danger is that in this fantasy world of projections, a hall of mirrors, those who are in power can very rapidly get cut off from the ordinary social feedback that helps all of us to maintain equilibrium with others. They may get addicted to power and find it hard to let go of the belief that they are free of weakness and inferiority. Precisely because they possess power, their subordinates may treat them like parental figures who know best and may fail to keep them in tune with other people's reality. Any pre-existing difficulties they may have had in acknowledging other people's views and experiences can then become exaggerated. In such circumstances, an individual's capacity for empathy and mentalising are liable to be tested.

Former MP and journalist Matthew Parris has described how Blair gave him the impression that he felt that his remarkable charm and power made him the one person on the planet who could reconcile George W. Bush, the French, the Germans, the UN and the anti-war protestors. On failing to deliver such promises, as Parris describes it, 'He goes into a sort of nose-tapping "watch this space" denial . . . any bank manager used to dealing with bankrupts with a pathological shopping habit who have severed contact with arithmetic will recognise the optimism.'[16] Blair insisted dogmatically that anyone who challenged his view of the Iraq war was 'crazy' and 'needs their head examined'. Donald Rumsfeld demonstrated a similar overconfidence at that time. He too believed that he had all the answers and had no need of other people's input. Rumsfeld felt he had no need to visit Iraq, to consult the army or to read the intelligence reports before waging war on that country.

People who have not had enough affirmation of their own growing self-hood as infants often struggle to recognise fully the value of other 'selves'. The more powerful they become in the external world, the easier it is to disregard those over whom they have power. Perhaps inevitably, the less power-ful become devalued and unreal, and the social emotions of empathy and guilt become more elusive. Frank Rich, eval-uating Bush's unsuccessful presidency in the *New York Times*, commented on Bush's 'bottomless capacity for self-pity', as revealed in Bush's comment that 'I was a wartime president and war is very exhausting . . . The president ends up carry-ing a lot of people's grief in his soul.'[17] What concerned Rich most was that Bush described feeling 'healed' and 'com-forted' by the men and women he met in military hospitals – but he didn't see his role as one of healing and comforting *them*.

Many narcissists find it difficult to acknowledge failure because they have not had enough supportive parental help in early life to deal with their limitations and mistakes. Instead they cling to what the psychoanalytic literature calls their 'infantile grandiosity' in order to avoid feeling weak and despised by an internalised critical or contemptuous parent. As Abse described it, Blair would often respond to criticism by widening his eyes, like a little boy who was indignant that anyone could doubt him, or by smiling sweetly as if to say, 'I didn't mean to, Mummy.' This might be all right for a child who has just hurt his sister in a pillow fight, but in the world of global politics it does not seem to be an adequate response. When NATO forces dropped cluster bombs on residential areas in Kosovo, killing innocent civilians, Blair's response was to say he 'didn't mean' it to happen.[18]

The psychotherapist Israel Charny outlines other common excuses used by those who are not well attached to other people to justify harmful behaviours:[19]

1) it wasn't my fault
2) it was only a prank
3) the victim deserved it or caused it
4) you can't judge me because you're just as bad
5) I did it for the group or the higher good
6) the victim isn't really human.

Although such justifications have a childish ring, and resemble the excuses made by young children in the playground, these are often the same underlying attitudes used in public life to justify wars or exploitation of other groups. Whilst 'the victim isn't really human' and 'the victim deserved it' has been a favourite of fascists and bullies the world over, 'I did it for the higher good' is a favourite of narcissists.

Tony Blair believed that he was acting for the higher good. Like many leaders, he used inflated language to promise great things – a 'strong society', 'dignity' and 'respect', and other abstractions that the journalist John Rentoul referred to as his 'vacuo-Olympian style'.[20] Blair used such rhetoric to claim the moral high ground and to invalidate any opposing views. By definition, anyone who disagreed with him must be against those values.

At one Labour Party conference, Blair made a speech designed to convince the assembly to abandon the word 'socialist' in its constitution. As another journalist, Peter Oborne, has described it, this was so unpopular that Blair didn't even attempt to make his case by means of argument.[21] Instead, he appealed to his audience to trust his decision, because he alone really knew what was best for the party – a strategy that was remarkable similar to his approach to the Iraq War. Bizarrely, in this speech Blair made a particular point of asserting his honesty, repeating 'Let us say what we mean and mean what we say' – the very thing he was not doing; again, it is echoed in his later claims about weapons of mass destruction. Whether he was engaged in deception or self-deception, Blair conveyed a sense of living in his own mental world, with little wish to engage in real dialogue with or encounter the disagreement of others.

Blair ensured that there was little opportunity for other people to affect his thinking by changing the way that politics was conducted in Britain. He transferred power from the House of Parliament and the Cabinet to a cabal of unelected advisers who shared his views. A similar preference for avoiding dialogue and relying only on a handful of advisers was practised by George W. Bush, whose policies became increasingly unilateralist as a result. Bush's mental isolation was expressed when he commented: 'The interesting thing about being the President is that I don't feel like I owe anybody an explanation.'[22] In fact, both Blair and Bush have stated that they felt accountable to God rather than to other people.[23]

## Disorganised emotions

People with 'personality disorders' sometimes have a similar difficulty in recognising and valuing other people's minds. Because their own feelings were not acknowledged in childhood, other people's feelings have not become quite real to them either. As the psychoanalyst Peter Fonagy has described it, people with this kind of psychopathology are stuck in the toddler mode of 'psychic equivalence' where the individual's own personal feelings are assumed to be 'the truth'.[24] This corresponds to an early developmental stage when the very young child who is afraid there is a monster in the cupboard has an unshakeable belief that there *is* a monster in the cupboard. His own thoughts and feelings are not yet one potential way of seeing things, but *the* way. At this level of development, it is difficult to grasp that ideas are just representations of reality – and there are always other ways of looking at things.

In this state of mind, conflict with other people is very hard to manage. When there is only one way of seeing things, only one person can be right. In a family that doesn't do 'mentalising' very well, the child's fear is that the other person will deny his feelings and will annihilate his psychological existence. Or they might treat him as 'bad' because he thinks differently from them. As I outlined in chapter five, when there isn't much mentalising going on, it is hard for negative feelings to be resolved in an amicable way. The key thing is to force the other person to accept your version of reality, so that you become the 'winner' and the other person the 'loser'. Clearly, this is easier to achieve when you have power, because then you are more likely to be able to insist that other people accept your version of reality. This suggests that power is likely to be particularly attractive to people who have not learned to mentalise well.

Children who grow up in families which do not recognise and acknowledge their feelings often become adults who have difficulties in recognising and acknowledging other people's feelings. But when children grow up with parents who also frighten them, the problems worsen. They don't know what to do when they experience negative emotions, because the person whom they need to protect and soothe them is the very person who is frightening or upsetting them. This could be a parent who is aggressive or abusive in some way or, alternatively, a parent who behaves in a frightened way herself: the problem is that neither is available to calm and soothe the child in a parental way. Children with this dilemma often develop what is known as 'disorganised' attachment. This is a severe form of insecure attachment in which the child has not been able to find a consistent technique for dealing with attachment stress. Without a workable strategy, the child gets overwhelmed by negative emotion and physiologically dysregulated (as infants, they have a high heart rate when left alone, and compared to other children recover slowly from arousal).[25] Research projects exploring the way such children represent their attachments to others in stories and artwork tend to find that they produce images of helplessness and chaos.[26]

One way that children gain mastery over their own experience of helplessness in the face of physical or emotional abuse is by attacking those who are weaker than themselves. In childhood, animals are often the most readily available victims, though siblings and neighbours may also be the target for bullying or 'sadistic re-enactments' of childhood mistreatment. According to a report in the *New York Times*, during his childhood George W. Bush was part of a group who enjoyed torturing animals: '"We were terrible to animals," recalled his childhood friend Mr Throckmorton, laughing. A dip behind the Bush home turned into a small lake after a good rain, and thousands of frogs would come out.

"Everybody would get BB guns and shoot them," Mr Throckmorton said. "Or we'd put firecrackers in the frogs and throw them and blow them up."[27]

Children who have experienced chronic exposure to mental abuses such as teasing, belittlement and humiliation often develop a paranoid outlook, and a tendency to view other people as hostile and dangerous. Theodore Millon, a psychiatrist who played a key role in defining personality disorders for the American Psychiatric Association's diagnostic manual, argues that children in this situation tend to view themselves as weak and worthless, and develop a 'timid, insecure, avoidant personality style', whilst others 'identify with the aggressor'.[28] It's hardly surprising that children subjected to hostility and rejection often become hypersensitive and are prone to believe that anyone who challenges their views is an aggressor.

Rudy Giuliani has been a prominent Republican politician in the USA who is known for his tough and intransigent persona – the very opposite of timid. He grew up with a father who had been in prison for armed robbery in his youth; his father ran a tavern and 'was not afraid to use his baseball bat to keep rowdy customers in line'. In this aggressive atmosphere, Rudy was a 'restless' baby, with a tic in one eye, prone to staying awake for forty-eight hours at a time. Both at Catholic school with nuns and at home with his mother, he was disciplined with corporal punishment. As a young boy, he was humiliated by his father, who dressed him up in a Yankees outfit and sent him out to play on the streets of 'Dodgers-crazed' Brooklyn. The local kids taunted him and on one occasion threw a noose around his neck as if they were going to lynch him; he was saved by his grandmother. 'To my father, it was a joke,' Giuliani has recalled. 'But to me it was like being a martyr.'[29]

Growing up with antagonistic adults does not stop people being reflective and empathetic in some spheres of their lives, but it often leads to great difficulty in thinking about other people's feelings whilst others are being hostile to them. When Rudy Giuliani took part in a radio phone-in show in 2007, one caller criticised his performance as Mayor of New York. The disgruntled caller had Parkinson's Disease, and was complaining that his Medicaid and food stamps had been cut off several times. Giuliani could not listen carefully and sympathetically to his critic's point of view. Instead, he immediately launched into a vicious attack, taunting the man contemptuously as if he were an aggressive enemy: 'What kind of hole are you in there? You're breathing funny . . . Why don't you stay on the line, we'll take your name and number and we'll send you psychiatric help because you seriously need it.'[30] In other words, he humiliated the caller in the same way that he himself had apparently been humiliated as a child. His aggression seemed to come out of the blue, but as Martha Nussbaum once put it, 'It is the past that so wells up, and not some shot of adrenalin.'[31]

Children who have lived with fear also often resort to becoming very controlling of other people as a way of trying to make their world safer. They can develop into adults who are so afraid of being rejected or punished by those to whom they are attached that they attack any evidence of separateness, particularly the partner having a mind of his or her own. These are the people who are so terrified of being abandoned that they destroy their partner's diaries, or restrict the other person's friendships and social contacts.

No one demonstrates this need for control more than auto-
cratic leaders, who – like the young children who seek
control over their parents – often use a mixture of manipulative charm along with a refusal to countenance other points
of view. When Benazir Bhutto was Prime Minister of
Pakistan, she became friendly with the journalist Christina
Lamb. Lamb enjoyed Bhutto's warmth and the girlie side to
her personality – she was known as Bibi or Pinky, enjoyed ice
cream and Mills and Boon romances. Bhutto's personal views
tended to be secular and liberal, and she clearly understood
Western thinking. However, when Lamb wanted to discuss
contentious issues such as the imprisonment of women for
having sex outside marriage, or public criticisms that her husband was enjoying kickbacks in return for government
contracts, Bhutto became angry and refused to engage with
Lamb's views. 'In Benazir's world, you were either with us or
against us,' Lamb observed.[32]

## Fundamentalist thinking

In recent years polarised black-and-white thinking has found
new respectability via the neo-conservatives. This movement
emerged in the 1970s as a reaction to the liberal, non-
judgemental, pluralist approach then becoming prevalent in
the universities. The neo-cons found such 'post-modern' rel-
ativism highly frustrating. They wanted to re-establish clear
values, and to be able to talk freely of 'good' and 'evil'.
However, their attempt to revive traditional values has become
a green light for a range of people, from fundamentalist evangelicals to public commentators, to give vent to extreme views,
and unleashed a groundswell of primitive moral judgements.

For example, US journalist Ann Coulter, described by Sam Tanenhaus as the chain-smoking, hard-drinking, blonde pin-up for the right,[33] felt emboldened to urge war against all Muslims after 9/11: 'We should invade their countries, kill their leaders, and convert them to Christianity. We weren't punctilious about locating and punishing only Hitler and his top officials. We carpet-bombed German cities, we killed civilians. That's war. And this is war.'[34]

Coulter indulged in child-like assumptions that all Muslims were a threat, no matter what their actual views or behaviour. She chose to dismiss them using the moral shorthand of 'evil'. Once written off, there was no need actually to engage with the Muslim community or the reasoning behind the attack, or to recognise that while some Muslims might support them, others might oppose them. By making all Muslims 'bad', Coulter implied that she and all Christians are 'good'.

This 'us and them' mentality has been described by ex-politician Avraham Burg as common in the Israeli world,[35] but is equally true of Islamic fundamentalists. Sayyid Qutb was an influential leader of the Muslim Brotherhood, who has been described as the inspiration for the current wave of Islamic jihadists. In the 1960s, he plotted to kill the Egyptian leader Nasser because he refused to turn Egypt into a theocracy. Qutb had a sincere vision of the sickness of the Western way of life, in particular its lack of respect for traditional family life and gender roles, and its gross materialism. He argued for a more moral and spiritual way of life, in tune with 'high ideals and values'. However, he could not imagine these values being established in a secular state; for him, the whole of society, its politics and religion, were all of a piece and no compromise with the Western way of life was possible. 'Islam is the only system which possesses these values,' he declared. Either one lived an Islamic life or not: 'The truth is one and cannot be divided; if it is not truth, then it must be false-hood.'[36]

Polarised thinking exists on all sides, and is engaged by all sides to mobilise wars. But it is regressive. It is proof of a tremendous difficulty in tolerating ambiguity and resolving conflicts with people by verbal means. Psychologically, it suggests a great difficulty in recognising and tolerating feelings of fear, vulnerability or inner 'badness'. These emotions are so intolerable that they must be projected onto others. Narcis-sistic rage at not having well been cared for as a child can find, through fundamentalist thinking, many targets which repre-sent the rejected 'Other': abortionists, Jews, immigrants, Arabs, Westerners, drug addicts or terrorists.

When children grow up feeling powerless and uncared for, they may become adults who are drawn to groups with authoritarian structures, such as political or religious sects. Their hope is that by submitting to something bigger and more powerful, they will become safe and cared for. Chris Hedges, himself the son of a Presbyterian minister, suggests that children who have not been well-loved find the author-itarian demands of a totalitarian leader familiar and even comfortable. They respond because it is a 'welcome repetition of an old pattern that can be followed without investment of a new emotional energy'. As adults, they may not have enough sense of self to genuinely give love to other people, or they may feel too hurt to invest in them emotionally; instead, their main drive is to be loved and taken care of by a parental force. As Hedges put it, within an authoritarian

structure people 'can bury their chaotic and fragmented personalities and live with the illusion that they are now strong,
whole, and protected'. They in effect return to 'a primitive
state, a prenatal existence, a return to the womb and a life of
submission'.[37]

At the same time, fundamentalist groups can meet real
needs for human connection. The progressive rabbi Michael
Lerner has noted how such faiths can offer a real sense of
community. He described the different social experiences he
had when attending a variety of liberal Jewish congregations
and Orthodox congregations. During the coffee and cakes
after the liberal services, he found that these more progressive
people tended to talk to their own friends and he was left feeling a little lonely. However, after Orthodox services, although
he had hated the messages he had heard, 'brimming with
anger or even implicit hatred at the Palestinian people, Arabs,
Muslims, or in a few extreme cases all non-Jews', he found a
warm welcome. People came up to him, wanting to know
who he was, whether there was anyone in his family who
needed a hospital visit or assistance, and 'even asked me if I
was single and wanted to meet someone'. Lerner found this
'nurturing and delightful'.[38]

However, there was a price to pay for belonging: Lerner
would be expected to set aside his discomfort at the hostility
to other groups. The sense of community he experienced was
actually a siege mentality, where antagonism to the 'out'
group cemented the 'in' group's sense of belonging. Care and
compassion was restricted to members of the in-group, which
required total loyalty.

The attack on a shared enemy not only glues the group
together, but also offers an outlet for buried childhood rage

at being neglected or hurt. There is satisfaction in venting rage on a safe target. However, this often involves ideological contortions. Hedges points out that the Christian Right 'finds its ideological justification in a narrow segment of the Gospel', based on the Book of Revelations, which is 'the only time in the Gospels where Jesus sanctions violence'.[39] Clearly, the Bible – like statistics – can be interpreted in many ways. Whilst the psychologist and philosopher Richard Ryder has suggested that 'Jesus today would be working for Medicins Sans Frontiers, Amnesty International or the Red Cross',[40] Christian fundamentalist interpretations of the Bible actively choose to focus not on Christ's message of love, forgiveness and compassion, but on a Manichaean world of good and evil, where violence and vengeance can be expressed – against non-believers. Similarly, Islamic jihadists interpret the Koran in a way that justifies suicide bombing and extreme forms of violence, ignoring other established interpretations which describe 'jihad' in very different terms – primarily as a struggle to be a good and righteous person. Traditional interpretations of the Koran stress that war is only acceptable to protect religious freedom, and otherwise is to be avoided. Both extremist Muslims and Christians use religion as a vehicle through which to express their inner demons on a wider stage.

Fundamentalist thinking is essentially closed; individuals cannot think for themselves, or evaluate data independently, without reference to the group-think. They are like the academic psychologists Michael Milburn's and Sheree Conrad's description of children living in punitive families, who 'never have a reason or opportunity to develop internalised moral standards or to think in a complex way about events around them. Instead, they retain the simplistic and concrete think-ing of early childhood, in which moral values are absolutes imposed by an external authority'.[41] Since the group is always right, there is no need to consider other points of view or to consider how other people feel. The psychologist Bob Altemeyer has analysed authoritarian forms of thought. He found that the fundamentalist does not feel obliged to be con-sistent, as the rational person would do. Fundamentalists allow their ideas to co-exist in separate compartments so they can simply pull one out and not worry about it contradicting another one – behaviour often found in young children, who do not yet have the mental maturity to deal with the uncer-tainty and complexity of reality in a more integrated way. As Altemeyer noted of the decision to go to war against Iraq, 'They liked the conclusion; the reasoning didn't matter.'[42] In a conflict with others, instead of putting things right with actual people, they simply ask God to forgive them – a form of 'cheap grace' as Altemeyer puts it – but once again, an example of difficulty in relating to others and their separate, different minds.

Altemeyer argues that what is crucial is that authoritarians, whether on the right or left, lack self-awareness. Culture wars – whether between Christian and Muslim, conservative and liberal, Strict and Permissive – are ultimately driven by emotions which derive a great deal of their power from being unconscious and out of awareness. This keeps people stuck in the primitive and childlike thinking of families that cannot value and acknowledge different points of view, but compete for the power to define reality. It is what the extreme evan-gelical James Dobson terms a 'civil war of values'. In this civil war, each side invalidates the other. There is no middle

ground between those who believe that there can be good
reasons to terminate pregnancies, and those who claim it is
'murder'. There is no compromise between those who think
women ought to stay in their traditional role in the family,
and those who think women should be free to work, divorce
and put their children in day-care. Each side's truths are non-
negotiable and their beliefs sacred to them. Each is afraid of
the other.

## A new direction

Recent American political leadership has exacerbated these
tendencies and has failed to show any lead in helping the
public to 'mentalise' and acknowledge each other's thinking.
However, there are hopeful signs of a desire to recover political balance and move away from regressive tendencies. We
now have a new President of the United States who conveys
emotional intelligence. Coming from a loving but complicated family, Obama describes a childhood with a mother
who was 'the kindest, most generous spirit I have ever
known', someone who was filled with joy and curiosity
about the world, open to other cultures and interested in
differences between people.[43] Her willingness to accept different points of view was exemplified by her attitude to her
ex-husband. Although he had left her in the lurch with a
baby, she brought up their son with affectionate and admiring memories of his father. She was also able to think of
others' feelings when she was under great stress. When she
was terminally ill, she helped her son to cope with his distress
and carry on with his life. It is easy to see many of these qualities in her son.

Similar stories are told by Nelson Mandela and Desmond Tutu, other world leaders who are notable for their empathy and concern for other people. They too claimed that they had absorbed their mother's values. Desmond Tutu was his mother's favourite as a child; he had health problems which drew out her empathy and kindness towards him. His Sotho and Nguni culture also passed on the values of interdependence, with mottos such as: 'A person is a person through other people.'[44] Tutu went on to initiate the Truth and Reconciliation Committee, which played such a powerful role in healing the divisions and enmity in post-apartheid South Africa.

Unlike the picture we have of Barbara Bush as a mother who constantly reprimanded and criticised her children, and by her own admission would 'scream and carry on' when they didn't do what she wanted, Nelson Mandela's mother has been described as 'gentle' and 'perceptive'. Mandela himself said, 'My mother and I never talked very much, but we did not need to. I never doubted her love or questioned her support.'[45] However, all three men had more problematic relationships with their fathers, despite admiring them. Mandela's father died when he was still a boy; Obama's returned to Africa after leaving his mother; and Tutu's father drank too much and abused his beloved mother when he was drunk. It is possible that these experiences may have fuelled their involvement in public life, by generating the drive to prove themselves as men.

It remains to be seen whether leadership informed by emotional intelligence can help to heal the world's conflicts. Certainly, Mandela's leadership achieved extraordinary change in South Africa through his empathetic stance and ability to engage with its white leaders as people – yet, at the same time, he failed to act on the rapidly spreading AIDS epidemic until after his presidency was over, a failure that he now acknowledges and regrets. He presided over ineffectual policies such as spending a fifth of the AIDS budget on a theatre troupe.[46] Despite his emotional intelligence, he behaved like so many other politicians before him, admitting that he had not spoken more about HIV and AIDS because black South Africans were conservative when it came to matters of sex, and he 'didn't want to lose the election'.[47] The result was that by the end of his presidency in 1999, maternal mortality was climbing and around 10 per cent of children were orphaned because of AIDS, whilst HIV had become a leading cause of death for older South African children (those over five years old) – figures which have continued to worsen in the last decade.[48] There are no guarantees of consistent wisdom.

Barack Obama has openly stated his intention to pursue empathy, promising a very different approach to the culture wars as well as to managing global conflicts. He has grasped that there can be no single winner of such conflicts. Instead, he gives priority to understanding the other's perspective, really hearing the other's feelings and giving them value. He promises to listen, 'especially when we disagree'. As he put it in his victory speech, 'Let us resist the temptation to fall back on the same partisanship and pettiness and immaturity that has poisoned our politics for so long.' He calls for a new ethos of service and responsibility, where each citizen resolves to 'look after not only ourselves, but each other.'[49] No matter how he and his advisers interpret this in practice or how his policies may turn out, there is at least a sense of turning away from the regressive polarised thinking of his predecessor.

It is tempting to hope that an exceptional leader will 'fix' things for us. However, even exceptional individuals are not omniscient, just as there is no perfect father or mother. In a truly mature political system, the electorate would surely be more capable of participating fully to make its views known. If we want a more just or caring world, we may have to look to ourselves, not to others, to supply it.

# 8. CAPITALISM? BEEN THERE, DONE THAT

> Not only are they rich and powerful, they feel that they
> deserve to be rich and powerful, because the free market is
> the highest good and they have worked the free market and
> benefited from it, and so has everyone they know. There are
> two things about them that you have to remember – that
> deep down they feel guilty and undeserving and that they
> live very circumscribed lives. Inside the office, inside the
> house, inside the health club, inside the corporate jet. Iraq
> is the size of California, right? But none of these guys has
> driven from L.A. to, say, Redding, in living memory.
>
> *Jane Smiley, 2007*

If we acknowledge that politicians are themselves limited by
their own emotional and moral development, it becomes more
difficult to entrust them with 'parenting' the nation state on
our behalf. In any case, moral guidance is a new role for politicians, one that in former times we left to priests – a class of
people whom most of the population believed were authorised
to represent God, the supreme 'Father'. Today, their claim to
authority is more tenuous, since religious leadership serves
only a minority of people in the West, albeit a substantial
minority in the USA. Instead, as society has become more

secular, we have begun to look further afield for guidance and direction – sometimes in the most unlikely places; we have even turned to musicians and actors, agony aunts and talk show hosts to make sense of the world. Why not politicians too? Yet there are real doubts about whether we want governments to take the lead in such intensely personal issues as morality and the family, and whether they are capable of it. Karl Rove, George W. Bush's adviser, argued in 2001 that the public did indeed want such leadership. As he put it, 'Compared to thirty years ago, Americans are more worried about moral values, the breakdown of the family and decline in civic life . . . The public wants government and individual elected officials to play a more active leadership role in dealing with declining values.'[1]

I suspect that when Karl Rove argued for the more active promotion of 'moral values', he had in mind a particular set of moral values associated with a particular kind of family. But neglectful or over-indulgent parents who largely fail to pass on social norms, or liberal families who promote women's freedom and rights to abortion and divorce, too, have their 'values' – even if they are not the independence, materialism and punishment for wrong-doing that comprise the Republicans' vision of successful citizenship. Every family has its own implicit values. In which case – since there is no consensus – how can the state be the arbiter of 'family values'? Do we even want the state to take on such a role?

## Role of the state

The functions of the state are always evolving, and what we expect from the state in any given period seems to be very tied up with the way the family is organised. In its early form, the state acted on behalf of monarchs and the aristocracy to preserve their property and power. Like a strict, authoritarian father, it beat and punished the nation to keep it in line – whilst at the same time fiercely repelling intruders to the family home. These punitive aspects of the state are less obvious these days, but the preservation of order is still a primary function of the state, as is defending national territory from outsiders.

As the population became better fed and better educated, power became more widely distributed. More representative forms of government were tolerated. The state extended its protection to a wider range of people. Instead of using brute force, new forms of control were developed using the law and administrative procedures. There was a gradual shift from private prosecutions paid for by the victims, often resulting in extreme punishments such as hanging, to the development of an organised police force and a system of public prosecution. By the eighteenth century, the state was managing ever more individual 'rights', which were established as people became more autonomous and based their relationships on contracts, rather than feudal obligations. In particular, it was the middle classes who demanded more and more abstract legal rights to protect themselves, their investments and their property. People increasingly relied on the law to solve their personal conflicts, and violent behaviour within the family declined.

The state was still seen as a paternal force, but perhaps it was now less of a feudal patriarch than a more rational and fair type of father figure. However, the state was not yet seen as a source of care or support for the general public. The old assumptions of a more rural or small-town way of life persisted – expectations that when people fell on hard times, got ill or could not make ends meet, they would depend on the people around them. For the more genteel, it was normal to turn to family and friends to borrow money or to get help with paying medical bills or with temporary accommodation. Further down the social scale, big landowners would often try to find work for anyone in their patch who needed it. People would turn to the state only in extreme situations, when the destitute would have to rely on the barest handouts from their local parish's poor relief fund, or would end up living in the workhouse. In some ways, it is this way of life that many conservatives still seem to hanker after.

The industrial way of life brought an end to this rough and ready tradition of mutual aid. Cities swelled with people, crammed into the equivalent of modern Third World 'shanty towns' without clean water, clean air or sanitation, struggling to survive on below subsistence wages. The city parishes could not cope with the huge numbers of distressed people. At the same time, the increasing dominance of 'laissez-faire' economic thinking, with its belief in free trade and competition, created a climate of opinion which worked against state intervention. Even when there were epidemics of cholera that led to thousands of deaths in the cities, campaigners for public health couched their appeals for donations in terms of 'enlightened self-interest'. They did not yet argue in terms of a right to good health or health care, only that it would be to the advantage of the wealthy employer to have a healthy workforce. Others resisted calls for public health measures on the grounds that it would interfere with their freedom. In August 1854 one *Times* correspondent argued that he would rather take his chance with cholera than 'be bullied into health'[2] – an argument still used today by those who complain about 'health fascism'.

## Resistance to the caring state

Resistance to expanding the scope of the state into a more interventionist, caring role was exemplified by a literary debate which took place in 1829 and 1830 between two major figures of the time: Robert Southey, the sensible and bookish Poet Laureate, and Thomas Macaulay, a smooth, clever, up-and-coming Liberal politician and future historian. Southey, a man in his late fifties, was shocked by the effects of the new 'manufacturing system' on people's health and mental well-being. Even though he had ditched his earlier radical ideals, and was writing for a conservative journal called the *Quarterly*, he saw modern conditions of work as no better than 'servitude' and he argued that the state should relieve the distress of the population. Thomas Macaulay, on the other hand, was then only in his late twenties and unlike Southey had grown up with industrial capitalism. He attacked Southey's views in a scathing piece in the more radical *Edinburgh Review*, claiming in a Pollyanna-ish way that things were not that bad; after all, people were actually better fed and clothed than in the sixteenth century and lived longer – statistics disputed by Southey. In a famous passage, Macaulay expressed his faith in progress: 'If we were to prophesy that in the year 1930 a population of fifty millions, better fed, clad, and lodged than the English of our time, will cover these islands . . . that machines constructed on principles yet undiscovered, will be in every house, that there will be no highways but railroads, no travelling but by steam, that our debt, vast as it seems to us, will appear to our great-grandchildren a trifling encumbrance, which might easily be paid off in a year or two, many people would think us insane.'[3] Macaulay's prophesy proved uncannily accurate in the long term. However, it is possible that both were right. Macaulay's optimism may seem well founded, but Southey's pessimism was too.

The manufacturing system did produce goods for everyone to enjoy, but there is little doubt that the workers who produced the goods paid for it with their mental and physical health. Children suffered terribly and many infants and small children died. The average life expectancy for factory workers in Manchester was seventeen years, compared to a professional man in the countryside who would expect to live an average of fifty-two years.[4] Yet, despite repeated outbreaks of cholera – which mostly affected the lower classes – there was an unwillingness to invest public money in health measures such as a sewage system. It wasn't until the long, hot summer of 1858, when the Thames stank so much of raw human waste that Members of Parliament were retching in their rooms overlooking the river, that action was finally taken: in other words, only when it affected the ruling classes themselves.

Privileged people like Macaulay were not overly troubled by empathy with the sufferings of the poor. Like most parliamentarians of his age, he had an aversion to public spending on behalf of others. He believed that '500,000 pounds subscribed by individuals for rail-roads or canals would produce more advantage to the public than five millions voted by Parliament for the same purpose.'[5] In other words, he thought that public works should only be undertaken if the public showed they wanted the service by paying for it directly – through a toll, or a subscription. This attitude persists in current conservative thinking, which is willing to encourage others to make provision for the common good, but does not want the state to be responsible for paying for it – or to borrow money to pay for it. It sees the function of the state above all as the facilitator of the market economy, the protector of free trade. The logical conclusion of such thinking would be to argue that everything must come through the market or not come at all – no matter what the consequences. This is such a stark prospect that few dare to go that far, and in practice most conservatives accept the need for state provision to meet many basic needs for policing, health and education.

### Needs or wants

One difficulty for the state is to differentiate between basic needs and optional 'wants'. The financial sector is devoted to stimulating consumer spending from which a profit can be made; left to its own devices, it doesn't distinguish between the need for a sewage system and the want for 'embryo lamb tongue pickled and served on the afterdeck of a sumptuous yacht', as the political philosopher Sheldon Wolin once put it.[6] In the marketplace, there are no needs, only wants – everything is seen as a 'choice' because everything is reduced to a financial transaction rather than a set of human relationships. For the market mindset, it would be impossible to decide for people what are needs and what are choices.

Yet people's needs are not that unique or mysterious: they can be identified and should be met. Any functional family, as Wolin has argued, knows instinctively that basic needs have to be met before whims and desires. The professor of law and ethics, philosopher Martha Nussbaum, has created her own long list of basic needs which includes: good health, a reasonably long life, freedom of movement, freedom to have sex and reproduce, being free to think and imagine, freedom to love without fear, abuse or neglect, freedom from assault and intrusion, freedom to have friendship and social interaction, concern for animals and nature.[7] Tim Kasser, the American psychologist, has a more succinct list. He sums up basic needs as anything that is necessary to 'survival, growth and optimal functioning'.[8] Beyond our basic needs for physical care such as sufficient food, shelter and protection from harm, he puts forward more psychological needs – to feel a sense of agency and competence, to feel connected to others and to express ourselves freely. Others may make their own version. However, there is a consensus that warmth and shelter, nutritious food, education and the opportunity to enjoy positive relationships with other people are the bottom line.

Macaulay would no doubt have objected that there is no such consensus. In particular, he would not have wanted the state to define it. He had a jaded view of the ruling classes, whom he saw as no wiser than anyone else. He intensely disliked the possibility that the state could become a patronising 'Lady Bountiful' or an intrusive 'Paul Pry', as he put it, 'spying, eaves-dropping, relieving, admonishing, spending our money for us and choosing our opinions for us'.[9] Like John Locke in earlier times, he did not want to be told 'what to read, and say, and eat, and drink and wear' by people he didn't respect. He felt 'there is no reason to believe that a government will have either the paternal warmth of affection or the paternal superiority of intellect'. His latter-day intellectual successor, the British academic Frank Furedi, takes a similar line. To him, as to Macaulay, the state is not a wise or benign parent, but a controlling, interfering, stupid parent who will restrict your freedom to no good effect. He resents the 'Thought Police' who treat us as 'biologically mature children', presiding over the minutiae of our lives. He concludes it is therefore best to avoid state intervention in people's lives, particularly in the personal sphere. 'State policy', he argues, 'is too crude an instrument to deal with the management of intimate emotional relations between parent and child. Parental anxieties and the complex relation between adults and children are not problems that are susceptible to public policy solutions. Why? Because the problems of human relationships are too specific and too personal to be tackled by policies which are by definition general in character'.[10]

The Southey attitude, on the other hand – which continues in liberal and socialist thinking today – is that public welfare cannot be left to chance, or to the unreliable benevolence of philanthropists, or to individual parents. Many things that are necessary to our well-being are more likely to be achieved collectively. We cannot individually build a sewage system, or a library; parks and roads and swimming pools and hospitals are things we all need to share, not purchase individually. We cannot rely on a local community to prevent child abuse; we need state policies and state-funded professionals to intervene. In fact, a fully socialist position is that the social good is so important that economic power must be subordinated to it.

Furedi argues that public authorities should only intervene in the family in exceptional circumstances – 'when a child faces real harm'– though he doesn't attempt to define this. He finds it patronising and authoritarian for the state to intervene in parenting, such as providing parenting classes or social and emotional learning in schools, since this undermines parental confidence and interferes with their own judgement. Although he claims to want the state to improve education and health care, he reacts even against the promotion of breastfeeding which he believes 'intimidates mothers'. Instead of building on decades of medical and psychological research and promoting proven aspects of good parenting, the state should leave parents to 'do their best' for their child.[11]

The idea that we could co-operate and organise ourselves to ensure that basic needs are met and the fruits of human creativity shared, has never achieved widespread acceptance. It is an idea that swims against the tide of laissez-faire economics which has unbounded faith in the self-regulating capacities of the market – 'leaving capital to find its most lucrative course, commodities their fair price, industry and intelligence their natural reward', as Macaulay put it – rather than in conscious and deliberate forms of social organisation.

## The delinquent economy

The problem is that, as a guide, faith in the laissez-faire economy turns out to be just as problematic as faith in the social democratic state as the instrument of the common good. If the state is an unimpressive parent, the economy is a positively delinquent one. In fact, it has little capacity for thinking at all – it runs on instinct. Like an animal with little higher brain function, it reacts purely with immediate profit in mind. This leads to short-sighted decisions such as farming fish without worrying about long-term sustainability, or producing fat-laden and sugary foods targeted at children, without concerning itself with the expensive health problems this will cause years down the line. Financial markets are not interested in assessing the social value of a particular business: they simply react to its current image and the likelihood of turning a profit in the mood of the moment. Corporations are in business to keep their gravy train rolling, and will constantly try to stimulate new needs in people, however detrimental that may be to individuals themselves or society as a whole. In pursuit of profit, they will dodge taxation, damage whole communities through unemployment, and pollute the environment with barely a second thought. As Robert Skidelsky has said, 'Such a system needs to be fabulously successful to command allegiance. Spectacular failure is bound to discredit it.'[12] However, periodically, the whole system has crashed disastrously – as now. Has that discrediting moment of spectacular failure arrived?

## Caring state

At moments of crisis, attitudes appear to change. For a brief while, it starts to feel like a wake-up call for the state and the economic system to respond to people's needs as well as wants. However, the usual course of events is that concern is short-lived, prompted only by the possibility of social unrest and destabilisation rather than by a commitment to 'caring'. The first major crisis that triggered a shift in political attitudes came in the late nineteenth century, in response to a collapse in food prices, when 'all industrial countries except the US started schemes of social insurance to protect their citizens against life's hazards'.[13] Next, during the economic Depression of the 1930s, the American government was finally compelled to respond to the desperate state of its people and to inspire hope with some basic forms of welfare, as well as greater regulation and control of the economy. In Europe, the Fascist solution attracted people with a very different way out of the economic misery of mass-inflation: Hitler promised the security of the authoritarian father who would take total charge of people's lives, rather than supporting them as a caring mother.

After the suffering caused by the Second World War, social pressure increased to provide a better life for those who returned from service to a war-torn Britain. 'Homes for heroes' was one slogan that was revived from the First World War, and there was a new and inspiring dream of a National Health Service for all. In the post-war period in particular, it really did start to look as if the state was willing to be a caring parent to a traumatised people. There was, for the first time, a real consensus that the state could do a better job than the market. The state expanded dramatically into providing welfare services and safety nets, as well as increased education and housing. The state started to 'care' for its people in a maternal fashion, finally taking some responsibility for the public good. In tandem, the consumer society took off – partly as a result of the new jobs created in the welfare state in health, education and house building. Basking in the well-satisfied glow of an economic 'boom', the state became a still more tolerant, progressive 'parent', passing laws that allowed more sexual freedom and more freedom of expression.

Families, too, became more tolerant and egalitarian, as I have described in chapter five. However, the good times did not last.

Economic growth began to falter in the 1970s. In Britain, this process was intensified by the collapse of its empire in the post-war period, up to the end of the 1960s. With the end of colonialism, the economy went global in a new way, as goods, services and capital became more mobile. Core industrial production such as ship-building, coal-mining and steel was increasingly diverted to the developing world where labour was cheaper and non-unionised. Unemployment in the UK rose, placing more demands on the welfare system. Suddenly the caring welfare state looked like an unaffordable luxury.

Faced with the terrifying possibility of failure and decline, bullied by businesses which demanded freedom to act as they wanted without regulation or else, leaders such as Thatcher and Reagan returned to the comfort blanket of neoclassical economic thinking. The neo-conservative dream was to bring back an idealised free market – free, that is, from the insatiable welfare state, and from the greedy demands of the trade unions, which thwarted attempts to compete with cheap sources of labour. They believed that if they removed restrictive trade union practices, as well as the state interference and regulation that was bogging the system down and making it unprofitable, economic growth would surely return.

To achieve this *volte face*, they had to bring a whole range of potentially critical, independent social institutions, such as the universities, local government and schools, under their control. Professionals had to be re-educated. They had to be made to understand that every activity must be directed towards wealth creation. In the UK, universities and schools were re-organised away from 'education' in the broad sense of the word, and were instructed to devote themselves to narrowly measurable outcomes and to producing skilled workers. Local government was only allowed to provide the services that central government dictated. Paperwork and regulation proliferated in the professions as central control tightened. Only the financial markets were allowed to be free from the grip of the state; for them, it was party time as regulation was loosened, and financial 'incentives' such as bonuses and payouts dramatically increased.

This ideological *coup d'etat* was shocking, but the ambush was so sudden that it succeeded in overturning cherished values with little effective resistance. Suddenly, nothing mattered except money. The shock was absorbed with the help of comedy and drama. The film *Wall Street* featured a trader who insisted that 'Greed is good'. My favourite representation was created by the British comedian and satirist Harry Enfield whose immensely popular cockney character 'Loadsamoney' waved his wads of cash in delight, holding up a mirror to the culture that was developing all around us. But eventually people adapted to it and learned to think the same way – 'me first'.

## Materialistic babies

This ideology permeated the family, too. The more tolerant social attitudes of the 1960s and 1970s could not be halted; the divorce rate continued to rise and there was a dramatic increase in single parent families across all social groups. At the same time neo-conservative economic policies began to affect those at the bottom of society, whose real wages declined, and more and more resorted to claiming state benefits. Despite attempts to crack down on abuses of the system, there was a massive expansion in benefit dependency in the 1980s. Many people got stuck there, feeling out of control of their lives, often depressed, and in some cases passing on the same lack of self-esteem to their children. According to a recent report by Jen Lexmond and Richard Reeves, researchers at the think tank Demos, a lack of confidence and control makes it difficult for parents to pass on the essentials of 'character' (defined in terms of their capacity for application, self-regulation and empathy) to their children. Their report suggested that those parents on the lowest incomes were the most likely to be 'disengaged' from their children, and the least likely to achieve the magic combination of warmth and firm discipline in their parenting.[14]

At the other end of the social scale, the rich got richer. Higher earners earned more. Meanwhile, those in the middle struggled to adapt to society's high material aspirations. Women were pulled into the economy, and many families became caught up in a financially precarious way of life which seemed to demand that both parents work long hours to maintain their standard of living.

## Selfishness increased

As the 1980s progressed, the working world became unashamedly hard-nosed and unempathetic. According to psychologist Michael Lerner, who has spent over thirty years at his Institute for Labor and Mental Health in California asking people about their experiences at work, people were positively encouraged to become selfish and materialistic during this period. His research describes how people learned to use other people and to curry favour with their managers to hold on to their jobs.[15] Over the next two decades, this culture established itself as the norm. Barbara Ehrenreich, a journalistic observer of the corporate world, confirmed this impression in her book *Bait and Switch*. She spent six months posing as a job-seeker in American businesses and found the same phenomenon: people being hired for their ability to display fake commitment and cheerfulness, even to the point of sycophancy.[16] Like the compliant babies who have to fit in with their parents' way of doing things to survive, these adults believed they had to compromise themselves to stay financially afloat.

The work culture of a corporation like Enron was extreme, but not untypical. In the 1990s, it introduced a bonus system which had no ceiling, allowing traders to 'eat what they killed'.[17] It stoked up competition between employees to keep them on the edge, using a performance appraisal system known as 'rank and yank' where employees might either be in line for a massive bonus or could equally well lose their job. This gave rise to a 'yes-man' culture where no one dared to challenge those higher in the system. Meanwhile, people in occupations at the bottom of the pile were being controlled in a more overt way. The success of Wal-mart, for example, arose from applying the 'scientific management' techniques that had proved so successful within the manufacturing industry in retail and distribution. This involved very precise control over the movements of workers so that costs could be predicted and minimised.[18] Workers were simply required to do exactly what they were told; to behave like components. Either way, compliance became the norm within the whole business world. As this situation left few who were willing to question or think for themselves, the powerful came to believe that they were invulnerable. In the bubble that was building in the 1990s, the chief executives of Enron convinced themselves it was OK to ignore the rules in order to achieve ever bigger pay-offs. They became a law unto themselves, unchallenged by their subordinates who were all desperate to stay in favour and win bonuses themselves.

Barbara Ehrenreich had expected the business world to be sharp, logical and efficient in its pursuit of profits. She was astonished to find instead that corporate culture was driven by insecurity, emotion and anti-intellectualism. She found it 'a culture addicted to untested habits, paralysed by conformity, and shot through with magical thinking.'[19] It seems to me that the same attitude to reality prevailed at Enron, where executives seemed to believe that if they declared a profit, hey presto!, like waving a magic wand, it would come into being. They got used to faking their accounts and deceiving their investors with their 'hypothetical future value' deals. But they were not alone. As we now know, false accounting and deception were rife in the financial sector too. Economic journalist and writer Ann Pettifor described how it worked: fees were paid to rating agencies for inaccurate ratings of their assets, then the assets were insured using the dodgy ratings, and then this 'insurance' was then used 'to entice investors like pension funds into buying their financial "assets". Market players, earnest central bankers and commentators call this misleading and fraudulent activity "mispricing risk". In fact it is simply unethical behaviour.'[20]

It is unethical because it is based on deceiving others and ultimately harms others. It is also behaviour that is familiar to any psychotherapist, who will have seen how people who have severe problems in their attachments to others often have great difficulty in taking other people's feelings and needs on board. The bankers operating in high finance lived in a bubble world: they could remain ignorant of other people's experiences and concerns. Likewise at Enron the senior executives, Skilling, Lay and Fastow, all lived in the same gated community, cut off from ordinary life, and were instrumental in promoting a company culture which had little empathy and compassion, not only for their workers but also for the public. Enron employees were heard to mock the 'Grandma Millies' of California who would have to pay higher bills because of Enron's manipulation of California's energy market.[21]

Governments of all stripes in this period turned a blind eye to the dubious ethics of such wealth 'generation', buying into the 'fairytale imitation of growth'[22] in the money markets as if it were real – or perhaps simply failing to understand the immensely complex financial juggling acts that were taking place. In the UK this crossed party lines. When New Labour replaced the Conservatives in 1997, it took on the mantle of worshipping business values. John Hutton, then its Business and Enterprise Secretary, assumed the role of indulgent parent, arguing that we should give unqualified admiration to the 'aspiration and ambition' of entrepreneurs and city traders: 'Rather than questioning whether huge salaries are morally justified, we should celebrate the fact that people can be enormously successful in this country.'[23] In the US too, as Ehrenreich found, it became increasingly difficult to put ethics before the paycheck. As one of her interviewees, Jeff Clement, put it, 'They think you can be evil all day and then go home and live the American dream.'[24]

## Trickle-down morality

Once 'do what you like' values are established by those in power, they can be more readily adopted by the whole population. If our leaders in business and politics were so confident that risks were not risky, why shouldn't we all join in the party? In the 1990s huge numbers of ordinary people abandoned caution and responsibility, succumbed to the temptations of unlimited credit and took out loans and mortgages, hoping blindly that they would continue to be able to afford them because growth would continue. Like the bankers who lent money they did not have, most of us believed we could spend money we had not earned, and indefinitely put off taking responsibility for the debts we incurred.

The economist Robert Higgs now criticises the American people for behaving in this rather infantile way. He portrays Americans as a spoilt bunch who had only themselves to blame because they wanted 'the impossible: home ownership for those who cannot afford homes, credit for those who are not creditworthy, old-age pensions for those who have not saved, health care for those who make no attempt to keep themselves healthy, and college educations for those who lack the wit to finish high school. Moreover, they want it now, and they want somebody else to pay for it.'[25] It is intriguing that his ire is reserved for ordinary people and for the state – which he described as the 'Hotel of Impossible Promises' – rather than financiers and what we might call their 'Casino of High End Gamblers'.

It is true, on the other hand, that when offered immediate and unearned material satisfactions, most people jumped on the bandwagon. We adapt to our social group; we follow the pack. As the eminent psychologist Philip Zimbardo has shown in his chilling analysis of the guards at Abu Ghraib prison in Iraq, systems are powerful because we *need* to belong to our social grouping.[26] When those in charge humiliated their own soldiers (for example, by taking nude photographs of female soldiers without their knowledge), they sent the implicit message that normal rules of conduct and boundaries no longer applied. It's not hard to understand why those same unsupported, exhausted soldiers, when asked in turn to 'soften up' their prisoners, would find it natural to take their own, more extreme, version of the humiliating photos. Survival demands that you fit in with your group, and survival takes precedence over empathy for others.

As Zimbardo also points out, our behaviour and personal identity is always shaped by those around us, in a broader sense: 'Some people make us timid and shy; others elicit our sex appeal and dominance. In some groups we are made leaders, while in others we are reduced to being followers – we come to live up or down to the expectations others have of us.'[27] The local culture and ideology are a powerful part of those expectations. When a 21-year-old soldier killed an Iraqi civilian who refused to stop at a traffic checkpoint, he explained: 'It was like nothing. Over here, killing people is like squashing an ant. I mean, you kill somebody and it's like "All right, let's go get some pizza."' When the Wörners established their financial success by displaying greed and lack of concern for others during early capitalism, it soon became disadvantageous for others to operate an ethically run business. If you don't act the same way as others, you will lose out. If you carry on saving whilst others are buying bigger houses and new kitchens and better cars, you will feel deprived. If all the young families around you are working long hours to pursue their ambitions and have chosen to buy homes they can't comfortably afford – and then, as a consequence, feel compelled to return to work soon after their baby's birth – it will come to seem retrograde to look after your own baby and forego the nicer home. It is difficult to hold on to different values when they are not supported by the wider culture. Good early development is not enough on its own; social structures must also continue to provide support for the values we want to prevail.

It is still possible for individuals with emotional integrity to be strong enough to resist the pull of the herd. As a young academic Philip Zimbardo led a team of researchers in conducting the Stanford Prison Experiment, a psychological study of the effects of becoming a prisoner, or prison guard, with students taking on both roles. Within the enclosed space of the experiment, the prisoner/guard identities soon became demarcated and students designated as 'prisoners' were being forced – by students designated as 'guards' – to walk around with a paper bag on their heads, being tripped up and treated aggressively. When Zimbardo's girlfriend at the time, Christina Maslach (a woman with a strong face and a big grin), came to visit him, she caught a glimpse of what was going on. As a fellow psychologist, she had been invited to conduct some interviews with some of the subjects of the experiment. She had not seen many of the more obviously humiliating activities, which included young people being forced to clean out toilets with their bare hands, but she had a gut feeling that the dehumanisation of the students was wrong. But no one else seemed to be reacting like she was: the parents of the students and other psychologists around the department seemed to have accepted the set-up. After leaving the 'prison', Zimbardo asked her what she thought. 'I think he expected some sort of great intellectual discussion about what was going on. Instead, I started to have this incredible emotional outburst. I started to scream, I started to yell, "I think it is terrible what you are doing to those boys!" I cried. We had a fight you wouldn't believe, and I was beginning to think, wait a minute, I don't know this guy. I really don't, and I'm getting involved with him?'[28] Perhaps because Maslach had not been involved in setting up the experiment, and was in a personal relationship with Zimbardo, she was able to be more in touch with her feelings than other colleagues who were more invested in the project. Although Zimbardo was shocked by her reaction, he cared about her feelings and paid attention to them. In fact, he was so upset that he decided to put a stop to the experiment immediately, finishing it after six days rather than the planned fourteen. She was impressed with his response: later she married him.

As adults we have a choice: we can choose to pay attention to our inner compass, or listen to the people around us. After all, there was someone at Abu Ghraib prison who handed in the degrading photographs of prisoners and raised questions; there was a whistle-blower at Enron. Many parents swim against the cultural tide and care for their own babies. Often, these are people who know what 'feels right' to them. But this is much easier to do if you have grown up in touch with your feelings, and confident in them. It is the people who are out of touch with their feelings who are easy to manipulate, and who are more concerned about fitting in with their social group. Lacking deep roots in their own sense of self, they look to others to provide them with a sense of identity as well as economic survival. One example in my own work is my client Peter. As a child Peter had been terrorised by his drunken father, while his chronically ill mother was unavailable to help him to manage his feelings or to know himself. The adult Peter whom I knew had a powerful and tough 'front' and appeared to be someone who knew who he was. Underneath, however, he was uncertain and unconfident, easily felt 'put down' by others, and tried desperately to fit in with his work colleagues. When asked to do something he didn't approve of, he found it impossible to say no. Such stories are commonplace, but the more people who are out of touch with their own feelings, lacking good early care, the more people who are willing to be carried along with the social current in whatever direction it is going.

## The current zeitgeist

Our political, cultural and business leaders do play a major role in setting the tone of the times. In the UK, politicians on both sides declare that the 'age of irresponsibility' is over or that they are 'pro-responsibility'. During the height of the economic crash, Gordon Brown declared that he wanted to turn away from selfish and reckless 'free market fundamentalism' towards a more sober and sensible way of doing business – 'markets need morals' after all, as he put it. Although there is still virtually no opposition to capitalism itself, since capitalism has 'won' as Francis Fukuyama once put it, nonetheless many

questions are currently being asked about what kind of capitalism we need. Is it possible to have a 'new political economy'
as the Conservative Jesse Norman argued,[29] perhaps a 'nicer'
capitalism, fashionably called a 'values-based capitalism'? Some
people are arguing that there are indeed more ethically acceptable ways of making money such as by 'greening' the
economy, whilst some corporations even believe there is
money to be made by figuring out the social good, innovat-
ing and developing new products in response to people's real
needs.

Yet the economic downturn has revealed in a stark fashion
that the state still understands its primary role to be the hand-
maiden of the economy and cannot move on from the
notion that people are primarily 'economic agents'. Like a
paternal 'breadwinner', current governments see their primary role and function as one of maintaining the economy,
because the unstated value by which we all live, the social
unconscious that drives us without our awareness of it, is that
material well-being is the goal of life. Just as parents often
have no idea that they are passing on values to their children
through their assumptions and their day-to-day behaviours,
so too our political leaders sustain our collective values
through their actions. In the current crisis, their primary aim
has been to help the banking system get back to its old ways,
unwilling to contemplate the possibility that banks could be
run differently, for the benefit of society as a whole. Like
many other people, my own pension has shrunk into oblivion during this crisis. Others are losing their jobs and homes.
Yet even in such extreme circumstances, it still seems impossible to imagine a different way of organising ourselves for
the common good.

## Well-being

New ways of thinking are emerging, but are not yet fully fledged. Since the 1990s, there has been a growing movement to suggest that 'happiness' or well-being is as important as gross domestic product and income. In the USA, an early influential voice was that of Mihaly Csikszentmihalyi, a psychologist originally from Hungary, who settled in the USA as a young man. He showed that real happiness came from 'flow', as he called it – from being absorbed in meaningful activities and relationships.[30] The American psychologist Martin Seligman has built on this work with his call for a 'positive psychology' designed to promote what he calls 'authentic happiness', a form of well-being which is implicitly anti-materialistic: building on people's strengths and encouraging them to notice what is good in their lives rather than fretting after what they do not have.[31] As I have described, in 2006, Daniel Kahneman articulated the case in economic terms.[32] He showed that above a certain income there would be no increase in well-being. His work was taken up by Richard Layard, and echoed by Tim Kasser, whose research on the psychology of materialism has also consistently challenged the prevailing belief system that wealth and possessions will bring happiness, referring to these values as the mental equivalent of junk food, incapable of satisfying and nourishing or meeting real needs.

Happiness, as defined by these thinkers, appears to be mostly biological and relational – it is about physical well-being, shared laughter, shared sexual pleasure, shared purpose and shared conversation. Yet these 'goods' are not on the political map. Kasser sees our current culture as a dystopia where there is 'a kind of famine of warm interpersonal relationships, of easy to reach neighbours, of encircling, inclusive memberships and of solid family life'.[33] As I noted in chapter one, Kasser found that materialistic teenagers tend to have more combative relationships, but this also works the other way: the poorer our relationships, the more materialistic we become. Kasser's findings confirm earlier work by the social scientists Patricia and Jacob Cohen, which showed that teenagers in enmeshed, punitive and inconsistent relationships with their parents were more materialistic.[34] Sadly, as Kasser puts it, 'when people follow materialistic values and organise their lives around attaining wealth and possessions, they are essentially wasting their time as far as well-being is concerned.'[35]

Kasser claims that materialism even undermines our cherished values of freedom and autonomy. 'How can this be?' he asks, since 'freedom and capitalism go hand in hand, so we are told.'[36] The answer lies in the fact that materialistic people, even those who might describe themselves as 'self-starters', are much more driven by what he calls 'extrinsic goals'. Focused on their status and how they look to other people, or concerned to avoid being blamed or criticised, they are in fact less *self*-directed than other people. As with the authoritarian personality in general, they are motivated by anxiety rather than by their feelings and interests. They are less likely to do things simply because they are pleasurable and absorbing – in other words, they experience less 'flow'. Yet for many, accessing their own feelings as their 'centre of gravity', as the paediatrician and psychoanalyst Donald Winnicott put it,[37] is not easy. The quality of care in infancy plays a large part in determining whether or not people develop in a way that is constantly uncertain and anxious, trying to adapt to others and find meaning in external sources, or deeply rooted in their authentic self.

## The intrusive state

I am fascinated by the fact that somehow people instinctively raise their children in a way that fits with the economic imperatives of the time, as well as in response to cultural initiatives. But it is easier to see this clearly when we look backwards; it is more difficult to see where we are today, or to picture how the development of a powerful global economy alongside relatively weak nation states will affect our personal lives and families.

Although we still seem to be in the grip of a work culture which encourages us to achieve economic goals regardless of their impact on our relationships, this may be changing. The assumption that the good life is primarily a materially comfortable life is losing ground. However, once a trend has taken hold, there is often an ideological battle to go through before it changes. In the 1960s and into the 1970s, there was strong opposition to women working. It took a great struggle over many decades to change attitudes. But now that the culture has more or less come to terms with women working, there is an equally defensive reluctance to consider the needs of young children, especially when this might involve real social changes. Change is never welcome; people prefer to stay with their familiar ways of doing and thinking. Whenever there are public debates about children and their care, the strongest feelings seem to be expressed by those who insist that women must have 'choice' and must not be told what to do. What emerges at such times is a fear of returning to an era where women were oppressed, gender roles were rigid, and sexual freedom was restricted. In many people's eyes, the state is seen as a potential instrument of social control, which may compel people to stay unhappily married or stuck at home doing childcare. The fear is that the state may become a means of enforcing a particular set of values over a reluctant population.

In response, people fiercely defend their right to bring up their children as they see fit, and resent intrusions by the state or experts. They will even deny the scientific evidence, some of which I have presented in earlier chapters, about the developmental needs of babies and children. They will complain about the dangers of the state's micro-management of people's lives, as do Frank Furedi and Jesse Norman. Norman says: 'If we are to have better public services and a better society, we need to rethink the shape and purpose of the state itself,' and argues that, instead of a centralised, bureaucratic, welfare state caring for people, the state should step aside and let charities do the work, allowing citizens to show their own 'fraternity and social responsibility'.[38] As someone who has co-founded a charity and worked in it, I am dubious about this solution. In my charity, the Oxford Parent Infant Project, as in many others, endless amounts of energy are spent fund-raising and worrying about how to survive financially, instead of caring for the clients. Skilled professionals give up their right to a decent salary and work for less than the going rate, subsidising the enterprise out of their own pockets, whilst the charity's management – the voluntary board of trustees – is largely restricted to those who can afford to give their time without financial reward. David Cameron's 'Big Society', full of dedicated volunteers is in practice more likely to be a place where those who care are financially exploited, whilst those who don't, carry on making money.

Opposition to state intervention in personal life is also often based on a view of the state as potentially coercive and intrusive, an insensitive parent who does not listen or respond to voters' real concerns or needs. Many people have no faith in the state as a potentially benign and supportive authority. Rather than turning to the state to ensure that we collectively meet people's basic needs, they prefer a model in which people rely on their own resources and choose how best to meet their own needs – with their own money. Frank Field, a former Labour minister in the UK, has even argued for people to have their own personal state welfare budgets which they can dip into when they choose. After all, the argument goes, people can choose whether or not they work hard and buy the services and goods they want, or they can choose to consume less and focus on their relationships. Why should the state have anything to do with such choices – why should the state dictate moral values, or attempt to impose its own version of utopia? Isn't this infantilising people?

Nowhere is state-intervention more keenly resisted than in how we bring up our children; many see state involvement as an unwarranted politicisation of parenting, invading an area of our lives where our deepest feelings lie. Even a psychotherapist such as Andrew Samuels believes that parents should be left alone to do it their way, claiming that he 'trusts people' not to be selfish. He is sanguine about the possibility that children might have difficult experiences along the way, since he believes that difficulties are grist to the mill of creativity and growth[39] – a similar argument to the one used in the 1950s by Sir James Spence, the paediatrician who argued that Wordsworth 'suffered from emotional upset, yet look at the poems he produced'.[40]

But our socialisation practices are not neutral matters of individual choice – they play a central role in creating culture. And unfortunately, individual parents rarely make informed *choices* about their parenting practices. Most of us simply reproduce the way we ourselves were parented – with a few minor variations. Certainly, my parents felt they were much more tolerant and easygoing than their parents had been; whilst their own parents had been fussy and controlling about tidiness and order, they allowed my brother, sister and I to turn tables upside down and pretend that they were boats, or make unholy mixtures from food found in the kitchen. When it was my turn to be a parent, I tried to offer my children the same freedom to explore but a greater sense of emotional security, which I felt had been lacking for me. But we can only try to improve the things that we are conscious of needing to change. The basic things we do with our children are deeply unconscious. It is more difficult to be sensitive and empathic to children if you have not experienced those things in your own relationships with your parents.

This is why many parents need help if they are to meet their children's needs adequately. People who have been neglected or mistreated to any degree in their own childhoods often find there is a gap between their conscious views of parenting and their instinctive reactions; it is easy to catch yourself, despite the best intentions, doing it the way it was done to you. In the past, generation after generation has blundered on, repeating the mistakes of their ancestors, whilst attempting at the same time to adapt to the evolving culture of the day. This is what you get when you rely on parents to 'do it their way' or 'do their best'.

However, science – after a couple of hundred years of avoiding emotion – has now finally penetrated into the sphere of human development and emotional life. We have a wealth of evidence about how humans develop; we now know what will promote individualism, independence and materialism – and what will promote social solidarity, empathy and co-operation. We know what children need to feel emotionally secure and confident, and what will lead to defensive behaviours. We know how important good self-regulation is and how empathy for others relies on it. We are beginning to understand the way that the brain itself develops in early life and how influenced it is by social experiences. All this relatively new information is becoming familiar to the highly educated layers of society and needs to be absorbed into widespread public awareness.

Although our 'major societal institutions are not founded on the tenet of helping others to develop' as Jean Baker Miller once said,[41] the new knowledge that we have means that this may be the moment to re-think that principle. Perhaps our institutions *can* now incorporate an awareness of real human needs and human development. The state has never fully embraced the possibility of being a maternal as well as paternal force. Although it has had its moments – such as the creation of the National Health Service – its caring functions have almost always been subordinate to its role as servant of the economy. But now we are in a new situation – economically, scientifically and in terms of our psychological knowledge – where for the first time in history we can enable and facilitate the kind of society we want.

More and more, established individualist values are coming up against the growing re-assertion of collective needs. But even if we want to give more weight to collective needs – a new culture that supports better care for children, as well as for other vulnerable groups such as the elderly and the international poor – how can change be effected? Is state coercion the only option or is there another way? Can we achieve a sufficient consensus to enable the state to carry out our collective will? How *does* a change in values come about? Does it come about through rational argument and democratic debate, the spread of scientific knowledge, pressure from the public and social movements from 'below', or through emotional manipulation via the media and social engineering?

# 9. THE PROCESS OF CHANGE

The democratic road is the hard one to take. It is the road which places the greatest burden of responsibility upon the greatest number of human beings.

*John Dewey, 1939*

Progress is improvement in how we treat each other.

*Walter Wagner, 2006*

There is a growing feeling that things have got to change – but how? Despite the pride that many Western nations take in being 'a democracy', few people feel any genuine sense that they can influence the events that affect them or participate in decision-making. According to the Power Inquiry, which in 2006 produced an independent report into the British people's lack of political participation,[1] most people feel that they have little influence – 'no choice in an era of choice'. Or, as Gore Vidal once put it, 'Democracy is supposed to give you a choice like painkiller X and painkiller Y. But they're both just aspirin.'[2]

In other words, we are 'managed' by politicians rather like the modern, enlightened parents who manage a child who is playing up and saying she doesn't want to get dressed, by saying, 'Would you like to wear your red jumper or your blue one today?' Politically we all too often find ourselves in the position of a child in relation to more powerful parents who at times may try to give us the illusion of choice and of being heard, but sooner or later revert to their default mode of Strict parent.

Our lofty conceptions of democracy – as the system most linked in people's minds to 'freedom' of various kinds, as well as to the belief that we are all sharing in power and making choices about our lives – are a far cry from the reality. The current practice is to use the electoral process itself as a kind of theatrical production to arouse emotions, rather than as an opportunity for a rational debate between equals about how best to allocate resources. In particular, visual media and the internet are used to stimulate people's unconscious right brain family 'frames' using emotionally loaded imagery, inviting them to identify with the hero or heroine of their choice. Perhaps it is inevitable that we should resort to such short-cuts, when many of our political choices are in reality too complex to be decided by a mass vote. However, we may need to reconsider how democratic processes might work in the light of what we now know about how our brains process political decision-making. Do we really want politics to be more like shopping than thinking – or could we find ways for politics to engage people emotionally while still enabling them to think?

Perhaps because we hold its original tenets dear, we are far too forgiving of our current version of democracy. The American political scientist James Q. Wilson, who has so much of value to say about morality, resorts to a lazy defence of capitalist democracy as the 'least worst' system humans have come up with. He is complacent about its failings, claiming that 'to the extent that a society is capitalist, it is more likely than its alternatives to sustain challenges to privilege. These arise from economic rivals, privately financed voluntary associations, and democratically elected power-holders; they operate through market competition, government regulation, legal action, and moral suasion. But they operate clumsily and imperfectly, and, in the routine aspects of ordinary morality, they may not operate well enough.'[3] Wilson claims with the cynicism of old age that all systems rest on greed and every kind of society will sooner or later throw up 'a profligate and self-serving elite'.

Wilson's complacency about the system's imperfections rests on his assumption that capitalism is synonymous with democracy, a view that is neither true today – since the development of an authoritarian capitalism in Chinese society – nor particularly historically accurate. In Britain, at least, democracy was not built into capitalism from the start. In fact, until the late nineteenth century, there was a terror that democracy would bring 'mob rule'. Electoral rights were only allowed belatedly, after the liberal state was firmly established: 'Democracy came as a top dressing' according to the political philosopher C. B. Macpherson.[4] He argued that it became tolerable to those in power only once it was clear that the lower classes wanted to join the market society, not to overthrow it.

## Individualistic democracy

Far from uniting the unruly electorate, in practice the idea of 'one person, one vote' tends to reduce human social collaboration to an isolated process, based on the idea of the self-sufficient, autonomous individual – a very close relative of '*Homo economicus*'. Politically, our power – such as it is – rests only on the cumulative force of a vote once every four to five years. Although this democratic process acts as a brake on the behaviour of politicians, who fear being ousted by the collective judgement of voters, politicians are still not accountable to us in any direct sense. Rather than granting the voter any real influence or participation in self-government, voting in many ways functions defensively as a safety valve for social unrest.

Our elevated, ideal version of democracy is also inextricably linked with human rights – rights such as the right to organise politically, to criticise government, to own property and to receive equal treatment with others under the law. In reality, neither universal rights nor votes are robust enough to alter the basic power structure, in which the people who have more wealth and influence are able to determine the nature of contracts, the way news is disseminated in the media or how political policies are shaped. As Martha Nussbaum has pointed out, abstract 'rights' are no good to people if they don't have the material or institutional resources to exercise them. Without adequate food, or a job, or a home, the right to free speech may seem less compelling. If you cannot afford a lawyer, the right to equality under the law may not have much traction. Nussbaum quotes the Dickens character in *Hard Times*, Sissy Jupe, who is asked by her teacher to admire a hypothetical nation with '50 millions of money' – 'Girl number twenty, isn't this a prosperous nation, and a'n't you in a thriving state?' Sissy replies in tears that she cannot answer the question until she knows 'Who has got the money, and whether any of it is mine.'[5]

Sissy correctly identifies her own lack of power and access to resources. Even if the nation is thriving, she might not be. Having rights, including the right to vote, does not ensure that Sissy's needs are met. A form of 'democracy' superimposed over an unequal society focused on making money cannot itself conjure up a sense of unity. When the question in people's minds is, 'What can I get out of this person?', or 'How can I advance my own material well-being?', the social pleasures of collaborating with others for the common good fade away. The other person becomes an adversary not a collaborator, and society is riddled with anxiety and resentment. The more inequality there is, the less trust between people there is likely to be, and less trust means a greater need for 'rights' as a defence against exploitation. But although 'rights' can be used to protect people's existing property and bodily integrity, they are almost always freedom *from* intrusions by other people and are much less often used to guarantee care or responsibility for others.

Feminist academic Carol Gilligan's pioneering work on morality in the 1980s has spearheaded a new way of thinking about rights. Her original view was that women's moral development was different from men's; her research suggested that women were guided less by rules and fairness than by empathy and care for others.[6] This perspective has subsequently been elaborated and critiqued by academics such as Joan Tronto, Selma Sevenhuisjen and Martha Nussbaum. Building on Gilligan's insights, they reject the defensively avoidant demand for 'rights' as an inadequate basis for political morality, and have begun to argue for an 'ethic of care' to be integrated into politics – for government itself to be reshaped around new principles, moving away from the focus on rights and rules which has predominated since the Enlightenment, towards more relational thinking. Without abandoning the importance of justice, such thinkers have argued that a morality based on universalistic principles of rights or justice is too abstract to be integrated with care, which is about responding to others' needs in a practical way.

They describe the essence of 'care' as a sensitivity to other people, a capacity to pay attention to them, and to be receptive and responsive to others, as well as taking responsibility for ensuring that other people get what they need if possible – in other words, the same values that are the foundation of secure attachments within the family. An ethic of care is about giving equal worth and responsiveness to every person and their needs – not just giving him or her 'rights' on paper.

## The powerful

The need for such an ethic becomes particularly pressing when one considers the enduringly large psychological barrier between those who live at the opposite ends of the economic spectrum. Those with more resources and more power have great difficulty in respecting those with fewer resources, or entering into their experience. For example, Gillian Tett, Assistant Editor of the *Financial Times*, who was one of the few journalists far-sighted enough to see the financial disaster approaching, described how bankers had come to live in their 'own little village' cut off from ordinary people. In her view, they see reality only at second hand, as if inside Plato's cave, looking at the 'flickering on the walls – or on their computer screens'. Tett believes that bankers have come to see themselves as 'masters, not servants', and are cut off from others in what she called a 'silo' mindset which assumed that each financier could do whatever they wanted and ignore what other financiers were doing, or how this affected society as a whole.[7] The more unequally wealth and opportunity are distributed, the less incentive there is for the rich and powerful to come out of their 'silo' to co-operate with the relatively powerless.

Too much power often leads to the illusion that you are not like others and can have what you want and do what you want without needing to think of others. Seemingly impervious to the vulnerability and anxiety that afflicts others further down the food chain, powerful people can become intoxicated with their freedom and addicted to acquiring yet more power. When they no longer have to respond to others or be constrained by others' needs, their sensitivity to others will inevitably be blunted.

The 2009 British parliamentary expenses scandal is an example of the 'silo' effect at work in politics. When the *Daily Telegraph* lifted the lid on politicians' expenses claims, one of the first cases to come to light was that of the British Home Secretary, Jacqui Smith. She, like many others as it subsequently became clear, had claimed a large sum of money from the taxpayer for her 'second home'; it in fact turned out to be her first, family home – a sleight of hand to claim more money. Yet as time went by, it became clear that this was a common practice in the House of Commons; in fact, there was worse to come as MPs were seen to be claiming public money for cleaning the moats of their grand houses, heating their swimming pools, as well as asking the public to fund their hair straighteners, silk cushions, digital cameras and even their attendance on 'intimate relationships' courses. Most serious of all, they used taxpayers' money for private property speculation, known as 'flipping'.

Jacqui Smith, however, was the first to make the notorious defence that she had 'abided by the rules'. Like the young children described in chapter three, Smith thought it was sufficient to conform, though clearly something in her was uneasy about it, because she had also consulted the relevant authorities before she made her claim to make sure that she could get away with it without being punished. In this she revealed a sort of limited tribal mentality that has characterised humans for most of our history, a way of thinking based on the need to co-operate with our immediate social group to survive.

Although Smith, who appears a practical and straightforward woman, is no doubt concerned about her constituents at other times, she did not make any mental link between many people's desperate struggles to keep their homes and make their mortgage payments during an economic recession, and her own behaviour in using public money to line her own pocket. In this she reflects Arsenio and Lover's description of the 'happy victimiser': a person operating at this level may well be capable of empathy for others, but doesn't manage to hold on to concern for others when driven by impulses to take what she wants. The behaviour of Smith and so many other politicians left the impression that their relationship with the people they represented was not invested with sufficient emotion to make them stop and think about their impact on others. It also raised a question: how can we put our well-being in the hands of these figures of authority when they are so disconnected from the rest of us?

## Moving away from democracy

For as long as *noblesse oblige* and other aristocratic values survived into the twentieth century (albeit in a diluted form), the illusion could be sustained that the powerful were born superior and fulfilled an obligation to take care of the lower orders, in the manner of remote parental figures. But in the twenty-first century, these attitudes are becoming a distant memory. According to the Power report, Joe Public is, on the whole, 'better educated, more affluent, expects greater control and choice over many aspects of life, feels no deference towards those in positions of authority, and is not as bound by the traditional bonds of place, class and institution that developed during the industrial era'. Those at the very bottom of the social scale, however, may be too poor, unqualified and marginalised to care; the Power Commission suggests they have 'only a limited and fragmented dialogue with those in power'.[8] In fact, the more educated and aware the population in general becomes, the more impossible it is to trust the state or to tolerate our dependence on leaders, who are invariably self-seeking or at the very least no better than we are. The end result? People withdraw from the voting process.

Currently, there is little sense that we, the public, have ownership of the government, or that society might be deliberately organised to share good things and provide for people's needs. In practice, the UK government is heading away from public participation, perfecting the art of 'spin' and manipulating public opinion. The independent campaigning journalist George Monbiot tells the story of how the UK government rigged its consultations on nuclear power. The government's Energy Review gave the people it consulted 'misleading' and 'inadequate' information. When Greenpeace took it to court, the High Court ruled that the consultation was unlawful and flawed. It then ordered the government to commission an opinion poll. The government did so. However, the poll was subsequently reviewed by the Market Research Standards Board, who found that 'information was inaccurately or misleadingly presented, or was imbalanced, which gave rise to a material risk of respondents being led towards a particular answer.'[9] The entire consultation was made a mockery by the government's compulsion to get the 'right' answer, rather than the real answer.

Increasingly authoritarian forms of 'managerial capitalism' have become the norm. In the UK, 'sofa government' by the Prime Minister and his non-elected friends has replaced collective government by Cabinet. In 1975, Cabinet met fifty-six times and received 146 papers, but in 2002, it met thirty-eight times and received four papers.[10] A similar phenomenon took place in the USA, as George W. Bush narrowed the democratic process down to himself and his close colleagues. By 2008, he was referring to himself as 'the decider' and had come to believe that he did not need to justify his decisions to others. Those at the very top seem to have become impatient even with the process of consulting their own colleagues, whose independent thinking might interfere with their strategies for managing the electorate. Power is concentrated in fewer and fewer hands.

In such a situation, many people would much rather see the reach of government into our lives shrink, not expand. They resent government power, increasing government infringements of liberty and government taxation; they feel government does not have their best interests at heart or may not be competent to deliver results. Some ask why they should defer to authorities which bitter experience – from the Watergate affair to Enron to the parliamentary expenses scandal – shows to be riddled with corruption. Others feel they are best placed to make their own decisions about how to manage their affairs and don't want government to interfere, particularly if they are high earners who resent high taxation, but sometimes even when they are not. There are also many people who resent Big Government because they experience a real sense of helplessness and difficulty in being heard, and are resorting to an 'avoidant' strategy – along the lines of 'Just let me have my own money and take care of myself'– the same strategy children use when they live with parents who don't listen to their feelings.

## The end of close-knit society

American democracy was founded when society was relatively small-scale. Most of the population was still rural and lived within strong communities, guided by religious values. It was relatively easy to make their feelings known to their representatives and there was little need for government intervention in people's lives; indeed, it was largely outside its scope. In such communities, shared values could be taken for granted. As John Adams said in 1798, 'Our constitution was made only for a moral and religious people.'[11] These religious ideals continued to guide society into the nineteenth century. But by the 1830s, when Alexis de Tocqueville wrote his book *Democracy in America*, the emerging industrial society had changed all this. As people's personal resources increased, they started to believe that they could be self-sufficient, leaving 'the greater society to look after itself'– or, at least, to be looked after by a political class who took on more and more responsibility for deciding and implementing the values of the whole society. Where once people had participated in political and social affairs and had argued as if it mattered, Tocqueville's view was that now, 'No longer do ideas, but interests only, form the links between men, and it would seem that human opinions were no more than a sort of mental dust open to the wind on every side.'[12] Already there was a nostalgia for the old way of life in impoverished rural communities where there were 'firm and lasting ties' between people and an obvious necessity to co-operate in practical matters.

Currently, Communitarian thinking – shared across the political spectrum from Blair to Cameron – harks back to these communities of old where neighbours called on each other and took responsibility for other people's children, offered help when times were bad, and so on. In our current way of living, most people don't even know who their neighbours are; when they run out of ingredients for their dinner, they are more likely to ring for a take-away than to go next door to borrow some food. As the environmentalist Bill McKibben puts it, the opportunity to feel grateful and connected to our neighbours is lost: 'We Americans haven't needed our neighbours for anything important, and hence neighbourliness – local solidarity – has disappeared.'[13]

Instead of neighbourliness, a larger-scale society has instead given us a sense of freedom. This has its merits; as Charles Leadbeater, the management consultant for 'innovation' has argued, there is a less attractive side of close-knit communities which is their intolerance of outsiders and their tendency to stifle creativity and difference. He suggests that instead of pursuing the chimera of a traditional idea of 'community', we should put our faith in an intensified pursuit of knowledge and education, which in itself will increase the possibility of democracy.[14] Even today, in our very different, technologically advanced, large-scale global culture, it seems that many still share the optimism of early theorists of democracy who hoped that reason and debate were the path to developing the capacity for self-government. Yet, desirable as his vision of an informed population sounds, it still rests on a perception of rationality, a 'left brain' process, as humans' most powerful modus operandi. It ignores the fact that people develop the desired capacities for responsible participation and care for others – the lynchpins of true democracy – not by demanding it, or arguing for it, but by having a *lived* experience of it – particularly in early life.

### Reason or emotion?

The philosopher Peter Singer has argued that humans are unique because we can see a bigger picture. Our higher faculties enable us to see the needs of the whole society, not just our own immediate family or group. Unlike other social animals, humans have something new in evolution: the ability to use rationality to overcome emotional responses – such as greed – to make more sophisticated evaluations and to reason that others 'have interests similar to our own'.[15] Increasingly, however, the scientific evidence points in a different direction – swinging away from the importance of moral reasoning towards the determining power of emotion in our moral behaviour. What this work points towards is that our potential for realising a caring society, for altruism, depends on our underlying moral development, and the feeling of connection with other people which comes, once again, from very early in life.

One recent attempt to explore the roots of moral potential has looked at the personalities of exemplary moral individuals. Are they particularly good at thinking and reasoning? What drove them to be brave and good? What the research has started to map out is that such people are actually more notable for their feeling than their thinking. For example, Elizabeth Midlarsky and colleagues made a study of Holocaust rescuers in 2005.[16] They compared those who had helped Jews – and had saved the lives of one or more Jews at great risk or cost to themselves (the 'rescuers') – with a group of similar Europeans who lived in the same areas or even next door, who had not offered any help even if it was requested (the 'bystanders'). Their final control group was a group of people from the same or similar neighbourhoods who had emigrated in the years leading up to World War II. They found that the bystanders and immigrants were remarkably similar in personality traits, though the immigrants were slightly higher on risk-taking. However, the rescuers (who had never before been interviewed or honoured) were different from both groups. They scored much higher on all the qualities that the researchers tested for: empathy, altruistic moral reasoning, social responsibility, risk-taking, autonomy, tolerance and self-direction. The most striking differences between them and the others were their high levels of empathy and sense of social responsibility.

Similar results were found in another recent study undertaken by Lawrence Walker and Jeremy Frimer.[17] They used a battery of personality tests on fifty Canadian adults given awards for exceptional bravery or caring. They found that

these individuals were more likely to have had secure attachments and a feeling of having had helpers in early life. They
were very self-aware and had a strong sense of agency and
responsibility, which they focused on helping and nurturing
others. In other words, their emotional development was
exceptional.

## The caring electorate

When we think about the creation of a caring society, clearly
an educated and rational population is not sufficient; what
matters just as much is the emotional maturity of its citizens.
The ability to take part in democratic processes actually
requires the development of psychological capacities that
come out of positive experiences of relationships – in particular, the capacity to listen to others undefensively, to be
flexible and to tolerate ambiguity. But these qualities tend to
emerge most reliably when individuals have the kind of deep
inner security formed in infancy. Without such psychological capacities, democratic engagement is tainted by anxiety
and fear, the need for control, the need to be 'right', to deny
feelings, and the tendency to be dismissive of others' suffering. When our emotional connection to others and ability to
recognise our own feelings in others is not particularly strong,
morality may falter. If we translate the 'bonus culture' or the
political expenses scandals into their childish equivalent – pic-
turing the scenario as that of the child who bullies and takes
advantage of younger siblings, commandeers their pocket
money and insists that they follow the unfair rules that she
herself had made up – a psychologist might well wonder
about the child's ability to relate and feel attached to others.

It is our failure to feel for others or stand alongside them in their difficulties that leads to selfishness.

How, as an electorate, can we help our public figures to stay connected and to feel emotionally invested in their relationship with the public? Are we choosing leaders based on the wrong criteria – their articulacy or ambition, rather than their personal moral development? Certainly this is one aspect of the problem. However, we should be wary of asking for idealised leaders and of projecting qualities onto ordinary people that they cannot possibly sustain. If the system allows powerful people to detach themselves from the constraints the rest of us experience, then there will be people ready to step forward and occupy that role.

It is hard to see how the average voter, who may not himself have a highly developed sense of empathy, would in any case be capable of identifying moral qualities in a potential leader – so perhaps we get the leaders we deserve. Until the values of social responsibility, empathy and altruism are more widely present in the culture as a whole, it seems unlikely that they will become the norm for our political leaders.

Jacqui Smith's behaviour was not unique in any way. She did not set out to cause harm, but simply kept other people's reality out of her awareness whilst she was thinking about her own desires. We all do this all the time, when we ignore the existence of starvation and suffering around the world and choose instead to buy the latest thing on our wish list. Corporate executives and business leaders automatically behave in the same way: they are concerned only for their bottom line, and are frequently willing to set aside other concerns such as public health or the quality of the lives of workers in their sweat shops. But it is the extent to which we allow ourselves to cut ourselves off mentally from others and to deny connection or responsibility for others, which allows inequality and suffering to continue.

As Roy Baumeister has pointed out, those who do bad things rarely see themselves as bad. He describes the 'magnitude gap', where the perpetrator thinks he may have harmed the other person at a level of, say, one 'damage point', whilst the victim feels harmed at a level of ten points.[18] Noam Chomsky puts it this way: 'It is very rare for people to justify their actions by saying "I'm doing this to maximise my own benefit and I don't care what happens to anybody else." That would be pathological.'[19] Instead, we tend to offer defensive rationalisations such as 'I did it in self-defence', 'they are grateful for a job', 'everyone's doing it' or 'I was only following the rules'.

When Philip Lawrence, a calm and softly spoken London head teacher went to the aid of a thirteen-year-old boy who was being severely beaten around the head by a gang of older local boys outside the school gates, he was not following the rules. He did not say, 'My responsibility only goes as far as the school gates.' He immediately went to intervene and was stabbed to death in the process. He felt for his student and responded, in his case a responsiveness that caused him to lose his life.

As the political scientist Fiona Robinson – another leading figure in feminist thinking about how to apply the ethics of care in the public realm – points out, the ability to act well emerges 'out of our personal and social attachments with others.'[20] It is this web of attachments that forms the foundation of the feminist thinkers' understanding of how an 'ethic of care' could work in practice. The model is once again a parental one – just as parents don't respond to their children because their children have 'rights' but because each child has intrinsic value, they want a culture that treats people in the same way. As they note: 'The world will look different if we move care from its current peripheral location to a place near the centre of human life.'[21]

Although often the practice of 'care' is associated with women, and with mothering behaviour in particular, these thinkers don't want to make 'care' something that belongs only to women, or to link it to the notion of 'good mothering'. The social scientist Selma Sevenhuisjen argues that everyone is capable of caring for others, and that everyone needs care – we are all interdependent and vulnerable at times, including men. In her thinking, care is very much about empathy, the capacity to 'think from the perspective of everybody', and to decide issues on the basis of who needs what, and how our choices affect others.[22] This does not necessarily mean that all needs can be met or that there are no conflicts between different people's needs. The key element is a thoughtfulness about what others feel and think and need. In psychological terms, this is close to a 'mentalising' perspective. Doing things in a caring way means doing it with others in mind, doing it with awareness of consequences for others, not basing decisions on 'my rights'.

## Changing government

How then could we develop an ethic of care in public life? There is a growing swell of opinion that wants to see a wider sense of responsibility to others, and awareness of others' needs built in to public policy. According to Fiona Robinson, a new, more relational, politics would decide policies on the basis of who is hurt by them, who has power and what relationships will be disrupted. It would demand that governments take responsibility for helping to develop the institutional structures that support care for others (including a consensus about global responsibility), whilst recognising that governments don't have magic wands and are limited by the available resources. Of course they can't *make* people healthy or emotionally well balanced, but they can deliver 'the social basis of these capabilities', as Nussbaum says,[23] with their policies on the family, their willingness to tackle poverty, policies on rape law, on psychological healthcare, on advertising and so on.

In other words, there would be a kind of re-framing of government's role in the light of a new moral consensus for a less selfish society. We could embrace the fact that we are now a large and complex society which needs 'Big' government, to hold us together around a shared vision. In the preface to Bertrand de Jouvenal's book *On Power*, the point was made that we can generate tremendous destructive power on a collective basis. It argued that 'It was not a spontaneously acting group of "scientists" who made the atomic bomb. It was a group of employees of the US who made the bomb, and the most important of them were scientists. But the decision to make it was the decision of President Roosevelt, as the decision to use it was the decision of President Truman. To state this is not to impute wickedness to either statesman; it is merely to call attention to the fact that only the state is powerful enough to do damage on this scale.'[24] The state has the potential to be enormously destructive, and at present almost always acts defensively. Most of our collective energy, as vested in the state, is currently used to keep capitalism going, to protect our financial interests or to defend the nation state at all costs. But why should that enormous collective power not be used constructively, to forge a more moral society?

The problem is that we don't yet have a shared moral vision. Religion is now a weak force in society, and the religion of materialism has taken its place. Some argue that psychology or the 'therapeutic' state is threatening to displace it, an exaggerated claim which is far from current reality. However, there are the first signs of a few green shoots of a new set of values, which have been 'forced on' in the hothouse of economic crisis. People are starting to think about what makes them happy. Policies are in place in the UK and the USA which recognise the social importance of early development and in giving children a good start in life. But there is no consensus as yet about what our priorities should be.

In any case, even if there were a vision of the common good, we would still have to rely on the state to realise it. Only the state is capable of mustering sufficient resources to break the intergenerational cycles of insecure ways of relating, only the state can shift agricultural policy away from meat-eating towards eating pulses, only the state can organise a universal health service or a new banking system or can collaborate to solve the problems of climate change.

But the difficulty is in finding consent for change. Many people hoped that politicians would show leadership with robust policies to tackle climate change, and help the population as a whole to understand why they were necessary. Such leadership has not been forthcoming. Whilst governments are sometimes willing to push through reforms which have a short-to-mid-term economic benefit, they rarely lead the way with progressive change that will place new financial burdens on the population. They are likely to act only when the pressure from the grass roots is strong enough and persistent enough to put their continued authority at stake. In other words, governments – and law-making – are still based on a defensive posture of mostly trying to limit harm rather than create good. When governments attempt to pursue more proactive policies for care and well-being, they are often accused of being a Nanny State. They depend ultimately on us, the mass of the population, to find a way to give the green light to the changes that are needed.

## Full-fat democracy

So if we want our leaders to take account of the wishes and needs of the electorate, we will need to make ourselves present more vividly. Currently, attempts to get politicians to listen are often adversarial: groups and individuals lobbying for their own causes speak out of frustration and powerlessness, often resorting to angry public demonstrations demanding to be heard. And the response is largely defensive: politicians try to manage the nuisance, and maintain their position, rather than really listening.

It is hard to see how this situation could improve without structural change in the way people are represented in parliament. For politicians to trust the electorate more and become more focused on representing our wishes accurately, they would need to become less oriented to pleasing the rich and powerful elite (their own parental authorities), and worry more about understanding and serving the public. This is unlikely to happen without reducing the power of politicians

and increasing the power of the public by insisting that
our voices are heard. It would involve the development of
more direct participatory democratic structures to increase
accountability and interaction with the electorate, such as
each MP holding a local annual general meeting and providing an annual report of his or her activities, as suggested
by the Power report. Other dynamic ways of stimulating
engagement might be through referenda and online interaction such as blogging, and social networks linking people
with each other and with their representatives, enabling
ongoing debate and *thinking* to take place. This is a rather
different proposition from the current Conservative party's
version of increased social engagement, which wants to
encourage local people to get involved in decisions about
local services – schools, new housing and social programmes – by allowing a little more room for local influence
on the details of such decisions.[25] This vision seems to hark
back once again to an ideal of village life where people
squabble amongst themselves to promote their own interests,
with echoes of the communitarians' moralising community
which knows other people's business and attempts to
pressurise people into 'good' behaviour. Of course, I would
not want to deny the value of local involvement in local
issues. But however useful it may be to increase such input,
this does not address the problem of real power and accountability at the national level. It does not enable people to
debate the questions that most matter to them, or to exert
influence over the bigger issues such as energy policy,
national planning strategies, childcare policies or the
protection of our civil liberties. If we really want to wake
people out of their political passivity, and engage them in

community activism, what is most needed is the opportunity to influence *national* policies.

Any measures which promote a more direct relationship between the public and our 'representatives', which ensure that the public's diverse voices ring in the elected politicians' ears, would make it harder for our views to be ignored. We don't need the political class to be Strict, remote parents any more; nor do we want them to be intrusive or over-protective parents. I believe that we want them to be 'authoritative' parents who listen and respond, who hold everyone's needs in mind and provide the structure which enables people to flourish. Instead of going towards a 'therapeutic state' which acts on behalf of the citizen in a relationship of parent and child in which 'the citizen recedes – the therapeutic self prevails', as the political philosopher Jean Bethke Elshtain fears, this might lead in the direction of her vision of a shared moral community of equals – a new civic brotherhood and sisterhood.[26]

The active involvement of citizens in democratic processes has never been guaranteed, just as emotional maturity is not guaranteed in human development. Mature citizenship and emotional maturity are both goals we may strive for, but find difficult to achieve. They are also linked, because a fully flowering democracy requires people who can argue for their own wishes whilst recognising other people's, and who have a well-developed sense of autonomy as well as an ability to co-operate. These capacities, as I have described in earlier chapters, flourish in secure families where people are confident that their needs will be met, and their voice will be heard.

In other words, participatory democracy that is more than a television spectacle is based on the same principles as the 'authoritative' family: being safe enough to speak freely and energetically for yourself, being sensitive enough to listen to others and take their views and feelings seriously. When there is conflict, instead of using coercion or intimidation as the Strict parent does, there is a willingness to process the tension together, to argue for different perspectives and communicate different experiences, whilst holding on to the value of the other person and his or her feelings. Isn't it time to stop worrying about whether psychological self-awareness has contributed to a 'me' generation or a 'therapeutic state', and to recognise that there are many new sources of psychological and scientific knowledge which can now help us to move on from the narcissistic society and to understand the links between the forms of our personal relationships and the kind of political processes we create?

# 10. AN UNSELFISH SOCIETY? THE MORAL MAKEOVER

The challenge in contemporary America is to create a nurturant society when a significant portion of that society has been raised either by authoritarian or neglectful parents.

*George Lakoff, 2002*

What is realistic is what happens. The moment we make it happen, it becomes realistic.

*George Monbiot, 2003*

One of the things that I have been trying to demonstrate in this book is that the inner life and the outer life are connected. Emotional life doesn't start at the front door of our homes (or the bedroom door, as some men might believe). It is part of everything. We are emotional creatures and we bring our emotional responses to our politics and economics as well as to our more personal relationships. They are what motivate us, and bring 'juice' to life. Our public behaviour – at work, in politics, in the media, in every profession – is driven by psychological forces, as well as our personal lives. The psychotherapist Julian Lousada and social work expert Andrew Cooper put it in more academic terms: 'Critical social analysis has always tried to reveal the individual psyche as shaped, constructed, or determined by social forces and processes. It has been less comfortable with methods of analysis that flow in the opposite direction, examining how social processes may be modelled on the amplification of dynamics most readily observed in the individual psyche.'[1]

The moral and emotional issues that we have to deal with as a society are the same as those we begin to grasp in the cradle: how we learn to pay attention to others and their feelings, how we manage conflict between people, and how we balance our own needs with those of others. Morality is about the way that we manage the interface between self and society, an interface that starts in babyhood and is learned from the actual practice of early relating. This gives early child-rearing a prime place in our cultural life. It is through these early, lived experiences with the adults around us that we form our social values and our tendency to be more or less selfish or to be more or less aware of others' feelings. It doesn't happen primarily through a rational process of moral instruction. What parent has ever had to instruct his child, 'When someone looks angry, that probably means you have upset them,' or 'They are smiling so you have done something right'?

In fact, we can't be fully rational until we understand our feelings – since our thoughts are an outgrowth of the way we interpret and elaborate our emotional states. The way that the inspirational author and neuroscientist Antonio Damasio has described it is to say that Descartes was wrong; we are not born thinking. *Being* comes first – and only later do we notice how our bodily feelings change, in relation to other people and events.[2] The process is one of ever-increasing complexity. First, we have bodily emotions. Then, as we form images of these bodily experiences and learn to link them together, they become the basis of representing our feelings. We can then use those representations to think about them. And only later still, do we learn the yet more sophisticated practice of thinking *about* our thoughts. But it has been a long struggle for human culture to become more aware of feelings. Throughout the twentieth century, even the discipline of psychology preferred to focus on cognition rather than emotion.

It has taken even longer to get children's emotions on the map. For example, in the 1940s and 1950s, parents were not allowed to visit their sick children in hospital. The child's distress at being alone, as well as ill, was seen as normal and inevitable: he's just a child, of course he will cry, that's what children do – after all, there are a lot of naughty and spoilt children. Hired by John Bowlby to help him investigate the impact on small children of separation from their parents, a couple of social workers called James and Joyce Robertson made a painfully vivid film of the children's distress and invited hospital staff to come and view it. The film acted like a mirror, inviting the hospital staff to see their behaviour and the children in a more objective light. However, the staff put up a tremendous resistance to seeing what the Robertsons were showing them and denied that it happened on their wards. Of course, no one likes to feel bad or to have their working practices challenged. The Robertsons were particularly crushed by the response of one doctor, Sir James Spence,

whom they had believed was an ally. At a meeting of paedi-
atricians, he attacked their film, saying, 'What is wrong with
emotional upset?'[3] It seems shocking now, yet the same arguments are still being made today. During a recent public
debate about a television programme (*Boys and Girls Alone*)
that had deliberately separated young children from their parents for a *Lord of the Flies*-type experiment, and had then
shown them crying in distress for their mothers, the producer,
David Dehaney, made exactly the same dismissive response:
'Kids do cry.'[4]

In the end, it took nearly a decade for sufficient numbers
of influential people to become convinced that children's distress at being separated from their parents in hospitals was
unacceptable and in some cases could have a lasting effect on
the child's emotional security. Finally, conditions in hospitals
were changed, and parents could visit their children – eventually even being encouraged to make overnight stays. This
process of change was a fight, amongst other things, to recognise that children have an inner self – an 'emotional
interiority', as the historian of childhood, Harry Hendrick,
describes it[5] – and feelings that matter. In many ways, the
same process is happening today in relation to babies.
However, if establishing respect for children's feelings is still an
unfinished battle, it is even more difficult to demonstrate the
significance of babies' emotions, particularly as they can't
name them.

As we have learned more about the process of emotional
development and the process of brain development as well, it
has become much clearer that we need a similar revolution in
our attitude to *babies*. They too have emotions. Their experiences count – not just to the individuals concerned but to

society. The way that babies are treated by the adults around them plays a profound role in perpetuating cultural attitudes and practices. And it is those first experiences of the social group – whether it is a traditional nuclear family, communal group, single parent, group of nursery workers or nanny – that have a disproportionately powerful influence on our lives, because they convey 'the way things are done' in this particular society. The baby soaks up the information without any conscious awareness that this is what he is doing, and fits in. Even his brain adapts, becoming equipped and ready to behave in certain ways rather than others. Mostly it is about copying the adults: if they are kind, thoughtful and empathetic, the baby will tend to learn how to be like that; if they are suspicious of other people and prone to aggression, the baby will follow suit, or become cowed. In the care of people who are intolerant of their own feelings, the baby is unlikely to learn much about his own. The earliest learning is about how to identify and manage feelings, as well as how to respond to other people.

## Emotional poverty

When babies are brought up insensitively, they will have brains that are adapted to unsatisfying relationships. While this is bad luck for them, it is not just a personal issue. When large numbers of people assume that it is normal for feelings to be ignored, they are likely to reproduce these attitudes in their own choices and may see nothing wrong with leaving babies to cry, or leaving seven-year-old boys in boarding schools. When people grow up experiencing their own feelings as difficult and unmanageable, they may assume that everyone finds life a struggle, or they may take it for granted that everyone relies on a supply of money, drugs, sex or food to feel better. If the adults in their lives rarely responded to their childhood needs, they may become adults who in turn don't feel much like putting themselves out for other people. Given enough people who think this way, the whole culture may shift.

People whose early years felt emotionally unsafe have 'bruised psyches' which can affect their behaviour in relationships. They are likely to be primed to react defensively to other people. For example, if they experienced their parents or social institutions as very demanding and perfectionist, they may readily be shamed by their own failures; if they were hurt by others in early life, they may be quick to feel resentment and anger. Further along the continuum, those who have had early experiences of emotional deprivation or maltreatment frequently develop an unconscious conviction that their needs cannot be fully met through relationships with others. Their vulnerable years have been such a painful experience that they try to avoid depending on others, and often try to control their relationships so that they are never abandoned or hurt again. Such people will not know how to put their faith in social bonds or in managing conflicts with others in a peaceful way. They are likely to find it difficult to trust the collective process of democratic decision-making.

Such experiences are not particular to low-income groups. They occur across the whole of society, a form of 'emotional poverty' which runs alongside economic poverty and intertwines with it but which has its own trajectory. Increasingly, researchers are demonstrating that some of the most pernicious effects of poverty come about through the increased stress that poverty puts on people: money worries, an unsafe environment,

lack of facilities all help to escalate feelings of insecurity. As in
the animal studies that showed the impact of 'unpredictable for-
aging' on monkeys, such stress can adversely affect their
offspring's brain development. However, in humans, we know
that, conversely, secure emotional attachments provide a protective effect. Some parents who live in poverty will be able to
withstand the impact of a stressful life because they have sufficient emotional resilience and confidence in others' helpfulness.
They may be able to protect their children by passing on a sense
of secure attachment. Baroness Patricia Scotland, for example,
a prominent black lawyer and government minister, grew up in
a large family in a poor part of East London. Yet she found
her parents 'inspirational' and said her mother 'instilled a strong
sense of self-worth in all her twelve children'. Others who grew
up with the double whammy of emotional poverty as well as
environmental poverty will find it much harder to protect their
children and often pass on their insecure patterns of relationship.[6] As a recent report for the World Health Organisation put
it, 'Because strong nurturant relationships can make for healthy
early childhood development, *socio-economic circumstances, despite
their importance, are not fate*'.[7]

We know from various sources of research which children
are most likely to be 'at risk'.[8] Although this phrase itself tends
to be associated with the lower classes of society, it is surprising how many of the conditions of being 'at risk' are
actually psychological. Although 'low income' and 'bad housing' do feature on the list, almost certainly because they
increase stress on families, the majority of risk factors are relational. They include 'having parents who are ambivalent
about being parents'. Whilst all parents have ambivalent feelings at times, those who are really uncertain about their ability

to inhabit the parenting role are those, I believe, who don't have the inner security and self-confidence to cope with the demands of children. 'Parental mental health problems' are also a given risk factor, and we know that the evidence points to emotional difficulties which may be genetically transmitted but also often originate in their own unsupported or maltreated childhoods. With such difficulties, they too are uncertain how to relate to others to get one's needs met, or how to meet their child's needs. 'Poor attachment' likewise has its roots in a lack of warmth or consistency in early relationships. There is often 'a history of anti-social behaviour' which I would interpret as poorly developed self-regulation and a tendency to act out rage with disappointing attachment figures. Finally, a 'poor education' is also a risk factor, perhaps because it would tend to inhibit the development of reflection and awareness, which are psychologically protective. Poor education also tends to limit children's potential, which is inherently frustrating.

Lists of 'risk factors' are rather aversive, because they seem to imply that poor social conditions inevitably lead to particular outcomes. There is a tendency to imagine that the less wealth and social power you have, the more likely you are to be 'at risk'. Certainly a lack of power makes you more vulnerable. But psychological damage runs through the whole of society like a sugary red vein in a stick of rock: it is not based on class, but on emotional habits that get passed down from one generation to the next. There are many people who act badly at times, who can't organise their lives well, who hurt others physically or psychically. Quite a few of these are hidden in well-heeled suburban neighbourhoods or splendid boardrooms, parliamentary chambers and classrooms.

In any early environment that cannot provide for children's psychological needs adequately, children's brains tend to become more sensitive to stress, more conditioned to see threats where none exist, and less able to integrate thoughts and feelings. However, parents are not the only source of trauma. The American psychiatrist Bruce Perry has warned of the dangers of allowing national conflicts – such as in Palestine, or Darfur or Rwanda – to remain unresolved, subjecting children to the experience of prolonged trauma.[9] Children who live in such environments of fear and terror will have compromised brains too. Their experiences could make it very difficult for them to hear others, empathise with others, and – crucially – resolve conflicts in the future. Thus vicious cycles will continue to be repeated unless the next generation are protected. This is likely to require diplomacy and psychological insight.

Successful societies, like successful families, depend on their members' ability to repair relationships when there have been ruptures or breaches between people. When this fails, wars and conflicts erupt, and the connection between people is broken; commonly, the enemy is dehumanised or written off. Whether in a marriage, a family, a social institution or conflicts between nations, the key to resolving persistent problems is to use empathy and mentalising to grasp the other person or group's motivations and feelings. The work of restorative justice, for example, aims to bring together those who have harmed others with those they have harmed, and to develop a dialogue rather than some form of punishment. It attempts to put people back into relationship with each other, by acknowledging that both parties have value and their actions have meaning. This approach insists on treating the aggressor as a person with a history who is more than the sum of his bad actions. Equally, the victim is given a chance to re-establish his or her personhood, after being dehumanised by the aggressor's behaviour, so that the damage done to his or her identity can be restored too. These are delicate negotiations which demand that all parties think about their own and others' feelings, instead of reacting impulsively. Under stress, these capacities are easily derailed.

## Building an unselfish generation

If we are going to build a less selfish society, we will have to address the sources of our selfishness. For many people, particularly those who have a religious faith, one important source is assumed to be the decline of the traditional family. In particular, the rise of the single-parent family is frequently seen as the cause of increased problems for children, who may not get enough financial security, attention or moral guidance in such a reduced and shrunken family form. Traditionalists believe that adults who leave their marriages are behaving selfishly in putting their own needs in front of their children's needs. They want to turn the clock back and re-establish marriage as an unbreakable, lifelong merger of two individuals, who come together to raise a family. There is some evidence that such a secure structure is beneficial for children, and, equally, evidence that divorce is painful and stressful for them.

As a selfish divorcee, I would not want to turn back the clock. However, I would not agree with those who reject these arguments on the grounds that their personal freedom is sacrosanct and in the hope that as long as they love their children, that should be enough. At their most excessive, such parents often reject the idea of having to make any sort of sacrifice – be it their career opportunities or their own personal happiness– or make any concessions to becoming a parent.

There is little real dialogue between these two extremes, yet both have valid points to make. I believe that the emotional difficulties of the parents are part of their children's experience and will have an impact on their children whether or not they stay together. In particular, research shows that parental conflict is very harmful to children, whilst some children can flourish in relatively unstressed single-parent homes. At the same time, I would not want to deny the misery that family break-up can cause, or question the fact that children benefit from stability and predictability, and also usually have strong bonds with both parents and want to live with them both.

My own experiences – as a parent and as a psychotherapist – lead me to think that what matters for a child's emotional health is not the particular *form* of family life, but above all for a child to have at least one permanent relationship with a loving, available adult who really listens and cares. My parents married young, had three children and stayed together until we were all grown up (when they did divorce). They did not argue with each other greatly, but were not emotionally close; instead, they went out a great deal and enjoyed a lively social life together. My own upbringing must have appeared very secure from the outside, but emotionally speaking, it was not. My father saw relatively little of us children, but he was emotionally warm and he enjoyed playing games with us occasionally at weekends. However, his presence also brought conflict, since he would deal with challenges to his authority with physical punishment. My mother had many talents and interests which she pursued, even when her children were infants. When she was not working outside the home, she tended to spend time with us only to teach us something, often criticising our social or academic performance. My grandmother was a more constant presence in the house during the week. She spent part of every day with us – cooking, cleaning and running the household – and then went home at night, after a day of grumbling incessantly at my mother or at us children. On the surface, an acceptable result for the traditionalists, since there was a stable home and married parents.

Yet none of these three adults paid much attention to the emotional state of the children. Empathy was missing. There was no 'mind-mindedness' in our home, and little talk or understanding about feelings. As far as I'm concerned, one really attentive, attuned parent would have been a lot better for me than three inattentive ones. And this is indeed what I found in the research on child development, and what has informed my own choices in relation to my children. When I became a parent in turn, I did not give a very high value to traditional marriage, as my parents had, but I did take the relationship between father and child more seriously than my parents' generation and encouraged and valued a much greater degree of emotional involvement than my father had had with me. My priority, however, was to adapt – and limit – my working life to ensure that I was available for my children as much as possible. No doubt my own children will react to the parenting they experienced in some new way.

The compromises that I cobbled together will be different from other people's compromises. Most people attempt to do what they think is best in their circumstances. Mothers, like anyone else, have wishes and needs of their own. Parenting frequently involves clashes between adult interests and children's interests. There is always conflict and ambivalence, and decisions are rarely transparent and pure. 'God is as much in the mess as the beauty,' as Thomas Moore said.[10] Not all needs can be met.

However, what is essential is that children's needs are fully weighed and considered, and that this consideration is based on the facts, not on wishful thinking. From a relational perspective, the question is 'How can I avoid harm?', not 'What are my rights?' From a developmental perspective, the question is 'how can I best help my child to develop?' Yet these are not necessarily the questions that are being asked, and the facts are often ignored in favour of what is politically or financially expedient.

## The nursery argument

Few areas of social policy today are more vexed that that of early childcare. Critics step in at their peril. However, it does seem to be central to the question of selfishness in society, since the quality of attention babies receive is crucial. If we take our current child-rearing practices to its logical outcome, leaving our babies with a random series of strangers from very early in their lives jeopardises not only their personal emotional stability but also social well-being. The risk is that poor early care will take us further down the road of creating individuals characterised by defensive self-sufficiency, who turn away from human contact as the greatest good, seeking comfort in the safer pleasures of food, drugs, gambling and passive entertainments.

Perhaps there is a deeper question facing us today: do we actually want a nurturing society, or a reflective society? There may be an unconscious imperative not to improve early care: if people were better nurtured emotionally, would they be willing to sustain capitalism? Perhaps there is a social momentum which demands our collective detachment from our own feelings and which keeps us focused on the material world. People who are well nurtured might be less interested in keeping up with fashion, buying the latest car or television, or emulating a celebrity lifestyle. They might be less obsessively concerned with expanding businesses and improving profits. And where would the food, gambling, entertainment and drugs industries be without human misery to drive them?

Certainly, the prevailing trends in child-rearing are not child-centred but work-centred and money-centred. Increasing numbers of parents believe that it is acceptable or even desirable to return to full-time work whilst their babies are still 'in arms'. This is strongly influenced by the availability of financial support during infancy. The current trend in the UK is to return to work when *paid* maternity leave expires. It is no accident that the countries with the highest rate of maternal employment are those which provide the least financial backing for parents during infancy. The Scandinavian countries are an exception, since they too have high rates of maternal employment, but within a flexible system of generous payments that enable parents as a couple to create their own personal formula to combine work and caring for their small children.

When parents look for childcare to enable them to work, they increasingly choose nursery day-care, often under the impression that this is the government-endorsed choice, even for babies. In the US, 12 per cent of three month olds are already in day-care centres, and by the age of fifteen months, this has risen to 21 per cent of US toddlers.[11] The same trend can be seen in the UK as the use of care in nurseries increases and the use of more personal childminders declines. Individual, responsive care for babies seems to be on the way out.

But the child psychiatrist Stanley Greenspan and philosopher Stuart Shanker warn that personalised care is a vital underpinning for a healthy society: 'Societies decline and regress when vast numbers of children are deprived of these co-regulated emotional interactions' – a danger which is more likely to be realised if children don't receive 'consistent nurture from loving caregivers who will be part of the child's life for years to come'.[12] They suggest that it is the quality of caregiving which is crucial: when caregivers come and go in an unstable way, or when they are stressed, perhaps have too many babies to manage comfortably on a given day as is often the case in day-care centres despite official ratios, or are just inadequately equipped to be parent-figures, there are real risks for children.

Certainly, recent evidence begins to demonstrate some of the consequences of failing to support parents in looking after their own children. New Zealand, Australia, USA and Britain are the countries that provide the least financial backing for babies and their parents; they are also the countries that have the worst social problems further down the line. These are the nations that suffer most with obese children, teenage pregnancies, bullying and poorer child well-being in general. On the other hand, countries such as Sweden, Norway and Denmark, which have made generous financial provision to support early parenting in a flexible way, have the best child-hood mental health.[13]

Although the eminent psychologist Penelope Leach, my colleague at the Association for Infant Mental Health, passionately agrees that early child-rearing is vital to the well-being of society, she takes a more relaxed view of parental participation in the workforce whilst their children are very young. She is sanguine about the inevitability of non-parental care in the earliest years, and looks back at the fantasy golden age of the family of the 1950s, concluding 'That is over,' or as my children would say, 'That is *so* over.' Leach takes a pragmatic view about the need for many women to work whilst their children are very young, and encourages women who are likely to feel lonely, anxious about their careers, or resentful of having no money, not to worry about staying with their babies but to get back to work, since they would be unlikely to do a good job if they feel trapped at home. There is a substantial body of research which confirms that a depressed adult who is losing her sense of self, or who feels stressed by a poor environment, or money worries, is in danger of becoming insensitive to her child. When parents are not enjoying being with their babies, obviously they will find it difficult to be responsive.

However, I am left wondering why the solution is for babies to be given to strangers, rather than to ensure that parents get what they need to feel supported. Why could we not ensure that mothers' (or fathers') jobs are protected so that they can pick them up again after a break? In Germany, either mother or father can opt to take extended unpaid parental leave over a three-year period, during which they cannot be sacked or lose their jobs. Why not develop more neighbourhood provision such as local parent cafés where entertainment, education and other community events take place, to make early parenting a more sociable and mentally stimulating activity? Why not provide therapeutic support for mothers who are depressed, which all the evidence (and my own clinical experience) shows is effective in lifting their depression? In my view, women should not be pushed into leaving their babies on such grounds.

To be fair to Leach, she does agree that non-parental care for babies is very problematic. She states that it is often not the kind of care babies need, and if 'done properly' would be pro-hibitively expensive.[14] Quality care depends on very high ratios of adult to child, basically replicating what might be available in a family. Nurseries generally provide the poorest quality of care for babies – they don't have enough staff to provide the continuous care babies need, and the staff that they do have are currently poorly paid and poorly trained. There is a massive turnover of staff – nearly 40 per cent – in day-care,[15] meaning that continuity of care is just not hap-pening even in enlightened nurseries with a 'key worker' system. When babies have to interact with a group all day long, rather than one-to-one care, it is stressful for them. Yet in the USA, she reports that there is a 'culture of silence and defeatism' amongst professionals, about the dismal quality of care in such places (only 9 per cent are rated as providing 'positive caregiving').[16] There is a terror of speaking up about the reality of the situation, because there is little hope of ever finding the funds to provide higher ratios or the infrastructure to provide better trained staff, which would enable babies to have close and secure (secondary) attachment relationships with their paid caregivers.

Rather than spend energy trying to achieve this unlikely and – even with the injection of all the cash in the world – not particularly optimum outcome for babies, I believe that there are better solutions to pursue. Why not provide a *right* to flexible working (as opposed to a right to ask for it) so that mothers and fathers can share looking after their babies and small children, whilst maintaining their working identities? After all, the research suggests that most women would prefer that either they or their partners should look after their own babies in the first couple of years, but ideally also have some part-time work.[17, 18] Increasingly, fathers too would like to play a more active role in their child's early life. In my view, this is the direction to go in, since it largely meets the needs of both babies and their parents. I think it is unlikely that trying to upgrade mass-produced nursery care will ever be able to provide the loving attachments babies need. That doesn't mean there would be no role for nurseries – their primary purpose would be to cater for children over two, which the research describes as beneficial for most children. A complete solution in the shared parenting route, to enable parents to be the primary caregivers for their babies, might also include the provision of, say, ten hours a week of subsidised free nursery or other alternative care from the early months onwards; this would help parents to juggle their flexible working lives between them – without being so long a separation that it would have a negative impact on their babies' well-being. The same hours should also be available if there is one full-time parent, to enable him or her to have a break from the demands of full-time caregiving.

These solutions are equally likely to be regarded as 'prohibitively expensive' either for the state or the employers, or both. However, they give both fathers and mothers a real choice of options, and they lift the burden of trying to achieve the impossible from parents' shoulders. Our current situation is unworkable. As a society, we have not yet adapted to the full integration of women into the workforce, or acknowledged that this poses a genuine dilemma for child-rearing. Historically, employers have never acknowledged that the working conditions they offered have affected the family and they have never taken any responsibility for their impact on the family. More recently, whilst bringing women in to play a central role in the labour force, employers have continued to treat child-rearing as an 'externality' – a cost that they regard as beyond their responsibility, like environmental pollution. But just as there is a growing demand to 'make the polluter pay', so too perhaps we could demand that employers must now use some of their profits to contribute to the social costs of employing parents of young children.

Although there are difficulties in meeting work responsibilities and childcare responsibilities all the way through childhood, my focus is unapologetically on the earliest years because these are so crucially important for establishing the emotional and moral development that underpins the rest of life. Babyhood is different in a number of ways. What babies are learning is primarily how to manage emotions and how to interpret the social world. They need individual guidance and feedback. Optimum development in babyhood therefore depends above all on the *quality* of their guiding relationships, as well as on relationships of sufficient duration to be able to hold the baby in mind and keep track of the baby's emerging self, shaping it and bringing it into being. The care that is needed at this stage of life is personal care, not impersonal care.

Penelope Leach rightly proposes that we should extend state funding for paid parental leave to at least twelve months, arguing that this would be 'value for money' in all sorts of ways. She doesn't spell out what these are, but there is little doubt that a secure early attachment has many long-term benefits not only to the individual concerned but also to society. The developmental psychologist Alan Sroufe has pursued an impressive long-term study of the same large group of families, starting in pregnancy and following them over decades at the University of Minnesota.[19] This shows that children who establish a secure attachment with a parent in infancy are set to do better on a whole range of measures in later life, only occasionally being derailed by difficult life experiences.

Leach argues for the value of one of the parents staying at home at the start of life to establish a bond with their baby. Despite its financial penalties, she encourages mothers to use their full nine months' maternity leave entitlement (in the UK) which she believes should be open to both parents (a sensible move which she points out would – even if not taken up greatly by men – help to restrain employers from discriminating against potentially fertile women employees). She points out that if parents establish a sensitive, responsive relationship with their baby in the first year, they will have built a solid foundation to their relationship, and will be more likely to be able to tune in to the child emotionally and later be more aware of what is going on for their child as he or she relates to other caregivers. This is certainly a valuable piece of the developmental jigsaw, but it may be optimistic to believe that nine months of more or less full-time parental care is sufficient.

If our policies support only very early parenting, they are still not fully acknowledging the depth and range of interactive experience which are also needed in the second year to establish the self-awareness and self-acceptance which leads to moral development – as I have described in earlier chapters. While it is true that the first year is the most intense form of care, based on the biological bond, in the second year the baby still needs to experience relationships with sufficient emotional depth to guide his or her moral development. This may be possible with a childminder or a nanny, and indeed in good arrangements, such carers may become part of the extended family, adding to the richness of the child's emotional repertoire. My family was lucky enough to stumble into such an arrangement with a wonderfully affectionate, fun-loving babysitter who developed a lasting relationship with my children, and who is still in touch with them now they are adults. When alternative caregivers are used to *supplement* the basic parental care, and the hours are gradually increased as the child gets older, the result can be beneficial for all.

However, many parents find that they don't have such reassuring experiences with the caregivers they use. The researcher Carol Vincent recently found that the London mothers she studied did not feel able to talk freely to their children's caregivers; nor was the idea of love or even 'care' on the agenda.[20] Instead, they felt obliged to fit in with the norms of the childminder or nursery, even if they disagreed with them; it was a seller's market. The reality for most parents is that choice is a myth. It is difficult to find childcare, so you have to make the best of what you can get. Quality care is often just not available or affordable. Working-class mothers, in particular, often have little choice of caregiver, and can only afford the nursery care funded by the state. For the under-threes there are no state-funded childminders.

Tacitly, government conveys its approval of nursery provision by offering it as the basic form of early childcare, particularly through its Children's Centres. This leads parents towards an unfounded assumption that nursery care in the first and second year of life is fine. The evidence is not presented to them, and when it does surface in the media is often batted away by commentators who — like parents — often believe what they want to believe. There is rarely any clear advice about the differences between what babies need and what pre-schoolers need, or a clear picture of the worst-case scenario — of babies spending long hours in poor quality day-care. It seems that political expediency blurs the picture and gives blanket approval to nursery care. But even a few months of good 'bonding' which are then followed by a period in mass-produced, low-grade 'caregiving' are not likely to give a baby the most favourable start in life. Indeed, the evidence is that when babies under two spend long hours in nurseries, they are stressed by the premature demands that are made on them, and are more likely to become aggressive and poorly regulated children.

## Love and sensitivity

In practice, many working mothers often feel uncertain about handing their young children over to strangers and worry about losing their closeness to their babies. Many of my own clients have expressed just such feelings of anxiety and ambivalence about allowing someone else to care for their baby.

Penelope Leach feels the need to reassure working parents that their baby will still love them best, even if they use others to care for their children in the working day. This is true, because only parents actually *love* their children and are permanently attached and committed to their welfare, and children can feel the difference between being deeply valued in an ongoing relationship, and temporary caregiving, however kind. But, although reassuring to parents, this doesn't mean that it is the best thing for babies to have limited access to their parents' loving care. Of course, if they have good enough childcare during the day (particularly if they are given the chance to form meaningful ongoing attachments) and then come home to sensitive, loving and attentive parents, they are just as likely to develop the capacity for secure attachment as a stay-at-home child. As Leach points out, the evidence is that having parents who are sensitive to their children's emotional needs is what matters most of all.[21]

However, it can also be more difficult for parents to be sensitively attuned to their baby if they spend limited amounts of time with him or her. If their contact takes place at the end of a long and tiring working day, it can be difficult to maintain sensitivity. As a businesswoman featured in Lynn Alleway's documentary *Quality Time* put it, rather unsympathetically, 'In the mornings I'm in a rush, in the evenings I'm tired and at weekends I'm exhausted. Life is such a rush. Children always mess about at the wrong moment, interrupting one's agenda'[22] – a sentiment which many fathers have expressed in the past. Parents of either gender who are caught up in their work to this extent no doubt do love their children as much as anyone else, but they are not necessarily sensitive to them. Love and sensitivity are not the same thing.

Being tuned in to another person is not something you can take for granted. Even in adult relationships, people who do not spend sufficient time with each other can find it hard to sustain their bonds. The evidence from decades of attachment research is that secure attachments are founded on being emotionally available and responding when the other person needs you, not just at some designated moment of 'quality time'. Whilst adults can sometimes manage to sustain relationships through verbal contact on the telephone, this is not what small children need. Although, as Leach suggests, familiar and safe 'secondary attachments' can keep a child afloat on an 'emotional life raft' until the child can be with his primary person again, it isn't really clear how long a particular child can hang on to that 'raft' – half an hour? A few hours? All day long? Some children may be able to keep afloat for longer than others, and younger children will find it harder than older children. And then of course some childcare experiences don't provide much of a raft at all.

When both parents are doing a demanding full-time job, and come home to a toddler who hasn't seen them all day, they may be just as stressed as the reluctant stay-at-home parent. Both experiences can erode the quality of parenting, and in turn this may affect their style of parenting. When people are stressed, they often find it easier to give in to their toddler's demands than to maintain firm, authoritative parenting. Or they are more likely to resort in moments of frustration and exhaustion to coercive forms of discipline to get some peace. These pressures have been more commonly experienced by working-class families in the past, but now the stress that undermines good parenting may be spreading to the professional classes.

## A social issue

Since it's this second year which is crucial for learning self-control and empathy, the quality of parenting at this stage is also of great importance to society. As Greenspan and Shanker argue, if we want a society where people can engage in democratic institutions, we will need to produce 'thoughtful individuals', people with 'well developed forms of empathy . . . coupled with the ability for being realistic and having a firm assessment of reality'.[23] Martha Nussbaum concurs that 'We will never have good institutions without compassionate people, so educating compassion is still crucial.'[24] Teaching compassion for self and others is not an academic exercise, however, but a practice, a way of behaving, a way of being, that is learned – largely outside awareness – from other humans. A big part of it is the attitude to emotions which is passed on, and whether or not a child's feelings are respected and heard, and his failures and weaknesses tolerated sympathetically. It is essentially about 'attentiveness, responsiveness, responsibility',[25] capacities which are first learned in the family. Less obviously, the ability to be attentive and responsive also depends on the development of the biological systems responsible for self-regulation, stress management and empathy, shaped through our earliest relationship experiences.

But how can we ensure that all children have the same chance to learn these skills, which are the key to social living, as well as to personal well-being? Parents whose own emotional regulation systems are not flourishing often struggle to teach these skills to their children; parents who are ashamed of their own flaws will not be able to help their children manage conflict and failure well. How can the endlessly repeating intergenerational cycles of anxious attachment and inadequate emotional development be interrupted?

## The Nanny State

Many people feel a strong resistance to state interference in private life and dislike the prospect of the state intervening in very early parenting. Frank Furedi, in his writings about parenting, fears that professionals intruding into such areas of private life are likely to do 'a lot of harm' and encourage 'emotionalism'.[26] Since he thinks that parents can be trusted to know what's best for their own children, he rejects the burgeoning industry in 'parenting skills' from the pre-school period onwards.

It is certainly difficult to draw a clear line between help and intrusion. As I have already conceded, it is hard to entrust the state with such a role when state officials are so unaccountable for their actions, even to parliament. On the other hand, Furedi's trust in all parents' abilities is also misplaced. Good parenting does not come naturally – what comes naturally, as the late psychotherapist Roy Muir once memorably said, is the way it was done for you. The evidence is that early parenting is challenging, and raises complex emotional issues and dilemmas; there is a real social need to intervene to help parents to help their children to greater emotional health than they might have enjoyed themselves. Showing parents ways of interacting that they cannot see for themselves can be life-changing, both for the parents and their children.

In my view, what is needed is the provision of universal psychological support services which target pregnancy and babyhood, the time when babies are rapidly learning and developing the social capacities that will influence their life chances. There need be no compulsion to take up these services, but it is important to ensure that they are universally available so that there is no stigma attached to using them.

This support, in my view, needs to include both basic emotional support and more sophisticated 'therapeutic interventions'. Although they are both needed, they are different. In a world where there is no local community watching over most of us any more, and often no parents nearby, support can make a huge difference to new parents. Warm human contact can lift a mother's depression and help her be more responsive to her baby. It can relieve the isolation of parenting, which is a huge factor in parenting difficulties; human mothers have never before reared babies single-handedly, and have always needed other adults to help them.

This support does not need to be complicated and can take many forms. However, in a highly mobile society where most people are employed, it is likely that it will in most cases have to be provided by the state. We have to pay for this collectively because our economic system has turned us into individual employees; the basis of society is no longer working families or extended families or local communities. In the UK, the state could expand the role of our unique profession of health visitors who could, with extra training, provide more support for psychological health. Doctors in local health centres could be more alert to any relationship difficulties between parents and their babies, inviting new parents to discuss how they are getting on emotionally as well as practically, during other routine check-ups. We could re-instate and expand the role of family centres (possibly adapting the current Children's Centres) in every local neighbourhood, which could provide social experiences which help to make early parenthood enjoyable, as well as practical benefits like book and toy libraries, second-hand baby clothes or even a stall for people to sell or barter the freshly grown food from their allotments. In the past, these forms of support were provided on the cheap, and then declined. Today, they are only likely to be well-used and enjoyed by all parents if they are widely available and of a high quality. But potentially, they could tip the balance in a positive direction for many parents with mild depression or other minor difficulties in establishing their relationship with their baby.

Unfortunately even this costly provision is unlikely to be enough by itself to make a difference to the insecure patterns of relating that so many parents inadvertently pass on. Particularly when parents have more serious difficulties in bonding with or understanding their baby, specialised help is needed. The parent-infant psychotherapy which I have been practising for over a decade is this kind of help. It works on two fronts. It helps parents to become more aware of their own patterns of relating which might be getting in the way of a good relationship with their baby, and it also helps them to become more in tune with their babies, sometimes through techniques such as video feedback, or using 'Watch, Wait and Wonder' which invites the parent to observe their baby's own activities in a 'wondering' frame of mind. The therapy session provides a space to step back and observe what is going on, with an expert and encouraging guide, and offers the parent help in changing habitual responses. Looking at a few minutes of video material of themselves with their baby, a parent has the chance to notice little details such as the way their baby's eyes follow them around, or the impact on the baby of being held in a tense way. As well as helping the parent to think about the meaning of the baby's expressions, it can give parents more confidence that they are capable of understanding their own baby.

Frank Furedi fears that professionals like myself will 'train a child how to feel' and will impose a politically correct way of feeling, or shape the child's sense of self in a way that is the private business of parents, not the business of professionals. I can understand this fear but it is wide of the mark. In practice, professionals do not have the time or funding to have such an impact on anyone. Much provision is limited to 'firefighting' and attempting to prevent neglectful and abusive parenting practices as best it can in limited time-frames. Where professionals are able to work in a more open-ended way, therapeutic approaches (and some parenting classes, too) are mostly about noticing and understanding feelings, both the parent's and the baby's, and learning how to tolerate them and respond to them.

Of course, there is a grain of truth in Furedi's objections, since those people who become more aware of their feelings, and more tolerant of them, are less likely to go down the route of insecure attachment, particularly the avoidant type of attachment which attempts to tough out difficulties and minimise feelings. Furedi may also be right in fearing that increased therapeutic intervention might produce a more emotionally homogenous outcome. The more emotionally aware people become, the more likely they are to become authoritative parents rather than Strict or Permissive ones. In this sense, greater availability of psychological supports and interventions such as parent-infant psychotherapy could shift the population towards a more emotionally sensitive culture which not everyone might enjoy. Furedi, for example, seems to be defending what he sees as a basic freedom to go to hell in your own way – to be miserable, to smoke, eat unhealthily and bring up children without thinking too much about it. I have a certain admiration for his chutzpah, but his belief that there is a right *not* to care for the self or others would be more convincing if it also involved a willingness not to use publically funded services to heal the resulting illnesses, antisocial behaviour and so on. It is even harder to go along with the idea that parents should have a *right* not to care well for their children.

Furedi also claims that there is no evidence that therapy works. This is simply untrue. There are many studies, targeting different aspects of the early relationship, which show that parenting interventions can relieve mothers' depression or improve their mental health, can improve family functioning, or the parent and baby attachment relationship itself.[27] Most conclude that therapeutic interventions help – although admittedly some are more effective than others. Whilst large-scale randomised controlled trials are still needed to provide more definitive evidence, one approach that has been thoroughly researched is David Olds' 'Nurse-parent partnership' model from the USA, which has a very solid track record and has been researched over a period of more than fifteen years.[28] It works by offering a combination of practical and psychological support through a pair of professionals who visit the home during pregnancy and over the first two years of a baby's life, and is currently being tried out by the British government with a few 'at risk' families (with accompanying scaremongering tabloid headlines about 'ASBO BABIES!'). There are many ways of intervening. Again, they all cost a substantial amount of money. But such social investment into human capital is likely to repay society many times over in the long term. In 2007, the World Health Organization stated in a report that 'Economists now assert on the basis of the available evidence that investment in early childhood is the most powerful investment a country can make, with returns over the lifecourse many times the size of the original investment.'[29] As Richard Layard pointed out, in the UK we are losing around 2 per cent of our GDP to depression[30] (in lost output as well as on incapacity benefits and mental health services) – a condition that frequently has its roots in infancy.[31] Robert Caldwell in the USA calculated that for every dollar spent on prevention in early infancy, nineteen dollars were saved in public expenditure further down the line.[32] More recently the New Economic Foundation has calculated that a massive investment in early intervention and nurture would – over twenty years – deliver significant *savings* to the economy in reduced spending on social problems.[33]

## A relational society

Whilst they have a practical element, all these solutions are primarily focused on providing psychological support for the task of assisting the psychological development of the young. This is necessary for two reasons: first, because the conditions of parenting have changed with affluence; the work of early parenting, in particular, has become more isolated and denigrated since the 1960s. Secondly, because the affluence we have achieved in the West means that we can now move on from the quest for material satisfaction towards other, more psychological sources of well-being.

If we are going to improve the quality of life, we have to put relationships back into a central position. We are so immersed in the capitalist culture that it's difficult to see it clearly as a particular phase of human history. However, there was a time when society was run on a different basis and it is likely that there will be a time when circumstances demand that things change yet again. As I have outlined in this book, our ancestors' intense drive for material improvements had the undesirable side effect of neglecting human relationships and endorsing selfishness, trapping people in a competitive set-up which has prolonged inequality and set people against each other. Few people at the time were wholly aware that this was the price they were paying for a more comfortable life. In the affluent West, it is beginning to dawn on us that for most people, further material improvements no longer make a significant impact on our happiness. We can now certainly afford to notice that in the process of building up our material wealth, we have lost out in other ways. Increasingly, people are aware that once they have achieved a reasonably comfortable life, there are other ways of feeling good such as being connected to others and doing pleasurable things with other people. These experiences, in turn, help to build up the social brain and enable us to develop our most human capacities in a way that the work-centred capitalist way of life does not. It turns out that unselfishness is often pleasurable too. When people start by doing one small thing for the benefit of others, they often discover this for themselves, and are able to build on it.

Industrial capitalism has bequeathed another undesirable side effect: serious damage to the climate. This provides another reason to change our priorities away from the heavy material consumption which is putting pressure on the earth's non-renewable resources. Yet it is difficult to know how to halt the relentless drive for personal and national financial growth since most of us find tremendous pleasure in the material world, in beautiful objects, in the things that make us comfortable and make life easier. Most developing countries today seek the conveniences that we can now take for granted, and it would be hypocritical to claim they are not important or have not improved the quality of our lives.

Our brains are also programmed to seek out fresh stimulation, and new things are a major source of pleasure. How, then, can we keep discovering new pleasures at the same time as limiting overconsumption? Green solutions are often portrayed – in the media, at least – as a sort of hair shirt. Individuals are exhorted to consume less, buy low energy light bulbs, use the car less, avoid air travel and so on; it often comes over as responsible but self-denying, like joining a slimmers' club. A different way of thinking about it, instead of merely denying ourselves some of our past excesses, is to consider whether we could create new forms of consumption which take pleasure in repairing and recycling materials. Perhaps we could learn to slow down and savour the more sustainable daily pleasures of relatedness, of community, of creativity and of nature? These, as the philosopher Kate Soper has suggested,[34] are arguably the real sensory satisfactions, unlike many of the goods currently on offer which, like our environment, are chemical, noisy, perishable, smell bad and lack beauty. Could we embrace a new way of looking at the world which re-defines wealth as being time-rich and relationship-rich?

Again, deciding we need to change our priorities away from the accumulation of things towards an appreciation of nature or relationships is a bit like telling an addict simply to stop. It won't happen until it takes account of the emotional drivers of our behaviour – such as the magnetic pull of being 'in' with the popular or powerful members of the social group. There is a growing recognition that people are more likely to change through persuasion, 'nudges' and popular cultural movements than through beating them with the stick of reason. Lower levels of consumption have to become chic and fashionable; altruism has to become 'cool'. As the environmental campaigner George Marshall suggests, this would involve re-framing our desires in terms of health and happiness, not money, and encouraging people to recognise that they can live *better* – not worse – with less. We could aim to free ourselves from the burden of acquiring more and more possessions, and pursue a 'lighter lifestyle', or have a shorter working week with more time to pay attention to our own and others' feelings.[35]

## The power of the social group

Social movements for change can have a powerful impact. The women's movement of the 1970s, for example, did succeed in changing society – not merely through its rational arguments for equality and justice for women, but also through the self-transformative power of women collectively re-thinking and re-framing their lives. The same psychological transformation is needed now if we are to move away from a selfish society towards a more relational, collaborative society. We need a new political movement that attempts to transform grass-roots thinking and feeling, as well as promote rational arguments for changes in policy. By creating a groundswell of people who are starting to live differently, giving more priority to relational values as well as environmental ones, the old values rooted in economic power may have to adapt. Without an active demonstration of popular will, such a sea change in values is unlikely to happen.

However, the problem of power remains. People who have it will not give it up voluntarily. As the theologian Reinhold Niebuhr pointed out long ago, 'As individuals, men believe that they ought to love and serve each other and establish justice between each other. As racial, economic and national groups, they . . . take for themselves, whatever their power can command.'[36] In the eighteenth century, the rising commercial classes developed the idea of democracy in order to serve their own interests; they wanted to transfer power from the landowners and aristocrats to the middle classes. Now it may be time to develop new forms of democracy to meet today's challenges, to fight for change simultaneously at the global level and at the very local level – which would allow power to serve new values beyond the purely economic. Extending democracy, whether at the local level to include more face-to-face discussion in local groups or in new online ways of debating and deciding, would in itself promote the value of relating to others and taking account of their needs as well as our own.

Any social movement for a more relational society, or politics based on the ethic of care, must recognise the importance of early child-rearing in helping to develop the capacities for empathy, compassion and sensitivity that such a society requires. At the current stage of debate, the social consequences of early caregiving have not been recognised. Instead, we find ourselves still in the midst of what have been described as the 'Mommy

Wars' – a conflict between the different social currents that pull mothers in different directions. One camp is happy with the 'new normal' that women must work on the same terms as men, whilst another feels that the loving mother/baby dyad should be supported, boosted by modern scientific knowledge that confirms that it is the foundation of social well-being. The antagonism between these groupings is currently a stumbling block in forging a new movement to turn society away from selfishness towards a more compassionate society.

## Mentalising the state

The argument of this book has been that we need an overhaul of our basic understanding of how society works, in the light of developmental psychology. If we ignore this dimension of human knowledge, we will miss out on a deeper perspective that explains much about human behaviour. For the first time in human history, we can use science to address non-material questions, to learn how we can make progress not only in technology and material well-being, but also in our psychological and moral capacities.

Developmental psychology helps us to understand how individuals are shaped by social forces, and particularly by the culture of the influential adults in our early lives. But it can also throw light on our understanding of the public realm. Some of the same processes are at work on the macro level of public life as at the micro level of the individual. On the micro level, individuals develop by gathering information from all parts of the body, and building up greater awareness and self-organisation, which culminates in the development of the higher brain. This is where they learn to identify feelings, and then to communicate about feelings with ever more consciousness of self and others. Individuals develop best when they feel relaxed in the care of competent, attentive adults – authoritative parents whom they can trust to respond to their needs and to maintain an adult overview of their best interests over the long-term. The developing child then feels safe to explore the world and learn how to relate effectively to others – by listening to others, valuing them and restoring relationships when conflict occurs.

At the macro level of whole societies, the state has many of the same functions as the higher brain. It, too, gathers information and provides both an overview of what the social group needs, as well as the executive power to make things happen. It has the capacity for foresight and long-term planning. All these are the equivalent of the prefrontal cortex of the individual. However, just as an insecurely attached child may have more difficulty in developing his or her higher brain capacities, so too a competitive and insecure society may not facilitate the development of more mature forms of social organisation. For instance, in highly unequal societies, the process of gathering information from all parts of the body politic is hampered: there is a tendency to pay attention only to the more powerful and vocal layers of society and to ignore the experiences of lower social and economic groupings. This can produce poor decision-making, just as ignoring bodily symptoms can lead to illness. Likewise, just as an individual who is driven by impulses for short-term gratification rather than long-term interests, will remain immature, so too societies may not develop into a mature form.

I have described how some individuals will be driven to achieve positions of power to recover their own self-esteem.

However, they may then confront the difficulty of holding on to power. When governments themselves feel insecure, because they are afraid that they will lose power, they often act in the same ways as insecure parents: they become dismissive of others' concerns, preoccupied with their own needs, and may become coercive or intrusive, instead of responsive, to the electorate. We might need to consider what we could do to make governments feel more secure and able to think of our long-term needs rather than focusing on their immediate need to survive.

Nonetheless, the family model is hard to apply to a global society – can we really all be one big family? Perhaps not – or not yet. But we can still apply the principles of developmental knowledge and family research. The concept of a caring society could involve behaviours that are desirable in families: people's needs and feelings being noticed, having attention paid to them, responding to them even when it doesn't suit you. It would involve dealing with conflicts by listening and working through disagreement and, most importantly, learning how to mend ruptures in relationships promptly. It would be hard enough to apply this on a national scale, but an enormous challenge to apply it globally, and to have to consider the consequences of all we do for the other peoples around the world.

There is now a much greater sense of urgency about creating a more empathic, and less selfish, society. We face a future where there may be new and very severe conflicts as people fight over land and water in a rapidly heating climate. We need to leap as fast as possible to a higher level of human development, using our foresight and empathy to be aware of the needs of the planet. We need to promote attachments between countries, not just between individuals, by linking people across continents by whatever means possible. We need to make the old model of self-sufficient states or self-sufficient people who don't intrude on each other become obsolete.

But if we are going to stand any chance of building a more co-operative global culture, the conditions of child-rearing must be addressed. It is now time to leave behind the model of harsh and strict parenting, and to endorse kinder, more nurturant values. Only adults who are able to empathise with others' experience will be able to extend that empathy further and further to people who are not personally known or part of the immediate community. Only adults who can manage conflict within the family will be able to take part in democratic processes that extend them to the global scene. This is now a pressing task, because we need to learn to care on a global scale, not just to care about our own families or nations. What is required is a global ethic as well as global laws. If we can have shared movies, music and food across the world, there is a possibility that we might also find a way to share moral values – such as non-violence, non-poverty and responsible consumption – and to develop a moral consensus on a global scale.

Selfish individualism is anachronistic. We no longer need it to build up the material base of society; in fact, it will destroy us if we cannot move on. Selfishness is essentially a narrow and fearful way of approaching life, based on insecurity. Of course we fear dependence on other people or on the state if we don't anticipate a caring response. But the answer to selfishness is to build a culture and society which makes collective care a much higher priority – a more balanced culture which recognises that we have social needs as well as individual needs. These are the needs that we cannot meet individually – for shared facilities, for high-quality housing in safe communities, for employment that allows employees time to raise their children as well as to enjoy other people's company. By doing a better job of meeting people's real social and emotional needs, narcissistic and materialistic urges will diminish.

This need not be a Nanny State which tells us what we want. If we had more developed democratic structures, we would have more power and agency, to express our own views and negotiate them with other people. The state would then serve us as a way of authorising and organising the realisation of policies, taking on the responsibility to provide and maintain those structures which are beyond the capacity of individuals to provide. Although it would have a parental function, it would not be that of the strict and authoritarian parent, nor the indulgent and permissive parent; it would become an authoritative parent, maintaining an overview of everyone's needs and considering their impact on everyone's psychological and emotional well-being, not only on their material well-being.

By changing the experience of early dependence on others into a positive experience for increasing numbers of children, there will be an increased capacity to extend concern to the wider community. As emotional literacy spreads, this in turn could affect the wider culture and the leaders we choose. The culture of the secure individual family can become the world culture – helping each other when necessary and working through conflicts without violence. Personal development and political progress are linked. The mature, unselfish society is based on the same things as the secure family: meeting basic needs, validating each other and working through conflict. Ultimately, our survival will depend on how we treat each other on a global scale.

# PERMISSIONS ACKNOWLEDGEMENTS

Quotation from 'In Those Years' © 2002, 1995 Adrienne Rich, from *The Fact of a Doorframe: Selected Poems 1950–2001* by Adrienne Rich. Reproduced by permission of the author and W.W. Norton & Company, Inc.

Excerpt from *Affective Neuroscience* by Jaak Panksepp © Jaak Panksepp, 1998, courtesy of Oxford University Press.

Excerpt from *Pigs at the Trough* by Arianna Huffington © Arianna Huffington 2003, courtesy of Random House, Inc.

Excerpt from *Ten Days in the Hills* by Jane Smiley © Jane Smiley 2007, courtesy of Random House, Inc.

Quotation from 'September 1st, 1939' from *Collected Poems* by W.H. Auden, reproduced by kind permission of Faber and Faber Ltd.

Excerpt from *The Age of Consent* by George Monbiot © 2003 George Monbiot. Courtesy of HarperCollins Publishers Ltd.

Excerpt from *Moral Politics* by George Lakoff © George Lakoff, 1996, 2002, courtesy of University of Chicago Press.

# NOTES

## Introduction

1 Michael Rutter, *Genes and Behaviour* (Oxford, Blackwell Publishing, 2006).

2 Beverley Hughes quoted in Lucy Ward, 'Appeal to parents on teenage births', *Guardian*, 26 May 2005.

3 Adam Smith, *The Theory of Moral Sentiments* (Edinburgh, Kincaid and Bell, 1759).

4 Martin Jacques, 'The death of intimacy', *Guardian*, 18 September 2004.

5 David Cameron, speech at Glasgow East by-election, 7 July 2008, www.telegraph.co.uk.

6 Jonathan Oliver and Isabel Oakeshott, 'Ethics Boy', YouGov survey, *Sunday Times*, 13 July 2008.

7 Fred Previc, *The Dopaminergic Mind in Human Evolution and History* (Cambridge University Press, 2009).

8 A useful overview of research can be found in Emma Adam, Bonnie Klimes-Dougan, Megan Gunnar, 'Social regulation of the adrenocortical response to stress in infants, children and adolescents', in Donna Coch, Geraldine Dawson, Kurt Fischer (eds.), *Human Behavior, Learning and the Developing Brain* (New York, Guilford Press, 2007). *See also* A. Wismer Fries et al., 'Neuroendocrine dysregulation following early social deprivation in children', *Developmental Psychobiology*, 50 (2008), pp.588–99.

9 In particular, I am thinking of Fiona Robinson, *Globalising Care* (Boulder, CO, Westview Press, 1999), Selma Sevenhuijsen, *Citizenship and the Ethics of Care* (London, Taylor and Francis, 1998), and Joan Tronto, *Moral Boundaries* (New York, Routledge, 1993).

10 Tronto, op. cit.

11 Ibid.

12 Usefully summarised in Arietta Slade, 'Parental reflective functioning: an introduction', *Attachment and Human Development*, 7:3 (2005), pp.269–281.

**Chapter One**

1 Richard Dawkins, *The Selfish Gene* (Oxford University Press, 1976).

2 Quoted in Robert Mackay, *Half the Battle* (Manchester University Press, 2002).

3 Louis MacNeice, 'London Letter, January 1941', in A. Heuser (ed.), *The Selected Prose of Louis MacNeice* (Oxford, Clarendon Press, 1990).

4 UNESCO, 1997, Declaration on the Responsibilities of the Present Generation Towards Future Generations, UNESCO ID:13178.

5 United Nations Development Programme, *Human Development Report* (New York, Oxford University Press, 2000).

6 Anup Shah, 'World Military Spending', www.globalissues.org/article/75/world-military-spending, 1 March 2009.

7 Robert Karen has produced a wonderful account of Bowlby's work, Robert Karen, *Becoming Attached* (Oxford University Press, 1998).

8 Meredith Small, 'The natural history of children', in Sharna Olfman (ed.), *Childhood Lost: how American culture is failing our kids* (Westport, Connecticut, Praeger Publishers, 2005).

9 Daniel Kahneman, 'Experienced utility and objective happiness: a moment based approach', in D. Kahneman and A. Tversky (eds.), *Choices, Values and Frames* (Cambridge University Press, 2000). See also D. Kahneman et al, 'Would you be happier if you were richer?', *Science*, 312: 5782 (2006), pp.1908–10.

10 Richard Layard, *Happiness* (Harmondsworth, Penguin, 2005).

11 National Institute of Mental Health, *The Numbers Count*, NIMH factsheet, 2008.

12 Derek Summerfield, 'Depression: epidemic or pseudo-epidemic?', *Journal of the Royal Society of Medicine*, 99:3 (2006).

13   Andrea Waylen, Nigel Stallard, Sarah Stewart-Brown, 'Parenting and health in mid-childhood: a longitudinal study', *European Journal of Public Health*, 18:3 (2008), pp.300–305.

14   Tim Kasser, *The High Price of Materialism* (Cambridge, MA, MIT Press, 2002).

15   James and Joyce Robertson, quoted in Karen, op. cit.

16   Gene-Jack Wang et al., 'Similarity between obesity and drug addictions as assessed by neurofunctional imaging', *Journal of Addictive Diseases*, 23:3 (2004), pp.39–53.

17   Peter Whybrow, *American Mania* (New York, WW Norton & Co., 2005).

18   Polly Toynbee and David Walker, *Unjust Rewards* (London, Granta Books, 2008).

19   Michael Hennigan, 'Executive pay and inequality in the winner-take-all society', 2007, www.finfacts.com. *See also* Henry Mintzberg, 'Beyond Selfishness', *MIT Sloan Management Review*, 44:1 (2002).

20   Joe Biden, speech at Miami Beach, Florida, 5 March 2009.

21   Layard, op. cit.

22   F. Leichsenring et al., 'Short term psychodynamic psychotherapy and cognitive behavioural therapy in generalised anxiety disorder: a randomised controlled trial', *American Journal of Psychiatry*, 166 (2009), pp.875–81. *See also* M. Haby et al., 'Cognitive Behavioural Therapy for depression, panic disorder and generalised anxiety disorder: a meta-regression of factors that may predict outcome', *Australia and New Zealand Journal of Psychiatry*, 40:1 (2006), pp.9–19.

23   F. Leichsenring and S. Rabung, 'Effectiveness of long-term psychodynamic psychotherapy: a meta-analysis', *Journal of the American Medical Association*, 300 (2008), pp.1551–65.

24   UNICEF, *An Overview of Child Well-being in Rich Countries*, Innocenti Report Card 7, Unicef Innocenti Research Centre, Florence, 2007.

25   Robert Putnam, *Bowling Alone: the collapse and revival of American community* (New York, Simon & Schuster, 2001). *See also* Richard Wilkinson and Kate Pickett, *The Spirit Level: why more equal societies almost always do better* (Harmondsworth, Allen Lane/Penguin, 2009).

26 National Family and Parenting Institute, *Teenagers' Attitudes to Parenting*, NFPI, 2000.

27 Robert Bly, *The Sibling Society* (Harmondsworth, Penguin, 1997).

28 Martin Jacques, 'The age of selfishness', *Guardian*, 5 October 2002.

29 Christopher Lasch, *The Culture of Narcissism*, 1st edn 1979, (London, Abacus, 1980).

30 Carrie Fisher, *Postcards from the Edge* (New York, Pocket Books/Simon and Schuster, 1987).

31 Jean Twenge and Keith Campbell, *The Narcissism Epidemic* (New York, Free Press/Simon and Schuster, 2009).

32 Lasch, op. cit.

33 Toynbee and Walker, op. cit.

34 Ibid.

35 Mike Davis, *Planet of Slums* (London, Verso, 2006).

36 Emmanuel Todd, *After the Empire* (London, Constable, 2004).

## Chapter Two

1 Diane Levin, 'Compassion deficit disorder? The impact of consuming culture on children's relationships' in Marci Green (ed.), *Risking Human Security*, (London, Karnac Books, 2008).

2 Boston Process of Change Study Group, 'The foundational level of psychodynamic meaning', *International Journal of Psychoanalysis*, 88 (2007), pp.843–60.

3 *Born Too Early: the kangaroo method*, film by Saskia van Rees and Richard de Leeuw, Stichting Lichaamstaal, 1987.

4 Rene Spitz, 'Hospitalism: an inquiry into the genesis of psychiatric conditions in early childhood', *Psychoanalytic Study of the Child*, 1 (1945), pp.53–74.

5 Maurizio Tirassa et al., 'Rethinking the ontogeny of mindreading', *Consciousness and Cognition*, 15:1 (2006), pp.197–217.

6 Douglas Watt, 'Consciousness, emotional self-regulation and the brain', *Journal of Consciousness Studies* 11:9 (2004), pp.77–82.

7 Candace Pert, *The Molecules of Emotion* (London, Simon and Schuster, 1999).

8 As quoted by Kate Ravilious, 'Lack of cuddles in infancy may affect development of the brain', *Guardian*, 22 November 2005.

9   Michael Kosfeld et al., 'Oxytocin increases trust in humans', *Nature*, 435 (2005), pp.673–6.

10  City traders who are not dealing with individuals but working off screens make more money when they are high in the male hormone testosterone. *See also* John Coates and J. Herbert, 'Endogenous steroids and financial risk taking on a London trading floor', *Proceedings of the National Academy of Science USA*, 105:16 (2008), pp.6167–72.

11  Penelope Leach, *Your Baby and Child* (London, Dorling Kindersley, 1978).

12  Daniel Stern, *The Interpersonal World of the Infant* (London, Karnac Books, 1985).

13  Stanley Greenspan and Stuart Shanker, *The First Idea* (Cambridge, MA, Da Capo Press, 2004).

14  Ed Tronick et al., 'The infant's response to re-entrapment between contradictory messages in face-to-face interactions', *Journal of the American Academy of Child Psychiatry*, 16 (1978), pp.1–13.

15  Jeffrey Cohn and Ed Tronick, 'Specificity of infants' response to mothers' affective behaviour', *Journal of American Academy of Child and Adolescent Psychiatry*, 28:2 (1989), pp.242–8.

16  Greenspan and Shanker, op. cit.

17  Gyorgy Gergely, 'The social construction of the subjective self', in L Mayes, P. Fonagy, M.Target (eds.), *Developmental Science and Psychoanalysis* (London, Karnac Books, 2007).

18  Greenspan and Shanker, op. cit.

19  M. de Haan and M. Groen, 'Neural bases of infants' processing of social information in faces', in P. Marshall and N. Fox (eds.), *The Development of Social Engagement: Neurobiological Perspectives* (Oxford University Press, 2006).

20  P. Shaw et al., 'The impact of early and late damage to the human amygdala on theory of mind reasoning', *Brain*, 127:7 (2004), pp.1535–48.

21  Adrian Raine and Yaling Yang, 'Neural foundations to moral reasoning and antisocial behaviour', *Social Cognitive and Affective Neuroscience* 1:3 (2006), pp.203–213.

22  Allan Schore, *Affect Regulation and the Origin of the Self* (Hillsdale, NJ, Lawrence Erlbaum Associates Inc., 1994).

23 Gerhard Dammann, 'Borderline personality disorder and theory of mind: an evolutionary perspective', in Martin Brune and Hedda Ribbert (eds.), *The Social Brain, Evolution and Pathology* (Chichester, Wiley Blackwell, 2003).

24 Harry Chugani et al., 'Local brain functional activity following early deprivation', *Neuroimage*, 14 (2001), pp.1290–1301.

25 Jean Decety, 'A social cognitive neuroscience model of human empathy', in Eddie Harmon Jones and Piotr Winkielman (eds.), *Social Neuroscience* (New York, Guilford Press, 2007).

26 Andrea Heberlein et al., 'Ventromedial frontal lobe plays a critical role in facial emotion recognition', *Journal of Cognitive Neuroscience*, 20:4 (2008), pp.721–33.

27 Kevin Ochsner and James Gross, 'Putting the "I" and the "Me" in emotion regulation', *Trends in Cognitive Sciences*, 20:20 (2005).

28 Daniel Siegel, *The Mindful Brain* (New York, WW Norton & Co, 2007).

29 M. Brower and B. Price, 'Neuropsychiatry of frontal lobe dysfunction in violent and criminal behaviour: a critical review', *Journal of Neurology, Neurosurgery and Psychiatry*, 71 (2001), pp.720–6.

30 M. Zanarini and F. Frankenburg, 'Pathways to the development of borderline personality disorder', *Journal of Personality Disorders*, 11:1 (1997), pp.93–104. *See also* M. Dozier and K. Stovall, 'Attachment and psychopathology in adulthood', in J. Cassidy and P. Shaver (eds.), *Handbook of Attachment* (New York, Guilford Press, 1999).

31 Donald Winnicott, 'Ego Integration in Child Development' in *The Maturational Processes and the Facilitating Environment*, 1st edn 1962 (London, The Hogarth Press, 1987).

32 D Lyons et al., 'Stress level cortisol treatment impairs inhibitory control of behaviour in monkeys' *Journal of Neuroscience*, 20:20 (2000).

33 Martin Teicher et al., 'The neurobiological consequences of early stress and childhood maltreatment', *Neuroscience and Biobehavioural Reviews*, 27:1–2 (2003), pp.33–44.

34 Schore, op. cit.

35 Jens Pruessner et al., 'Dopamine release in response to a psychological stress in humans, and its relationship to early life maternal care', *Journal of Neuroscience*, 24 (2004), pp.2825–31.

36  Jaak Panksepp, *Affective Neuroscience: the foundations of human and animal emotions* (Oxford University Press, 1998).

37  Schore, op. cit.

## Chapter Three

1  Ben Okri, *The Famished Road* (London, Vintage Books, 1992); quoted in Heather Montgomery, *An Introduction to Childhood* (Chichester, Wiley Blackwell, 2009).

2  Donald Winnicott, *The Child, the Family and the Outside World* (Harmondsworth, Penguin, 1964).

3  Alan Macfarlane, *Marriage and Love in England 1300–1840* (Oxford, Basil Blackwell, 1986).

4  *Hello!*, issue 1033, 3 August 2008.

5  Julie Daggett et al., 'Parents' attitudes about children', *Journal of Family Psychology* 14:2 (2000), pp.187–99.

6  M. Pajulo et al., 'Prenatal views of baby and parenthood', *Infant Mental Health Journal*, 27:3 (2006), pp.229–50.

7  Gordon Moskowitz, *Social Cognition* (New York, Guilford Press, 2004).

8  Charles Zeanah et al., 'Adolescent mothers' perceptions of their infants before and after birth', *American Journal of Orthopsychiatry*, 57:3 (1987), pp.351–60. *See also* J.Contreras et al., 'Pregnant African-American teenagers' expectations of their infants' temperaments', *Journal of Applied Developmental Psychology*, 16:2 (1995), pp.283–95.

9  Peter Fonagy, Howard Steele and Miriam Steele, 'Maternal representations of attachment during pregnancy predict the organisation of infant mother attachment at one year of age', *Child Development*, 62:5 (1991), pp.891–905. *See also* Diane Benoit et al., 'Mothers' representations of their infants assessed pre-natally: stability and association with infants' attachment classifications', *Journal of Child Psychology and Psychiatry*, 38:3 (1997), pp.307–13.

10  Lloyd de Mause, *The History of Childhood* (Northvale, New Jersey, Jason Aronson, 1995).

11  Jonathan Haidt, TED talk on YouTube, 2008.

12  William Arsenio and A. Lover, 'Children's conceptions of socio-moral affect: happy victimisers, mixed emotions, and other

expectancies', in M. Killen and D. Hart (eds.), *Morality in Everyday Life* (Cambridge University Press, 1995). *See also*, Judith Smetana and J. Braeges, 'The development of toddlers' moral and conventional judgements', *Merrill-Palmer Quarterly*, 36 (1990), pp.329–46.

13  Robin Briggs, *Witches and Neighbours* (Harmondsworth, Penguin, 1996).

14  Ben Wilson, *Decency and Disorder* (London, Faber and Faber, 2007).

15  Briggs, op. cit.

16  It is worth noting that when modern Native American Navajo babies are strapped onto a wooden board while their mothers are travelling or working, their mothers always compensate with a period of intense interaction with the baby afterwards; *see* James Chisholm, *Navajo Infancy* (New York, Aldine, 1983).

17  Daniel Etounga-Manguelle, 'Does Africa need a cultural adjustment program?', in L. Harrison and S. Huntington (eds.), *Culture Matters: how values shape human progress* (New York, Basic Books, 2001).

18  Gary Gregg, *The Middle East: a cultural psychology* (Oxford University Press, 2005).

19  Christina Zarowsky, 'Trauma stories: violence, emotion and politics in Somali Ethiopia', *Transcultural Psychiatry*, 37:3 (2000).

20  Barbara Rogoff, *The Cultural Nature of Human Development* (Oxford University Press, 2003).

21  Meredith Small, *Our Babies, Ourselves* (New York, First Anchor Books, 1998).

22  Rogoff, op. cit.

23  H. Keller, S. Voelker and R. Dzeaye Yovsi, 'Conceptions of parenting in different cultural communities: the case of West African Nso and northern German women', *Social Development*, 14:1 (2005).

24  Heather Montgomery, *An Introduction to Childhood* (Chichester, Wiley Blackwell, 2009).

25  Batja Mesquita and Dustin Albert, 'The cultural regulation of emotions', in James Gross (ed.), *Handbook of Emotion Regulation* (New York, Guilford Press, 2007).

26  Ibid.

27  Seth Pollak et al., 'Physically abused children's regulation of attention in response to hostility', *Child Development*, 76:5 (2005), pp.968–77.

28  Jane Goodall, *Reason for Hope* (London, Thorsons/Harper Collins, 2000).

29  Leonard Rosenblum et al., 'Adverse early experiences affect noradrenergic and serotonergic functioning in adult primates', *Biological Psychiatry* 35:4 (1994), pp.221–7. *See also* Jeremy Coplan et al., 'Behavioural, monoaminergic, neuroendocrine and neuropeptidergic alterations in grown nonhuman primates exposed to unpredictable early rearing: relevance to human anxiety', *European Neuropsychopharmacology*, 5:3 (1995) p.353.

30  Sarah Stewart-Brown and Andrea Waylen, *Parenting in ordinary families: diversity, complexity and change* (York, Joseph Rowntree Foundation, 2008).

31  Mags Gavan and Joost van der Valk (producer/directors), *Saving Africa's Witch Children*, Channel 4 *Dispatches* programme, 12 November 2008.

## Chapter Four

1  Norbert Elias, *The Civilising Process* (Oxford, Blackwell Publishing, 1994).

2  *See* Dennis Smith, *Norbert Elias and Modern Social Theory* (London, Sage Publications, 2001) for an overview.

3  Simon Schama, *The Embarrassment of Riches* (London, Collins, 1987).

4  Keith Thomas, *The Ends of Life* (Oxford University Press, 2009). *See also* Keith Thomas, *Religion and the Decline of Magic* (London, Weidenfeld and Nicolson, 1971).

5  Allan Schore, *Affect Regulation and the Origin of the Self* (Hillsdale, NJ, Lawrence Erlbaum Associates Inc., 1994).

6  Agnes Heller, *Renaissance Man* (London, Routledge and Kegan Paul, 1978).

7  William Shakespeare, *Henry VI*, part III, l.1594.

8  Ficino, quoted in Heller, op. cit.

9  Robin Briggs, *Witches and Neighbours* (London, HarperCollins, 1996).

10  Niccolò Machiavelli, *The Prince*, 1532 (Harmondsworth, Penguin Books, 1999).

11  René Descartes, *Discourse on Method*, 1637 (Upper Saddle River, Prentice Hall, 1956).

12   Ellen Meiksins Wood, *The Origin of Capitalism* (London, Verso, 2002).

13   Christopher Friedrichs, 'Early capitalism and its enemies', *Business History Review* L:3 (1976).

14   Margaret Jacob and Matthew Kadane, 'Missing – now found in the eighteenth century: Weber's Protestant capitalist', *The American Historical Review*, 108:1 (2003).

15   Ibid.

16   Carol Stearns, 'Lord help me walk humbly: anger and sadness in England and America 1570–1750', in Carol and Peter Stearns (eds.), *Emotion and Social Change: towards a new psychohistory* (New York, Holmes and Meier, 1989).

17   Richard Tremblay, Willard Hartup, John Archer, *Developmental Origins of Aggression* (New York, Guilford Press, 2005). *See also* D. Hay et al., 'Toddlers Use of Force: a precursor of serious aggression', *Child Development*, 71:2 (2000).

18   Robert Sussman, Paul Garber and J. Cheverud, 'Importance of co-operation and affiliation in the evolution of primate sociability', *American Journal of Physical Anthropology*, 128 (2005), pp.84–97.

19   Kate Keenan et al., 2004, 'Evidence for the continuity of early problem behaviours, *Journal of Abnormal Child Psychology*, 26:6, pp.441–52.

20   Lloyd de Mause, *The History of Childhood* (Northvale, NJ, Jason Aronson, 1995).

21   John Locke, *Some Thoughts Concerning Education*, 1693 (Oxford University Press, 1989).

22   Jean-Jacques Rousseau, *Emile*, 1762 (London, J.M. Dent, 1993).

23   Ibid.

24   Maria and Richard Edgeworth, *Practical Education* (London, Joseph Johnson, 1798).

25   Mary Wollstonecraft, *Vindication of the Rights of Women* (London, Joseph Johnson, 1792).

26   John Brown, *Estimate of the Manners and Principles of the Times*, 2 Volumes, 1757–8 (London, David and Reymers, 1757).

27   C. B. McPherson, *The Political Theory of Possessive Individualism: from Hobbes to Locke* (Oxford University Press, 1962).

28  Karl Marx, *The Communist Manifesto*, 1848 (London, Longman, 2005).

29  Lasch, op. cit. *See also* Adam Nicolson, *Arcadia* (London, Harper Perennial, 2009).

30  Jonathan Haidt, 'The emotional dog and its rational tail', *Psychological Review*, 108:4 (2001), pp.814–34.

31  Jorge Moll et al., 'Neural correlates of moral sensitivity', *Journal of Neuroscience*, 22:7 (2002), pp.2730–6.

32  Joshua Greene et al., 'An FMRI investigation of emotional engagement in moral judgement', *Science*, 293 (2001). *See also* Jorge Moll et al., 'The neural basis of moral cognition', *Nature Reviews Neuroscience*, 6 (2005).

33  Alain Berthoz, *Emotion and Reason*, tr. G. Weiss (New York, Oxford University Press, 2006).

34  Michael Koenigs et al., 'Damage to the prefrontal cortex increases utilitarian moral judgements', *Nature*, 446 (2007), pp.908–911.

35  Jorge Moll and Ricardo de Oliveira-Souza, 'Moral judgements, emotions and the utilitarian brain', *Trends in Cognitive Sciences*, 30:10 (2007).

36  Karl Polanyi, *The Great Transformation*, 1st edn 1944 (Boston, Beacon Press, 2001).

37  Thomas Carlyle, *Past and Present*, 1st edn 1843 (Teddington, The Echo Library, 2007).

38  Francis Place, *The Autobiography of Francis Place 1771–1854*, ed. Mary Thale (Cambridge University Press, 1972).

39  Ibid.

40  Ian Donnachie, *Robert Owen: Owen of New Lanark and New Harmony* (Edinburgh, Tuckwell Press, 2000).

41  Ibid.

42  Horace Bushnell, *Christian Nurture*, 1847 (Eugene, OR, Wipf and Stock, 2001)

43  Ibid.

44  Samuel Johnson, *The Rambler*, 1750 (Whitefish, Montana, Kessinger Publishing, 2008).

45  Quoted in Philip Greven, *The Protestant Temperament: patterns of childrearing, religious experience and self in early America* (University of Chicago Press, 1977).

46 George Orwell, 'Those, those were the days', in Sonia Orwell and Ian Angus (eds.), *Collected Essays, Journals, Letters* (Harmondsworth, Penguin, 1970).

**Chapter Five**

1 *Bringing Up Baby*, Executive Producer Tanya Shaw, Channel 4, December 2008.
2 Lionel Shriver, *Guardian*, 9 March 2006.
3 George Lakoff, *Moral Politics* (University of Chicago Press, 2002).
4 Elizabeth Roberts, *A Woman's Place* (Oxford, Blackwell Publishing, 1996).
5 Tim Kasser, *The High Price of Materialism* (Cambridge, MA, MIT Press, 2002).
6 Ibid. *See also* Lisa Ryan and Suzanne Dziurawiec, 'The relations of maternal and social environments to adolescents' materialistic and prosocial values', *Developmental Psychology*, 31 (2001), pp.907–914; Ken Sheldon and Tim Kasser, 'Coherence and congruence', *Journal of Personality and Social Psychology*, 68 (1995), pp.531–43; Ken Sheldon and M. Flanagan, 'Extrinsic value orientation and dating violence', unpublished essay 2001, quoted in Kasser, op. cit.
7 Tim Kasser and Virginia Kasser, 'The dreams of people high and low in materialism', *Journal of Economic Psychology*, 22:6 (2001), pp.693–719.
8 Diana Baumrind, 'Effects of Authoritative Parental Control on Child Behaviour', *Child Development*, 37:4 (1966), pp.887–907.
9 Erica Hoff et al., 'Socioeconomic status and parenting', in M. Bornstein (ed.), *Handbook of Parenting* (Mahwah, NJ, Lawrence Erlbaum Associates Inc., 2002).
10 Richard Ferber, *Solve Your Child's Sleep Problems* (New York, Fireside/Simon and Schuster, 1985)
11 Gina Ford, *The Contented Little Baby Book* (New York, NAL Trade, 2001).
12 Barbara Rogoff, *The Cultural Nature of Human Development*, (Oxford University Press, 2003).
13 John and Elizabeth Newson, *Patterns of Infant Care in an Urban Community* (London, Penguin, 1963).

14  Christine Everingham, *Motherhood and Modernity* (Milton Keynes, Open University Press, 1994).

15  Judith Smetana, 'Parenting styles and conceptions of parental authority during adolescence', *Child Development*, 66 (1995), pp.299–316.

16  Douglas Symons, 'Mental state discourse, theory of mind and the internalisation of self-other understanding', *Developmental Review*, 24:2 (2004), pp.159–88.

17  Gordy Slack, 2009, salon.com, quotes Marco Iacoboni, www.mobile.salon.com.

18  Martin Hoffman, *Empathy and Moral Development* (Cambridge University Press, 2001).

19  Betty Repacholi and Alison Gopnik, 'Early reasoning about desires: evidence from 14 and 18 month olds', *Developmental Psychology*, 33 (1997), pp.12–21.

20  Grazyna Kochanska et al., 'Effortful control in early childhood: continuity and change', *Developmental Psychology*, 36:2 (2000), pp.220–32. *See also* G. Kochanska and A. Knaach, 'Effortful control as a personality characteristic of young children', *Journal of Personality*, 71:6 (2002), pp.1087–1112.

21  Elizabeth Meins et al., 'Rethinking maternal sensitivity', *Journal of Child Psychology and Psychiatry*, 42 (2001), pp.637–48.

22  Elizabeth Meins et al., 'Maternal mind-mindedness and attachment security as predictors of theory of mind understanding', *Child Development*, 73 (2002), pp.1715–26.

23  Ibid.

24  Arietta Slade, 'Parental reflective functioning: an introduction', *Attachment & Human Development*, 7:3 (2005), pp.269–81.

25  Peter Fonagy, Gyorgy Gergely, Mary Target, *Affect Regulation, Mentalisation, and the Development of the Self* (New York, The Other Press, 2002).

26  Deborah Laible and Ross Thompson, 'Mother–child discourse, attachment security, shared positive affect, and early conscience development', *Child Development*, 71 (2000).

27  Deborah Laible and Ross Thompson, 'Mother child conflict in the toddler years', *Child Development*, 73 (2002).

28  Susanne Denham et al., 'Preschool emotional competence: path-

way to social competence?', *Child Development,* 74 (2003), pp.238–56; and S. Denham et al., 'Parental contributions to preschoolers emotional competence', *Motivation and Emotion,* 21:1 (1997), pp.65–86.

29  Ross Thompson et al., 'Understanding values in relationships: the development of conscience', in M. Killen and J. Smetana (eds.), *Handbook of Moral Development* (London, Psychology Press, 2006).

30  Seth Pollak and Pawan Sinha, 'Effects of early experience on children's recognition of facial displays of emotion', *Developmental Psychology,* 38:5 (2002), pp.784–91.

31  Marjorie Beeghley and Dante Ciccetti, 'Child maltreatment, attachment and the self system', *Development and Psychopathology,* 6 (1994), pp.5–30.

32  Mary Main and Carol George, 'Responses of abused and disadvantaged toddlers to distress in age-mates', *Developmental Psychology,* 21:3 (1985), pp.407–410.

33  Martha Stout, *The Sociopath Next Door* (New York, Broadway Books /Random House, 2005).

34  Grazyna Kochanska et al., 'Pathways to conscience: early mother child mutually responsive orientation and children's moral emotion, conduct and cognition', *Journal of Child Psychology and Psychiatry,* 46:1 (2004), pp.19–34.

35  Vic Seidler, 'Rescue, righteousness and morality', in P. Oliner, S. Oliner et al. (eds.), *Embracing the Other* (New York, New York University Press, 1992).

**Chapter Six**

1  With thanks to the person who sent this poem to me; unfortunately, I have not kept her name.

2  Betty Friedan, *The Feminine Mystique* (London, Gollantz, 1963).

3  Lee Comer, *Wedlocked Women* (Leeds, Feminist Books, 1974).

4  Barack Obama, *The Audacity to Hope* (Edinburgh, Canongate, 2007).

5  Tine Rostgaard, 'Setting time aside for the father: father's leave in Scandinavia', *Community Work and Family,* 5:3 (2002).

6  Sue Miller, *The Senator's Wife* (London, Bloomsbury, 2009).

7  Adrienne Rich, *Of Woman Born* (London, Virago, 1977).

8  Ivana La Valle et al., *Maternity Rights and Mothers' Employment*

*Decisions*, Research Report 496, Department of Work and Pensions, 2008.

9   Pat McGovern et al., 'Mothers' health and work–related factors at eleven weeks post–partum', *Annals of Family Medicine*, 5 (2007), pp.519–27.

10  Kate Figes, *Because of Her Sex* (London, Macmillan, 1994).

11  Ed Tronick, *The Neurobehavioural and Social-Emotional Development of Infants and Children* (New York, W.W. Norton & Co, 2007).

12  BBC Whistleblower programme, Jane McSorley (Producer/ Director), March 2008.

13  DFES, *Every Child Matters*, Public Service Agreement Targets 2005–8.

14  Penelope Leach, *Child Care Today* (Cambridge, Polity Press, 2009).

15  Denise Riley, *The War in the Nursery* (London, Virago Press, 1983).

16  DFES, Early Years Foundation Stage, 2007.

17  Kathy Sylva et al., *The Effective Provision of Pre-School (EPPE): Findings from Pre-School to end of Key Stage 1*, DCSF, 2004.

18  Edward Melhuish et al., 'Type of childcare at 18 months, part II', *Journal of Child Psychology and Psychiatry*, 31 (1990). *See also* National Institute of Child Health and Development, *The NICHD Study of Early Child Care and Youth Development* (Washington, DC, US Department of Health and Human Services, 2006).

19  Jay Belsky, 'Quality, quantity and type of child: effects in child development in the USA', *Occasional Paper* 37 (Berlin, Liberal Institute, 2008).

20  Ibid.

21  Clancy Blair et al., 'Relating effortful control, executive function and false belief understanding to emerging maths and literacy ability', *Child Development*, 78:2 (2007), pp.647–63.

22  Department for Children, Schools and Families, *The Children's Plan*, 2007. *See also* Department of Health, *Child Health Promotion Programme*, 2008.

23  Scott Montgomery et al., 'Breastfeeding and resilience against psychosocial stress', *Archives of Disease in Childhood*, 91 (2006), pp.990–4.

24   Valerie Walkerdine and Helen Lucey, *Democracy in the Kitchen* (London, Virago, 1989).
25   Quoted in Celia Dodd, *The Independent*, 22 April 1996.
26   Brigitte and Peter Berger, *The War over the Family* (London, Anchor Press, 1983).
27   Elizabeth Beck-Gernsheim, 'From "the family" to "families"', *Soundings*, 35 (2007).
28   Ibid.
29   Kate Stanley, 'The New Conservatives and family policy', in Jon Cruddas and Jonathan Rutherford (eds.), *Is the Future Conservative?* (London, Lawrence and Wishart, 2008).
30   Jennifer Roback Morse, *Love and Economics* (Dallas, Texas, Spence Publishing Company, 2001).
31   Laurence Thomas, *The Family and the Political Self* (Cambridge University Press, 2006).

**Chapter Seven**
 1   Susan Jacoby, *The Age of American Unreason* (New York, Pantheon Books, 2008).
 2   Drew Westen, *The Political Brain* (New York, Perseus Books/ Public Affairs, 2007).
 3   Michael Lewis-Beck et al. (eds.), *The American Voter Revisited* (Ann Arbor, MI, University of Michigan Press, 2008).
 4   George Lakoff, *Moral Politics* (Chicago, IL, University of Chicago Press, 1996).
 5   Thomas Sowell, *A Conflict of Visions* (New York, Basic Books, 2002).
 6   James Davison Hunter, *Culture Wars* (New York, Basic Books, 1991).
 7   Carl Bernstein, *A Woman in Charge: the life of Hillary Rodham Clinton* (New York, Vintage Books, 2008).
 8   Margaret Thatcher, speech to the Conservative Women's Conference, 1986.
 9   Oliver James, 'So George, how do you feel about your Mom and Dad?', *Guardian*, 2 September 2003. *See also* Oliver James, *They F\*\*\* You Up* (London, Bloomsbury, 2007).
10   James, 'So George', op. cit.

11  Ibid.

12  Leo Abse, *Tony Blair: the man who lost his smile* (London, Robson Books, 2003).

13  John Rentoul, *Tony Blair* (London, Little Brown, 2001).

14  Abse, op. cit.

15  Heather Nunn, *Thatcher, Politics and Fantasy* (London, Lawrence and Wishart, 2003).

16  Matthew Parris, 'Are we witnessing the madness of Tony Blair?', *The Times*, 29 March 2003.

17  Frank Rich, *New York Times*, 4 January 2009.

18  David Runciman, *The Politics of Good Intentions* (Princeton University Press, 2006).

19  Israel Charny, *Fascism and Democracy in the Human Mind* (Lincoln, NE, University of Nebraska Press, 2006).

20  Rentoul, op. cit.

21  Peter Oborne, *The Rise of Political Lying* (London, Free Press, 2005).

22  Bob Woodward, *Bush At War* (London, Pocket Books/Simon and Schuster, 2003).

23  David Owen, *The Hubris Syndrome* (London, Politico's Publishing, 2007).

24  Peter Fonagy et al., op. cit.

25  Gottfried Spangler and Karin Grossman, 'Biobehavioural organisation in securely and insecurely attached children', *Child Development*, 64 (1993), pp.1439–50.

26  Sheri Madigan et al., 'Naïve observers' perceptions of family drawings by 7 year olds with disorganised attachment histories', *Attachment and Human Development*, 6:3 (2004), pp.223–39.

27  Nicholas Kristof, *New York Times*, 21 May, 2000.

28  Theodore Millon, *Disorders of Personality: DSM-IV and beyond* (New York, Wiley, 1996), quoted by Aubrey Immelman, Unit for the Study of Personality in Politics, *New York Observer*, www.csbsju.edu/USPP/articles/Giuliani-NYObserver.html (1999).

29  Ibid.

30  Rudy Giuliani Mocks Parkinson's Victim, www.youtube.com, 22 February 2007.

31  Martha Nussbaum, *Upheavals of Thought* (New York, Cambridge University Press, 2001).

32   Christina Lamb, 'My life with Benazir', *Sunday Times*, 30 December 2007.

33   Sam Tanenhaus, *Slate*, 24 July 2003.

34   Ann Coulter, 'This Is War', *National Review Online*, 13 September 2001.

35   Avraham Burg, *The Holocaust is Over* (Basingstoke, Palgrave Macmillan, 2008).

36   Sayyid Qutb, *Milestones (Ma'alim fi'l-Tariq)*, 1964 (Islamic Book Service, 2006).

37   Chris Hedges, *American Fascists* (London, Vintage Books, 2007).

38   Michael Lerner, *The Left Hand of God* (New York, HarperCollins, 2006).

39   Hedges, op. cit.

40   Richard Ryder, *Putting Morality Back Into Politics* (Exeter, Societas, 2006).

41   Michael Milburn and Sheree Conrad, *The Politics of Denial* (Cambridge, MA, MIT Press, 1996).

42   Robert Altemeyer, *The Authoritarians* (Winnipeg, MB, University of Manitoba Press, 2007).

43   Obama, op. cit.

44   John Allen, *Rabble Rouser for Peace: the authorised biography of Desmond Tutu* (London, Rider and Co./Ebury Press, 2006).

45   Nelson Mandela, *Long Walk to Freedom* (London, Abacus/Little, Brown, 1994).

46   Paul Zeitz, 'Lessons from South Africa's experience of HIV/AIDS', *The Lancet*, 370: 9581 (2007), pp.19–20.

47   John Battersby, 'Mandela: I failed SA's Aids challenge', www.iol.co.za (2003).

48   The Presidency, *Situational Analysis of Children in South Africa*, UNICEF Report 2009.

49   Barack Obama, Remarks of President-Elect Barack Obama: Election Night, 4 November 2008, www.barackobama.com.

**Chapter Eight**

1   Karl Rove, the Karl Rove initiative, 2001.

2   G. Roberts, *Shaping Modern Hereford* (Almeley, Logaston, 2001)

3   Thomas Macaulay, 'Southey's Colloquies', 1830 review of 'Sir

Thomas More; or, Colloquies on the Progress and Prospects of Society' by Robert Southey, in Lady Trevelyan (ed.), *Critical and Historical Essays: the complete writings of Lord Macaulay, Part 2* (Whitefish, MT, Kessinger Publishing LCC, 2004).

4 Thomas Jordan, *Victorian Childhood* (Albany, NY, State University of New York Press, 1987).

5 Macaulay, op. cit.

6 Sheldon Wolin, *Politics and Vision* (Princeton University Press, 2006).

7 Martha Nussbaum, *Women and Human Development* (New York, Cambridge University Press, 2000).

8 Tim Kasser, *The High Price of Materialism* (Cambridge, MA, MIT Press, 2002).

9 Macaulay, op. cit.

10 Frank Furedi, *Paranoid Parenting* (London, Allen Lane/Penguin, 2001).

11 Ibid.

12 Robert Skidelsky, 'Where do we go from here?', *Prospect*, 154 (January 2009).

13 Ibid.

14 Jen Lexmond and Richard Reeves, *Building Character* (London, Demos, 2009).

15 Michael Lerner, *Surplus Powerlessness* (New York, Humanity Books/Prometheus, 1991).

16 Barbara Ehrenreich, *Bait and Switch* (London, Granta Books, 2006).

17 William Thomas, 'The Rise and Fall of Enron', *Journal of Accountancy* (April 2002).

18 Simon Head, 'Inside the Leviathan', *New York Review of Books,* 16 December 2004.

19 Ehrenreich, op. cit.

20 Ann Pettifor, 'The credit crunch and the Green New Deal', *Soundings*, 41 (2008).

21 Richard Oppel, 'Word for Word: Enron traders on Grandma Millies and making out like bandits', *New York Times*, 13 June 2004.

22 John Ralston Saul, *The Unconscious Civilisation* (London, Penguin, 1997).

23  Andrew Grice, 'Hutton's call to "celebrate" millionaires receives an icy reception from the TUC', *Independent*, 12 March 2008.

24  Ehrenreich, op. cit.

25  Robert Higgs, 'Ticking time bomb explodes, public is shocked', *The Beacon Blog*, The Independent Institute, 10 September 2008.

26  Philip Zimbardo, *The Lucifer Effect* (London, Rider/Random House, 2007).

27  Ibid.

28  Kathleen O'Toole, 'The Stanford Prison Experiment: Still powerful after all these years', *Stanford University News Service*, 415 (1 August 1997), pp.723–2558.

29  Jesse Norman, *Compassionate Conservatism* (London, Policy Exchange, 2006).

30  Mihaly Csikszentmihalyi, *Flow: the psychology of optimal experience* (New York, Harper Collins, 1991).

31  Martin Seligman, *Learned Optimism* (New York, Pocket Books/Simon and Schuster, 1998). *See also* www.authentichappiness.sas.upenn.edu.

32  Daniel Kahneman et al, 'Would you be happier if you were richer? A focusing illusion', *Science*, 312: 5782 (2006), pp. 1908–10.

33  Robert E. Lane, *The Loss of Happiness in Market Democracies* (New Haven, CT, Yale University Press, 2000), quoted in Kasser, 2002, op. cit.

34  Patricia and Jacob Cohen, *Life Values and Adolescent Mental Health* (Mahwah, NJ, Lawrence Erlbaum Associates Inc., 1996).

35  Kasser, 2002, op. cit.

36  Ibid.

37  Donald Winnicott, 'Anxiety associated with insecurity', in *Through Paediatrics to Psychoanalysis: Collected Papers*, 1st edn 1975 (London, Karnac Books, 1987).

38  Norman, op. cit.

39  Andrew Samuels, speaking on *The Moral Maze*, BBC Radio 4, February 2009.

40  James Spence, quoted in Robert Karen, *Becoming Attached* (Oxford University Press, 1998).

41  Jean Baker Miller, *Towards a New Psychology of Women* (London, Penguin 1976).

**Chapter Nine**

 1  Power Inquiry, *Power to the People*, Joseph Rowntree Charitable Foundation, 2006.
 2  Gore Vidal, Interview with Martin Amis, *Observer*, 7 February 1982.
 3  J. Q. Wilson, *The Moral Sense* (London, Free Press/Simon and Schuster, 1993).
 4  McPherson, op. cit.
 5  Nussbaum, 2000, op. cit.
 6  Carol Gilligan, *In a Different Voice* (Cambridge, MA, Harvard University Press, 1982).
 7  Gillian Tett, 'Take Three' interview in *CAM* (2009).
 8  Power Inquiry, op. cit.
 9  George Monbiot, *Guardian*, 10 February 2009.
10  Andrew Turnbull, Cabinet Secretary's Valedictory Lecture: Full Speech, on www.guardian.co.uk, 27 July 2005.
11  John Adams, Address to the Military, 11 October 1798.
12  Alexis De Tocqueville, *Democracy in America*, 1835/1840, tr. G. Lawrence (London, Fontana Press, 1994).
13  Bill McKibben, personal correspondence, 4 July 2009.
14  Charles Leadbeater, *Civic Spirit* (London, Demos, 1998).
15  Peter Singer, *The Expanding Circle: Ethics and sociobiology* (Oxford University Press, 1981).
16  Elizabeth Midlarsky, Stephanie Fagin Jones, and P. Corley, 'Personality correlates of heroic rescue during the Holocaust', *Journal of Personality*, 73:4 (2005).
17  Lawrence Walker and Jeremy Frimer, 'Moral personality of brave and caring exemplars', *Journal of Personality and Social Psychology*, 93:5 (2007).
18  Roy Baumeister, *Evil: inside human violence and cruelty* (New York, Henry Holt & Co Inc., 1999).
19  Noam Chomsky, Interview with Kate Soper, *Red Pepper*, August 1998.
20  Fiona Robinson, *Globalising Care* (Boulder, CO, Westview Press, 1999).

21  Joan Tronto, *Moral Boundaries* (New York, Routledge, 1993).
22  Selma Sevenhuisjen, *Citizenship and the Ethics of Care* (New York, Routledge, 1998).
23  Nussbaum, 2000, op. cit.
24  Bertrand de Jouvenal, *On Power* (Boston, MA, Beacon Press, 1962).
25  David Cameron, 'The Big Society', Hugo Young speech, www.conservatives.com, 10 November 2009.
26  Jean Bethke Elshtain, *Democracy on Trial* (New York, Basic Books, 1995).

**Chapter Ten**

 1  Julian Lousada and Andrew Cooper, *Borderline Welfare* (London, Karnac Books, 2005).
 2  Antonio Damasio, *Descartes' Error* (New York, Penguin Putnam/HarperCollins, 1995).
 3  Quoted in Robert Karen, *Becoming Attached* (Oxford University Press, 1998).
 4  *The Television Show*, Channel 4, 7 March 2009.
 5  Harry Hendrick, 'Optimism and hope vs anxiety and narcissism: some thoughts on children's welfare yesterday and today', *History of Education*, 36:6 (2007), pp.747–68. Lori Irwin, Arjumand Siddiqi, Clyde Hertzman, 'Early Childhood Development: a powerful equalizer', report of the World Health Organisation Commission on the Social Determinants of Health, WHO, June 2007.
 6  Ilan Katz et al., *The Relationship between Parenting and Poverty*, Joseph Rowntree Foundation, 2007.
 7  Irwin, Siddiqi and Hertzman, op. cit.
 8  Child Health Promotion Programme: Pregnancy and the First Five Years of Life, Department of Health, 2008.
 9  Bruce Perry, interview in *New Scientist*, 10 February 2007.
10  Thomas Moore, *Care of the Soul* (London, Piatkus Books, 1992).
11  Leach, 2009, op. cit.
12  Greenspan and Shanker, op. cit.
13  Richard Wilkinson and Kate Pickett, *The Spirit Level:* why more equal societies almost always do better (London, Allen Lane/ Penguin, 2009).

14  Leach, 2009, op. cit.

15  Ibid.

16  Ibid.

17  Alison Booth and Jan van Ours, 'Job satisfaction and family happiness', *Economic Journal*, 118:526 (2008).

18  Catherine Hakim et al., *Little Britons: financing childcare choice* (London, Policy Exchange, 2008).

19  Alan Sroufe et al., *The Development of the Person: The Minnesota Study of Risk and Adaptation from Birth to Adulthood* (New York, Guilford Publications, 2005).

20  Carol Vincent et al., 'Childcare, choice, and social class', *Critical Social Policy*, 28:1 (2008), pp.5–26.

21  Leach, 2009, op cit.

22  Lynn Alleway, *Quality Time*, BBC2, March 1996.

23  Greenspan and Shanker, op. cit.

24  The Chronicle of Higher Education, Colloquy Live, at www.chronicle.com/colloquylive/2001/10/nussbaum (2001).

25  Fiona Robinson, *Globalising Care* (Boulder, CO, Westview Press, 1999).

26  Frank Furedi, *Therapy Culture* (London, Routledge, 2003).

27  Sarah Stewart-Brown, 'Improving Parenting: the why and the how', *Archives of Disease in Childhood*, 93 (2008), pp.102–4; K. Armstrong et al., 'Promoting secure attachment, maternal mood and child health in a vulnerable population: a randomised controlled trial', *Journal Paediatric Child Health*, 36:6 (2000), pp.555–62; C. Heinicke et al., 'Relationship based intervention with at risk mothers', *Infant Mental Health Journal*, 20:4 (2000), pp.349–74; Michael Guralnick, 'Effectiveness of early intervention for vulnerable children: a developmental perspective', *American Journal of Mental Retardation*, 102:4 (1998), pp.319–45.

28  David Olds, 'The Nurse Family Partnership: from trials to practice', Federal Reserve Paper, www.earlychildhoodrc.org/events/presentations/olds.pdf (2007).

29  Irwin, Siddiqi and Hertzman, op. cit.

30  Layard, op. cit.

31  Sue Gerhardt, *Why Love Matters* (London, Brunner Routledge, 2004). *See also* A. Poobalan et al., 'Effects of treating postnatal

depression on mother–infant interaction and child development',
*British Journal of Psychiatry*, 191 (2007), pp.378–86.

32  Robert Caldwell, *The Costs of Child Abuse vs Child Abuse Prevention*, Michigan Children's Trust Fund, 1992.

33  Stephen Spratt et al, *Backing the Future* (London, New Economic Foundation, 2009).

34  Kate Soper, Talk given at 'Left Futures', event organised by *Soundings*, 30 June 2007.

35  George Marshall, 'Change the message to save the planet', *Guardian*, 15 October 2007.

36  Reinhold Niebuhr, *Moral Man and Immoral Society* (New York, Charles Scribner's Sons, 1932).

# INDEX

# NOTE ON THE AUTHOR

Sue Gerhardt is a practising psychoanalytic psychotherapist. She wrote the bestselling *Why Love Matters: how affection shapes a baby's brain*, an accessible account of the neuroscience of early development.